City Themes

Christopher Brook is Lecturer in the Faculty of Social Sciences at The Open University. His recent books include *A Global World?* (1995, co-edited with James Anderson and Allan Cochrane) and *Asia Pacific in the New World Order* (1997, co-edited with Anthony McGrew).

Kathy Pain, formerly a Staff Tutor in Geography, is now an academic consultant in the Faculty of Social Sciences at The Open University. She is co-author, with Andrew Blowers, of 'The unsustainable city?' in *Unruly Cities?* (Book 3 in the course series).

UNDERSTANDING CITIES

This book is part of a series produced for DD304 *Understanding Cities*. The other books in the series, copublished with Routledge, are:

City Worlds, edited by Doreen Massey, John Allen and Steve Pile

Unsettling Cities: Movement/Settlement, edited by John Allen, Doreen Massey and Michael Pryke

Unruly Cities? Order/Disorder, edited by Steve Pile, Christopher Brook and Gerry Mooney.

The books form part of the Open University course DD304 *Understanding Cities*. Details of this and any other Open University course can be obtained from the Courses Reservations Centre, PO Box 724, The Open University, Milton Keynes, MK7 6ZS, United Kingdom: tel. (00 44) (0)1908 653231.

For availability of other course components, contact Open University Worldwide Ltd, The Berrill Building, Walton Hall, Milton Keynes, MK7 6AA, United Kingdom: tel. (00 44) (0)1908 858585, e-mail ouwenq@open.ac.uk.

Alternatively, much useful information can be obtained from the Open University's website, http://www.open.ac.uk.

City Themes

edited by
Christopher Brook and Kathy Pain

The Open University

The Open University
Walton Hall
Milton Keynes MK7 6AA

First published 1999 by The Open University

Edited, designed and typeset by The Open University

Printed in Great Britain by the Alden Group, Oxford

ISBN 0 7492 7781 5

1.1

CONTENTS

THE OPEN UNIVERSITY COURSE TEAM

John Allen *Senior Lecturer in Economic Geography*

Sally Baker *Education and Social Sciences Librarian*

Melanie Bayley *Editor*

Andrew Blowers *Professor of Social Sciences (Planning)*

Christopher Brook *Lecturer in Geography*

Deborah Bywater *Project Controller*

David Calderwood *Project Controller*

Margaret Charters *Course Secretary*

Allan Cochrane *Professor of Public Policy*

Lene Connolly *Print Buying Controller*

Michael Dawson *Course Manager*

Margaret Dickens *Print Buying Co-ordinator*

Nigel Draper *Editor*

Janis Gilbert *Graphic Artist*

Celia Hart *Picture Research Assistant*

Caitlin Harvey *Course Manager*

Steve Hinchliffe *Lecturer in Geography*

Teresa Kennard *Co-publishing Advisor*

Siân Lewis *Graphic Designer*

Michèle Marsh *Secretary*

Doreen Massey *Professor of Geography*

Eugene McLaughlin *Senior Lecturer in Criminology and Social Policy*

Gerry Mooney *Staff Tutor in Social Policy*

Eleanor Morris *Series Producer, BBC/OUPC*

John Muncie *Senior Lecturer in Criminology and Social Policy*

Ray Munns *Cartographer*

Kathy Pain *Staff Tutor in Geography*

Steve Pile *Lecturer in Geography and Course Team Chair*

Michael Pryke *Lecturer in Geography*

Jenny Robinson *Lecturer in Geography*

Kathy Wilson *Production Assistant, BBC/OUPC*

External Assessor

John Solomos *Professor of Sociology, University of Southampton*

External Contributors

Ash Amin *Author, Professor of Geography, University of Durham*

Stephen Graham *Author, Reader in the Centre for Urban Technology, University of Newcastle upon Tyne*

Kerry Hamilton *Author, Professor of Transport, University of East London*

Mark Hart *Tutor Panel, Reader in Industrial and Regional Policy, University of Ulster*

Susan Hoyle *Author, Research Associate in the Transport Studies Unit, University of East London*

Linda McDowell *Author, Director for the Graduate School of Geography and Fellow at Newnham College, University of Cambridge*

Ian Munt *Tutor Panel, Researcher, London Rivers Association*

Phil Pinch *Tutor Panel, Senior Lecturer, Geography and Housing Division, South Bank University*

Jenny Seavers *Tutor Panel, Research Fellow, Centre for Housing Policy, University of York*

Nigel Thrift *Author, Professor of Geography, University of Bristol*

Sophie Watson *Author, Professor of Urban Cultures, University of East London*

Introduction

Congratulations on reaching the final component of *Understanding Cities*. We hope that your journey through the course has been stimulating, surprising and thought-provoking. In your studies so far, you have been introduced to many narratives about the ways in which cities are structured and restructured over time, and about the diverse ways in which cities are lived and experienced. The course has adopted a specifically spatial perspective. We have seen how a city's spatial character is shaped by, as well as shapes, the complex patterns and rhythms of people's lives. We have also seen that cities have multiple characters and spatialities for different people, depending upon who we are and how our lives connect into, or are disconnected from, the networks, flows and rhythms which constitute cities.

The focus for this book is to prepare you for the *Understanding Cities* course essay which you are required to submit as the examinable component of your assessment. Writing this course essay will provide you with an opportunity to reflect on your own understanding in the context of one of three themes – urban social issues, the urban economy or the urban environment. These themes represent key elements of city life and the future of cities will be crucially determined by their social, economic and environmental relations. None of these areas will be new to you but they will be new as a focus for study. So, this last component of the course will require you to use the information you have acquired so far in an active way, in thinking through your responses to a particular question on one of the three themes. The actual questions for the course essay are provided in the Course Essay Question Booklet.

In reality, as we have argued in the course, social, economic and environmental aspects of city life are interconnected in complex and shifting ways through the spatial relations within and between cities. While, many economic, social and environmental aspects of city life have been examined in the course, they have not been singled out for special attention and, until now, issues have not been organized under these specific themes. As a result, you will find that all are given an uneven prominence as you re-trace the book chapters, readings, television programmes and audiocassettes. Although you will be focusing on only one of the three themes in your course essay, you will also need to be aware of the ways in which your chosen theme interrelates with the other two for a full understanding of urban issues and of achieving sustainable cities.

In writing the course essay we want you to use your imagination as you think through spatial relationships that are associated with your particular chosen theme. This will mean using the geographical or spatial lens, introduced in the Course Guide, to re-think the city narratives presented in the course. As you review the book chapters, readings, activities, TV programmes and audiocassettes, you will need to think about the particular connections and disconnections, tensions and intensities thrown up by this new slant on the city.

The central purpose of the course essay is therefore to give you the opportunity to stand back from what you have learned so far and to make new and different connections between the course ideas.

City Themes is the fourth book of the *Understanding Cities* course and its purpose is to help you in this new and, hopefully, rewarding enterprise. Its organization and character is, accordingly, rather different from the previous three volumes. While Books 1, 2 and 3 comprise the substantive study texts for the course and were designed to start you thinking about how cities work, and why the spatiality of these processes is so crucial to this understanding, this final book seeks to advance that understanding through 'active' review. Rather than going back through the various course components and course ideas in ways that you are used to doing for previous assignments, we want you to take the review one step further. In essence we want you to progress and apply your understanding of course materials and arguments as you explore your chosen city-related theme.

Chapter 1 sets out the overall context for this active review and provides practical guidance to help you in planning and writing the course essay. This chapter provides the main starting-point for this work. It explains what is expected of you, then takes you through the various stages of course essay development. It also provides guidance on skills, together with practical tips to help you get the most out of your investigation so that you can achieve a higher grade for the essay and thus for your course assessment overall. However, the course essay is not just about assessment and skills development. As we have indicated, investigations of this kind should be stimulating, even fun! While there are constraints to work within, there is considerable scope for you to draw out materials and ideas in ways that interest you.

Chapters 2, 3 and 4 introduce the three themes, and help you begin to connect these themes with the rest of the course. Each chapter reviews the course materials with one of the themes in mind: that is, each looks selectively at the book chapters, TV programmes and so on, using society, the urban economy or environment as a focus. In addition, the chapters provide some new material to allow the themes to be studied in a substantive way and give you a resource to work on independently: sometimes there are areas to consolidate and gaps to fill; sometimes there are avenues worth pursuing in further depth. Perhaps most importantly for you, the theme chapters give you a base from which to begin working on the course essay, showing what is covered by each theme, and giving you the information to decide which question to choose.

A key challenge for Chapters 2, 3 and 4 is to start you on the right track exploring social, economic and environmental issues for yourselves. But more than this, the course essay will give you the opportunity to think about city futures. The desire to imagine cities in a visionary way goes back to experiences of the earliest cities in history. City utopias have frequently been imagined as the spatial manifestation of an ideal society. Indeed, ideal city spatial configurations have been seen as a way to create the utopian society.

Such visions are not situated on one pathway. Multiple trajectories are possible. Every day, individual and collective behaviours can – and do – change what happens in cities. Individual visions and actions can, together, help to construct a scenario for the positive future of cities. In the course essay, we want you to engage with this additional challenge. We want you to take one theme and use course arguments to explore not just the many tensions, paradoxes and rhythms of city life, but ultimately, and more positively, how it may be possible to make cities more humane, liveable and sustainable places. In the Course Guide, Phil Pinch notes how past utopian solutions failed 'because of an ignorance of the complexity, diversity and interdependent nature of city life'. Any attempt to find solutions must therefore take full account of the diverse spatial character of cities and their complex webs of wider connections. For example, we need to consider how local economic fortunes of cities are tied together but in unequal ways; how environmental 'footprints' of local urban change can sometimes be traced to other parts of the world; how the social lives of city groups can be juxtaposed yet at the same time disconnected.

In sum, *City Themes* gives you guidance in applying your geographical and spatial imagination and in taking further steps towards independent learning and research. The ideas and arguments developed in Books 1, 2 and 3, and in the associated television series and audiocassettes, will have given you a strong analytical and material base from which to work, while the course assignments have required you to link together course materials, text and images, in a variety of ways. This earlier work involved you in careful sifting and selecting of appropriate information and images and in developing your ideas in a focused and logical way; these are important base-line skills in research. Such skills are 'transferable': they can be used in a wide range of settings and not just as part of this course. So far, your assessed work has been relatively segmented, with assignments tied to a particular set of book chapters or part of the television series. For the course essay the arguments and potential sources are course-wide while the three new organizing themes bring an added dimension. The themes and course arguments open up all kinds of avenues for exploration, avenues which we hope will spark an interest of your own and lead to further study outside the course.

Christopher Brook and Kathy Pain

CHAPTER 1

The *Understanding Cities* essay: a guide

by Christopher Brook

1 *What is the course essay?*

The course essay is your final and most substantial piece of work on the course. In terms of course understanding and skills development it is something you have been building towards over the year. It is designed to allow you to take a fresh look at course ideas and materials by selecting and focusing on *one* of three themes – urban social issues, the urban economy and the urban environment. These themes are elaborated in turn in Chapters 2, 3 and 4, but first it is important to take a closer look at what you will be asked to do in the course essay itself so that you know what is required in undertaking this active review of the course.

The skills we want you to develop through working on the course essay have already been mentioned in the Course Guide (section 5) and in the Introduction to this book. Essentially the course essay is designed to enable you to demonstrate your understanding of course arguments by *applying* them to a comparatively fresh set of themes. These themes will be explored using existing course sources – the specially written chapters and associated readings, the TV programmes and audiocassettes – supported by some new text and readings in Chapters 2, 3 and 4 of this volume. The earlier materials will need to be carefully sorted and reworked to focus on the theme of your choice. You can, if you like, also include your own examples from outside sources but this is not essential for achieving a high grade. While the independence of your investigation is in some ways constrained, the work will depend crucially on *your* ability to select, marshal and deploy appropriate information and ideas from across the course. In doing so, you will also have demonstrated that you are sufficiently at ease with course arguments to apply them in a relatively independent manner. These are significant skills which can be used outside your narrower course work. In a very real sense, then, the course essay represents an important step towards independent research.

Because the course essay is a key part of course assessment, it is understandable if your initial reaction is one of slight trepidation. You may be wondering whether you can cope with the extended word length (3500–4000), or you may be concerned about what is expected of you and whether you can make penetrating links between course arguments and your chosen city theme. While such concerns are reasonable, particularly at this early stage, we should like to assure you that personal investigations have their positive side: they can be exciting and rewarding to undertake. Now, clearly there will be course guidelines and expectations to keep in mind, but there is also plenty of scope for you to select and develop your investigation in the way in which you want. The themes and course arguments open up all kinds of options for exploration – options which may spark an interest of your own and lead to further study outside the course. So, while keeping in mind what is expected, we do want you to develop your particular interests and get involved, extending your understanding that much further through applying the taught ideas.

2 *Course arguments and themes*

What we are asking you to do, then, is to show your understanding of course materials by organizing them around a fresh theme. The themes were played down in the structure of the course books and television programmes, and until now have not been discussed in a sustained and up-front way. In a very real sense, you will undertake an active review of the course: by organizing material along different lines you will be involved in selecting and marshalling ideas and examples for yourself. *But we are asking you to do more than use social, economic or environmental themes as a new organizing device for your studies. We also want you to approach these themes using course arguments* which have been developed through the study texts and the TV series. So let's recap briefly on those arguments.

First, the course stresses the importance of **'thinking spatially'** about the ways in which cities develop and operate. In Chapter 4 of Book 1 Doreen Massey explores this notion in some detail and begins to unpack some of its elements. For instance, she shows how 'thinking spatially' is important in allowing multiple (and contested) images and stories about a city, or parts of a city, to co-exist. These multiple views of what a place is like, and how it has developed, will reflect the many different experiences and networks of interests of those coming into contact with that place. She also explores what she terms the 'generative effect' of a city's spatial layout and differentiation. Can you remember what she meant by this? Essentially, the existing spatial patterning of cities and their positions within wider world networks will influence the actions of those living there and shape what happens next. Where we live in a city confers certain locational advantages and disadvantages; a city's position in relation to diverse wider networks of economic and political power also shapes its opportunities and can give it 'initial advantage' (see, for example, the discussion of Chicago's development in Chapter 1 of Book 1). In sum, 'thinking spatially' provides us with greater insight into how cities work; whatever the local issue, we are soon forced to make diverse connections to other parts of the world and recognize that it will often be seen very differently by different groups.

ACTIVITY 1.1   In order to check your understanding, try to illustrate the following aspects of 'spatial thinking' using examples from any of the six TV programmes. The TV Guide will also be useful here. ◆

Spatial thinking	Examples from TV
The co-existence of multiple views …	
The generative impact of spatial patterns …	
Viewing urban issues/changes in a wider context …	
Linking local juxtapositions in urban space to wider connections …	

A second set of course arguments deals with a series of **tensions** about the way in which cities work, their geographical character and our experiences of them. These tensions were presented as paradoxes since their impact is often as ambiguous as they are uncertain, and can affect different groups in different ways. The TMAs and in-text activities should have given you plenty of opportunity to think through these tensions using a range of examples. The three tensions that perhaps received most discussion are:

- *community and difference:* how 'communities' appear increasingly difficult to identify in places that are home to such a variety of groups, with such a variety of wider connections; how some people come to the city to escape community while for others there are pressures to construct community; how huge inequalities and differences within the city make it difficult to get together to develop communal actions.

- *movement and settlement:* how cities are both a place of settlement and also a focus for intense interaction and movement; how increasing interaction and movement also brings increasing pressure for security of settlement; how, as some barriers fall, others are constructed.

- *order and disorder:* …

ACTIVITY 1.2   Now it's your turn. Try using your own words to show you are comfortable exploring this tension:

The tension of 'order and disorder' prompts thoughts like … ◆

A third set of arguments running through the course has been concerned with the **intensity of social relations** and the manifestation of this in the organization and physical character of a city. You were introduced to the notions of 'felt intensities' (the impact of crowding and intense interactions on the rhythms of city life and its built form) and 'open intensities' (how these interactions connect to other cities and how the cities must be viewed in a wider world context). The three theme chapters that follow provide examples of how these open and felt intensities have social, economic and environmental expression.

ACTIVITY 1.3   Make some preliminary notes on how *you* see the intensities of city life being linked to its social, economic or environmental character. Take just *one* of these general aspects of the city and think about how the notions of 'open intensities' and 'felt intensities' might apply. Don't worry about being too precise at this stage. You will be able to check the applicability of your initial thoughts as you work through the relevant theme chapter. ◆

	Social / Economic / Environmental aspects of cities
Open intensities	
Felt intensities	

In sum, each course essay question will be asking you to work back through the course materials with one of the three **themes** *(social, economic, environmental)* **and** *with these* **arguments** *('thinking spatially', applying urban tensions, the intensification of social relations) in mind.* Table 1.1 shows diagrammatically what is involved. You will have a choice between three theme questions, and you will be asked to select and marshal course materials both by theme and by course argument. The question may also include a component that asks you to make a judgement about these arguments.

TABLE 1.1   *Options for the course essay*

THEMES	COURSE ARGUMENTS		
	Thinking spatially	Urban tension, e.g. – community/difference – movement/settlement – order/disorder	Intensification of social relations
1 Social			
2 Economic			
3 Environmental			

The course essay is thus about application and research as well as review. This is in line with our broader expectation for the course: that you should complete the year confident of your ability to apply ideas in *Understanding Cities* to urban issues you see around you, and that your application can be substantive and penetrating. The course essay also provides an opportunity for you to practise basic *research skills* such as selecting appropriate information from a wide range of materials, and building your investigation in a coherent and focused way (see section 5.3 of the Course Guide). Finally, it should help you in the skill of *using course materials and ideas for yourself.* That is, you will have developed a 'transferable skill' which is useful outside the confines of this course.

3 *Selecting a topic*

Choosing between the topic areas is a matter of personal choice. It is difficult to give more than general guidance on this but you may wish to consider the following when making your selection.

First, and rather self-evidently, choose a topic area you think you will enjoy investigating. Given it will be the dominant focus of your work for some five weeks, it needs to be of sufficient interest to you to sustain quite prolonged and in-depth analysis. For example, you may have found particularly interesting the discussions of environmentally related topics in the course so far, or perhaps you were stirred by book chapters or TV programmes with more of an economic or social flavour. Alternatively, you may decide to choose a topic area which links well with other courses you have studied, or which builds on interests outside the OU. For whatever reason, choose an area for which you feel some enthusiasm.

Secondly, before making your choice, you should study carefully *all three* theme chapters and their readings to check each theme's scope and confirm to yourself that your initial interest extends to the detail. Initial reactions are useful but it is important to check that you are happy working across the full subject matter of that theme. The 'flip side' of this is that you may find that an area which was apparently of less interest to you – urban economics perhaps – suddenly comes to life when you read up on the relevant theme. So make full use of the theme chapters and readings, and allow yourself to be surprised before making your selection.

Finally, be aware of the *context* in which each theme is to be explored. Not only do the course essay questions ask you to choose between themes but also between course arguments. As has already been explained, each question will be angled to engage with certain course arguments: you will need to make sure you are clear on the breadth and nature of those arguments, so that you will be able to use them for yourself. Select on the basis of which arguments you find most interesting as well as on the basis of theme.

4 *Getting started on the course essay*

Once you have chosen your course essay question, what is the next step? To most students the hardest part of any essay work is just getting started. Over the year you have had some practice at this with your TMAs, but given the extra significance and length of the course essay it is as well to note the various steps involved. You may have your own particular approach, but it is probably useful to have a general checklist of the basic necessary steps. They are:

1   Clarifying the question

Your first task is to clarify what the question is asking you to do. You will, of course, have thought about this when choosing between options, though maybe only in outline and without thinking through the detail. Suppose one part of the course essay asked:

> In what ways does 'thinking spatially' help us to understand environmental issues within cities?

This question may look reasonably straightforward, but even so you will need to note the key terms and phrases – 'thinking spatially', 'environmental issues', 'within cities'. They set out the *scope* of the question, and you need to work within these parameters. You might find it useful to underline these words/phrases to register them clearly in your mind. You will also need to note any command word or phrase asking you to 'do things'. Here you are asked 'In what ways … ?', but you could just as easily be asked to 'discuss', 'assess' or 'analyse'. A complete listing of command words and their meanings can be found in Appendix A.

2   Jotting down ideas

Having noted the scope of the question you need to think about the things you want to discuss. The 'notes' following each of the course essay options may help you to get started on this but you will also have your own thoughts from your review of relevant course material, prompted by the guidance in Chapters 2, 3 and 4. Here it is usual to spend time *brainstorming* ideas, listing ideas which the course essay question prompts for you.

ACTIVITY 1.4   Take the sample question above and make a short list of ideas and questions that it prompts for you. ◆

When you have jotted down a few ideas, turn to Appendix B of this chapter. There I have set out what I consider to be important points. Don't worry if some of your ideas are different from mine; the ideas I have included are certainly not the only relevant ones. The important thing is that, like mine, your ideas draw out some aspect of the sample question, and don't lead to tangential discussion. In other words, the ideas need to engage with, or interrogate, the question.

3 Mind maps

You could set out these lists of ideas as a 'mind map' (sometimes termed a 'spider diagram'). My attempt is shown in Figure 1.1. The advantage of mind maps like this is that they get you thinking about how your ideas connect together, something that could be useful when you start writing and need to give your discussion a clear structure and logic. The one slight danger with a mind map is that it can tie you prematurely to a quite narrow set of connections, with other ideas and relations rather played down. No doubt in Figure 1.1 there are many more connections that could have been made, and of the links that have been made some may be more important than others. Because of this, it may be helpful to experiment with more than one mind map so that different arrangements of ideas are considered.

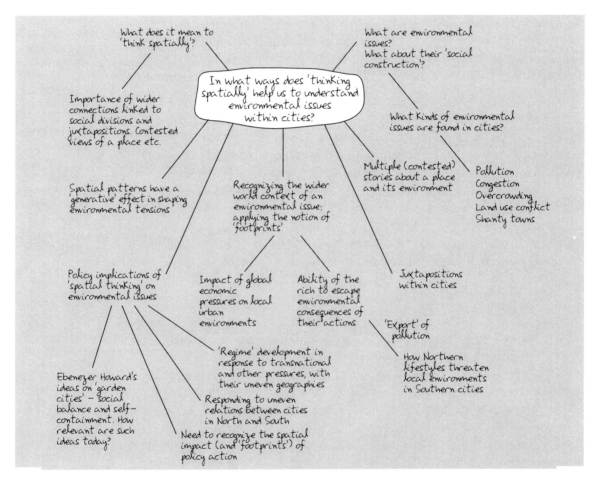

FIGURE 1.1 *Sample mind map for 'In what ways does "thinking spatially" help us to understand environmental issues within cities?'*
Note: This mind map shows the kind of ideas and their relations you might consider when answering the sample question above; it is not intended as a prescription on what to cover and how. Other mind maps could be constructed on the same general topic area.

5 *Structuring your ideas*

Unlike the traditional essay, we ask that you divide your course essay into identifiable sections which connect together in some logical way. In a standard 1500–2000 word TMA there is less need for formal structure and signposting of this kind: you can set out your plans at the beginning of the essay and, as long as you hold to those plans, the reader should be able to follow your train of thought without too much difficulty. However, with longer presentations it becomes less easy to hold the reader's attention using a pure essay format. It is also easier for the writer to get side-tracked into more tangential arguments and for the essay to lose direction. One advantage of using section headings is that they 'flag up' key elements in your argument and force you to keep thinking about the overall structure of your answer; this will help you to ensure a logical sequence of enquiry and maintain a strong focus on the question set. *If you remain uncertain on what to do, I suggest you look at how book chapters in this course use section headings to make clear the developing focus of enquiry and to reinforce chapter coherence.*

What you decide for section headings is a matter for personal choice. *Where possible, though, try to get your section headings to address the course essay question in some way.* If the headings engage with the question, what you write under each heading is more likely to be on track. The ideas listed while brainstorming can provide a useful basis for heading selection as long as they were carefully focused in the first place.

How would this work for the sample question above? If I was constructing an answer, my building-blocks would include:

- Introduction – what do we mean by 'environmental issues'?, what is 'spatial thinking'?
- Impact of urban spatial patterns on environmental issues
- The importance of viewing local environmental issues in a wider context
- How 'thinking spatially' sheds light on the contested character of environmental issues
- What are the policy implications of 'thinking spatially' about these matters?
- Conclusion – why 'thinking spatially' is important to understanding environmental issues … how far can 'spatial thinking' assist the search for solutions?

My sub-headings would, of course, need to be more 'snappy' than those above. In this illustration I might choose, for instance, 'Spatial thinking and the environment', 'The generative impact of spatial patterns', 'Urban environments in a wider context' and so on. Choosing sub-headings may seem like an unimportant task, but in fact they require careful thought. On the one hand, you want to grab the reader's attention; on the other you want to reflect the discussion in that section and its appropriateness to the course essay question.

6 *Selecting support materials*

Having decided on the general structure of your essay and key points you wish to raise, you must think about the range of course materials you can usefully draw on to support and illustrate these ideas. *Try to draw on each course component* – from the TV series and audiocassettes as well as the three main texts and this final volume. For all course essay questions you will find no shortage of relevant course materials to draw on. To underline this point here are just some of the potential sources for the sample question:

– theme chapter on urban environmental issues: **Bk 4 Ch. 4**

– elaboration on 'thinking spatially': **Bk 1 Ch. 4, Course Guide** and **AC 1 Side B**

– how a city's spatial form is 'generative' of environmental issues: **Bk 1 Ch. 2** (section 3)

– the impact of transport networks in shaping patterns of congestion and pollution: **Bk 2 Ch. 2**

– the complex geography of 'city-nature formations' and their impact on contested stories and images of a city's relations with the environment: **Bk 2 Ch. 4**

– the externalities produced by the juxtaposition of different land uses: **Bk 3 Ch. 5** on nimbyism (section 4.2)

– the environmental impact of exporting urban planning models from one city to another: **Bk 3 Ch. 6** (section 2)

– the impact of 'ecological footprints' caused by city development and the significance of 'spatial thinking' in planning for sustainable development: **Bk 3 Ch. 6**

– Readings and extracts associated with book chapters. For example: Sit **(Bk 2 Extract 2.2)** on the character of Beijing transport and its impact; Simon **(Bk 2 Extract 4.1)** on the environmental impact of Mexico City's distinctive geography; Wolch *et al.* **(Bk 2 Reading 4A)** on urban wildlife; Harvey **(Bk 3 Extract 6.2)** on the need for environmental justice …

– **TV** programme on Mexico City

– **AC** 2 Side A

– Relevant 'snippets' of newspapers and magazines you may have collected.

Because there is so much material to choose from, your task may seem a little daunting. Hopefully the next three chapters will provide some reassurance on this. Each should give you a head-start in finding relevant material for the essay of your choice. The next stage is to manage your time carefully, and to select first those materials that seem most useful and interesting. The fifteen or so potential sources for the sample question (listed above) can then be seen as an important initial stage, a way of narrowing down the potential material to form a base from which to narrow and select further. You need to make your task manageable, while at the same time getting on with the more practical tasks such as re-reading relevant texts and taking more detailed notes. You can't cover every last potentially relevant example, and we don't expect you to. However, as a general rule of thumb, try to select something from *each* course component, i.e. from Book 1, Book 2, Book 3, the selected theme chapter, and at least one TV programme and audiocassette. It is also important that you make use of chapter readings as well as chapter texts.

Given the range of potential sources, it is crucial to select carefully between these materials and to make sure their relevance is clearly shown. The ideas and examples that you will want to use in your course essay are unlikely to be set out in a nice 'ready to use' way in the book chapters, readings, guides and media notes: *they will need reworking so that their relevance to the question is clearly shown*. The materials you use may have been written with slightly different questions in mind or may draw in other less relevant points and examples. The skill you must show is that of '*application*': you must show that you are able not only to select potentially relevant sources but also that the relevance is made clear and unequivocal; that the course materials are *applied* to the question in hand. For example, if you were answering the sample question you would need to do more than include a general discussion of urban environmental issues; you would also need to make clear how it relates to 'thinking spatially'.

As a general rule, however, stay clear of including extensive discussions of single case studies. 3500–4000 words may appear to provide opportunity for such work, but if you do so, you run the risk of including less relevant material as well as side-tracking the main line of argument. If a large part of the course essay is given over to one or two detailed case studies, you may find yourself adding material which is germane only to the case studies themselves and not to the points you are discussing. Historical background to environmental issues in Mexico City or Beijing may be interesting in itself but how much will it add to a discussion focusing on links between environmental issues and 'spatial thinking'?

We also suggest that, where possible, your arguments are supported by more than one example. A range of illustration will provide more solid support for your ideas by showing more diversity of application. A single example will show the idea works for one particular set of circumstances, but if you want to make clear that it has a 'wider currency' you will need varied illustration. Furthermore, many ideas are subject to questioning and debate, and you may need to underline this point by providing both examples *and* counter-examples. Either way, full and appropriate illustration will add significantly to the depth of your analysis.

Given that there is so much text material from which to choose, there may be pressures to play down information from TV programmes or the maps, photos, tables and figures that accompany book chapters, media notes and the theme chapters. These non-text sources are valuable for examples and ideas and we encourage their use, the TV programmes in particular. Finally, while there are dangers in overwhelming the essay with diagrams and tables, they can be very effective when used selectively and their relevance is made clear. Similarly, selective use of maps could be very useful in supporting examples of, for instance, the impact of a city's spatial form.

6.1   CHAPTER READINGS AS A KEY RESOURCE

The readings placed at the end of each book chapter (including the relevant 'theme chapter' in this book) are key sources for your course essay, and you should make full use of them; the same goes for extracts included within chapters. A key difference between the readings/extracts and the book chapters is that the former were written with another purpose in mind. One important implication of this is that a reading or extract may be of relevance to more than one chapter and could be useful in elaborating a range of course ideas, not just the points signalled by chapter activities or cross-references. *Try, then, to use the readings and extracts as key course resources, to be used in different ways, rather than as part of a particular chapter.* In this context you may find the index at the back of each book helpful in finding your way around the readings/ extracts and connecting ideas in different ways. While you may have to work harder in drawing out connections than you would for purpose-written material, there is also a great diversity and richness in the readings and extracts which you should make use of.

6.2   USING OUTSIDE SOURCES

The book readings and extracts may start you thinking about using outside sources. This is something we very much encourage though it is not essential to attain a high grade. While those who do make appropriate use of outside sources will be credited, those who stick to course materials will not be penalized. One of the main advantages of your making connections outside the course is that you are forced to go further in using course ideas *for yourself.* To a large extent you are already applying course ideas and materials, particularly when drawing in the non purpose-written readings, but using outside sources takes you a notch further in developing these ideas with confidence. Even with the readings there has been pre-selection and some editing, but with non-course sources you're on your own! The more you can make these wider connections and use newspaper articles, TV broadcasts, books and other outside materials to show relevance of 'thinking spatially' etc., the more likely it is that these ideas will stick in your mind when you move on from this course.

In the Course Guide it was suggested that you assemble a file of course-related cuttings from newspapers, magazines etc. to make the course 'come alive' and connect with day-to-day experience. Hopefully you have been able to do this over the year, and some of you may have been sufficiently prepared to collect in the general area of your course essay option. If you have started a course essay file, you will need to think carefully about what can usefully be included given the 3500–4000 word limit. Remember, too, that you will need to be very clear in showing relevance: don't leave ideas and examples from your file to 'speak for themselves'. You should show that your own sources are included in the full knowledge of course arguments and not in an attempt to evade them. Any outside source will almost certainly not be written with course arguments in mind. So it will be up to you to make that link very clearly yourself.

7 Checking your essay presentation skills

At this stage of a Level 3 course you should be well practised in essay presentation skills, and although the format and length of the course essay is rather different, the same basic presentation needs still apply. Nevertheless given that much rests on this particular piece of work, it is worth listing some key essay presentation skills which have not already been referred to above.

- Your course essay must include an introduction and conclusion: section 9 on 'What the scriptmarker is looking for' includes a brief note on what is required.

- It's important that you check through your final draft for basic things such as sentence construction and grammar, making sure your ideas are clear and the argument is easy to follow. Try reading it out aloud or asking a friend to read it. Remember that if the person marking your essay has to stop, for any reason, and perhaps go back over part of the essay, there is a strong chance that the flow of argument will be lost. Given that you will have spent several weeks on this piece of work, it would be a pity to lose its full impact because you missed out on the final polishing.

- Make sure that you have drawn on materials from across the course and from the different course components. It is important to show that you can work confidently with the three main texts and TV series, and that your course interests are not narrowly focused.

- Where possible you should develop ideas in your own words and certainly you should avoid excessive quotation from other sources. Using own words makes you check that you are comfortable with what is being discussed and the ideas once elaborated will stick in the mind more readily. When you do need to quote, make sure you reference the original source and page number (see Redman *et al.*, 1998, section 8.3). Remember that plagiarism – the writing out of other people's work (from whatever source) as if it were your own – is a serious offence.

- Remember to include a full list of references to sources you have used. If you are unsure of how to set out references, the quick solution is to look at the end of any book chapter. If you want more detail on basic principles, you should consult Redman *et al.* (1998), Chapter 8 and Appendix D. It is also important that all sources you use are referenced at the appropriate point(s) within your course essay with the full reference listed at the end in the bibliography.

8 *Scheduling your work*

With around five weeks formally allocated to the course essay, it is important to organize your time effectively. You will find there is quite a bit to do and it is worthwhile making an early start and not letting things slip. To leave all the work to the last couple of weeks would court disaster. Some of you will have experience of extended essay and project-type work, but many will find the thought of a course-wide investigation of some 3500–4000 words a little daunting. In the circumstances, some general advice on scheduling your work seems appropriate.

Start with a realistic assessment of your commitments and time available over the period and then set out your own personal study schedule. These may seem pretty basic steps, but it is important to be clear about what's involved and match the various elements to the actual time you have available. There are a number of key stages to consider.

FIGURE 1.2   *Balancing task against time (adapted from Giles and Hedge, 1994)*

Stage 1: General review and theme selection

We suggest you allow yourself *one week* to study the three theme chapters before *finalizing* your choice of course essay. You might start by skim-reading the themes to get a general sense of the scope of each issue area. Also look back at the Course Guide and Book 1 to clarify key course arguments attached to the questions. Before making your selection you need to be happy with both the issue and the way the question has been focused. That said, don't spend too much time on this initial selection: *move on to Stage 2 as soon as you can.*

Stage 2: Marshalling relevant material

The next stage is to go carefully through the course materials with the question you have chosen in mind. You will probably need *one or two weeks* to explore, and select from, the widest possible range of course sources – chapters from all three books as well as the relevant theme chapter, associated readings, TV programmes and audiocassettes. Remember to use the book indexes to help track down relevant sources. You will find it helpful to write notes which show how potential sources might link to the course essay question. It is also important to keep an accurate record for your reference list of where these sources can be found.

Stage 3: Drafting your course essay

Don't expect that things will fall neatly into place first time round. It will take time to develop an effective 3500–4000 word course essay, one where arguments and their relevance are set out clearly, and develop logically, and with ideas and examples drawn from a range of DD304 sources. So allocate time to planning the structure of your course essay (which may include experimenting with different structures) and to the review and revision of drafts. For work of this kind it is not unusual to complete two or three drafts, as well as fine-tuning of particular sections along the way. Our suggestion is that you allocate around *two weeks* to drafting and finalizing your work.

In practice you may find that these stages do not form a simple linear sequence. For example, you may find that, after starting to marshal materials with a particular option in mind (Stage 2), you decide the question is not for you and select a new option (Stage 1). And you will almost certainly wish to return to the marshalling material stage (Stage 2) while you are drafting your course essay (Stage 3): there are always those extra details to track down and additional examples to incorporate. So jumping around between these stages is to be expected; indeed it is part and parcel of the process of research and setting out ideas. In the 'skyscraper' course plan in the Course Guide Phil Pinch used the notion of 'lifts' to show this more complex interaction between course essay stages (see also Figure 1.3). At various points (floors) in your work you may wish to jump from one stage (lift) to another!

FIGURE 1.3

9 *What the scriptmarker is looking for*

Remember that the course essay replaces the unseen examination more usually taken at the end of an OU course and thus will supply 50 per cent of your course marks. Given the significance of the course essay to your final grade, it is important that you know what kind of things the scriptmarker (examiner) will be looking for and, in broad terms, how marks will be distributed (see also the Course Essay Question Booklet on feedback). There are four main criteria that will guide how the course essay is graded.

1 Using course concepts and arguments in effective and appropriate ways

An essential part of the course essay is the development of so-called 'application' skills. You will be expected to show that you are sufficiently comfortable working with concepts and arguments from the course books and TV programmes to be able to use/apply them for yourself when exploring your chosen theme. You will need to show not only that you fully understand these ideas but that you can unpack them and rework them in ways appropriate to your particular discussion.

2 Showing the relevance of your ideas

You need to make clear how the ideas and examples you use relate to the particular focus of the question selected. And you must show this relevance throughout. It is not sufficient to address the question in your introduction and conclusion, but not follow it up by linking back to the question through the main body of your course essay. The scriptmarker will expect you to make clear the relevance of your discussion throughout your answer. Also, take care not to leave your ideas to 'speak for themselves'; however self-evident you think the relevance is, you must spell it out.

3 Developing a coherent course essay structure with effective use of subsections

The scriptmarker will be looking closely at the way in which you organize your answer. The points you raise must be linked together in a meaningful way, so take care not to jump from point to point with little thought about the overall direction of the course essay. They will be looking for how the different parts of your discussion connect together to form a coherent whole and whether there is a logical and well-signposted progression of ideas. You will, of course, be developing your own structure and we would expect your subsection headings to reflect the content of each subsection.

4 Drawing on a range of course materials and components

You should aim to use ideas and examples from a variety of course sources. The scriptmarker will want to see evidence of your ability to marshal relevant material not just from different book chapters but also from the different course components – TV as well as text, readings as well as materials specifically written for the course. The more you can draw these materials together in support of your chosen theme (and the way you are asked to approach it), the more you will be credited.

Other inmportant points that the scriptmarker will consider are:

5 The quality of your introduction and conclusion

In the case of the introduction, they will look at how you set out your plans for the course essay, make clear the scope of the question and define key terms. For the conclusion, they will be looking at how you draw ideas together and at the effectiveness of summary remarks.

6 The effectiveness of your referencing system

The scriptmarker will want to see the discussion carefully referenced and detailed sources provided if you use quotations. At the end of the course essay you must also supply a full list of the references used. Again, Chapter 8 and Appendix D of *The Good Essay Writing Guide* (Redman *et al.*, 1998) make clear what is required.

7 Length of course essay

The scriptmarker will expect you to make full use of the word limit of 3500–4000 words, *but not to exceed it.*

10 *Over to you ...*

Hopefully this chapter will have helped you to start on your course essay and given you some idea about what is expected. The rest is up to you! We hope you are able to select an option that interests you, and enjoy the challenge of thinking through course arguments in some depth and applying them to thematic issues. We also want you to address the final aim of the course, that is, to use course arguments to explore how one might make cities more liveable and sustainable places. Whether you choose the social, the economic or the environmental option, we want you to think about how course arguments can further your understanding of the challenges facing cities, and how governments and other agencies can best manage city futures. As the Course Guide makes clear, these arguments 'sharpen awareness' of the diverse impacts of spatial differences and the environment both on what goes on within cities and on uneven relations between cities. If they are an integral part of understanding cities, it must also be part of any serious search for solutions.

We hope your work on the course essay will not mark the end to your 'thinking geographically' about cities. The fact that you have used this particular way of thinking, and the ideas and arguments it prompts, for yourself, and in a substantive and relatively independent way, means that it is likely to stick in your mind. So, if you have the opportunity, try it out on other urban issues and experiences outside the course. Or perhaps you can take these ideas with you to other courses. 'Thinking geographically' is as transferable to other contexts as the more general research skills you have begun to develop.

References

Allen, J., Massey, D. and Pryke, M. (eds) (1999) *Unsettling Cities*, London, Routledge/The Open University (Book 2 in this series).

Giles, K. and Hedge, N. (1994) *The Manager's Good Study Guide*, Milton Keynes, The Open University.

Massey, D., Allen, J. and Pile, S. (eds) (1999) *City Worlds*, London, Routledge/The Open University (Book 1 in this series).

Northedge, A. (1990) *The Good Study Guide*, Milton Keynes, The Open University.

Pile, S., Brook, C. and Mooney, G. (eds) (1999) *Unruly Cities?*, London, Routledge/The Open University (Book 3 in this series).

Pinch, P. (1999) *Course Guide* for DD304 *Understanding Cities*, Milton Keynes, The Open University.

Redman, P. *et al.* (1998) *Good Essay Writing: A Social Sciences Guide*, Milton Keynes, The Open University.

Note

Redman, P. *et al.* (1998) *Good Essay Writing: A Social Sciences Guide* is *only available from* Eddington Hook Ltd, PO Box 239, Tunbridge Wells, Kent TN4 0YQ. (Freephone orderline: 0800 0182 799; Fax: 01892 549481; Enquiries: 01892 517439.)

Appendix A
Process and command words
in essay questions

Account for	Explain, clarify, give reasons for.
Analyse	Resolve into its component parts. Examine critically or minutely.
Assess	Determine the value of, weigh up (see also Evaluate).
Compare	Look for similarities and differences between; perhaps reach conclusions about which is preferable and justify this clearly.
Contrast	Set in opposition in order to bring out the differences sharply.
Compare and contrast	Find some points of common ground between x and y and show where or how they differ.
Criticize	Make a judgement (backed by a discussion of the evidence or reasoning involved) about the merit of theories or opinions or about the truth of facts.
Define	State the exact meaning of a word or phrase. In some cases it may be necessary or desirable to examine different possible or often used definitions.
Describe	Give a detailed account of …
Discuss	Explain, then give two sides of the issue and any implications.
Distinguish or differentiate between	Look for differences between …
Evaluate	Make an appraisal of the worth/validity/effectiveness of something in the light of its truth or usefulness (see also Assess).
Examine the argument that …	Look in detail at this line of argument.
Explain	Give details about how and why it is …
How far … ?	To what extent … ? Usually involves looking at evidence/ arguments for and against and weighing them up.
Illustrate	Make clear and explicit, usually requires the use of carefully chosen examples
Justify	Show adequate grounds for decisions or conclusions; answer the main objections likely to be made about them.
Outline	Give the main features or general principles of a subject, omitting minor details and emphasizing structure and arrangement.
State	Present in a brief, clear way.
Summarize	Give a concise, clear explanation or account of … presenting the chief factors and omitting minor details and examples (see also Outline).
What arguments can be made for and against the view that … ?	Look at both sides of this argument.

Source: Redman *et al.* (1998); adapted from Cole and Harris (undated handout material)

Appendix B
Brainstorming the course
essay: an example

'In whay ways does "thinking spatially" help us to understand environmental issues within cities?'

The ideas and sub-questions which the sample question prompted in my mind were:

- What does it mean to 'think spatially' about urban issues? What different aspects are there to 'thinking spatially'? – impact of a city's spatial form, impact of uneven webs of wider connections, impact of multiple views of a place.

- What do we mean by 'environmental issue'? Aren't environmental issues also social issues, in that they are socially constructed and have a social impact? What kinds of environmental problems are found in cities – issues of congestion, pollution, conflicting land uses etc.? Why are local environmental issues sometimes viewed in different ways by different groups? Isn't the definition of 'environmental problem' as well as its solution often subject to political debate?

- What of the impact of spatial patterns in shaping the character of local environmental tensions within cities? For example, doesn't the particular way in which major transport arteries are laid out within a city have uneven environmental consequences for local communities? What of the local environmental impacts of a new office development etc.? What of the environmental advantages/disadvantages facing different kinds of residential neighbourhood?

- Why do local urban environmental issues often need to be viewed in a wider world context? Won't the construction of a new transport link or office-block have wider as well as local environmental effects? Aren't some local environmental issues really about the 'footprints' of decisions taken outside that area, perhaps in other parts of the world? Does production and consumption of cities in the 'North' threaten local environments of cities in the 'South'?

- Why is 'thinking spatially' useful to understanding the contested nature of environmental issues and the multiple stories about a place? Why do different groups sometimes view the same local environmental issue in rather different ways?

- Doesn't 'thinking spatially' force us to recognize the increasing difficulties of delivering environmentally sustainable solutions to local urban problems? Aren't our own local environmental concerns exacerbated by the 'footprints' of urban processes elsewhere? Doesn't the increasing spatial connectedness between as well as within cities make it more difficult for local urban communities to seek solutions alone?

- Can we get closer to resolving environmental tensions by making more use of 'spatial thinking' in planning and governance? How useful were Ebenezer Howard's ideas in applying spatial ideas to reduce urban environmental tensions? Do increasing environmental pressures within cities suggest a dystopian future, and can 'spatial thinking' do any more than help to explain these pressures?

CHAPTER 2
Social consequences of city life

by Jenny Seavers

1 *Introduction*

By this stage in the course you will probably have a whole set of new ideas, and even more questions! Well, this chapter is designed to let you explore some of these questions in detail and, in particular, questions about urban *social* issues. Each time we switch on the news we are confronted by clips of film coverage showing images such as children on city waste-tips eking out a living by gathering rubbish, or urban unrest as groups march through the streets trying to make their voices heard. We are bombarded with images of conflicts generated by different groups vying for rights to space within the city, and pictures of shiny, opulent skyscrapers surrounded by poverty and slums. Perhaps, like me, you feel an element of dismay when you see the news, that – with all the technology and so-called 'advancement' society has made – there remain such glaring inequalities in our cities. One of the things that has struck me throughout the course is that these inequalities are depicted not just in cities across the globe, at a distance from our own space, they also characterize the cities where we do or might live: for example, the riots in British cities during the 1980s, or the conflict between different groups in Belfast. Not only this, the connections between our cities and the more distanced cities we see on the news mean that what goes on in one place often affects the lives of the people living in those other cities.

Throughout, the course has explored the various ways of understanding and making sense of cities today and how some of these problems of unrest and inequality arise as people from different cultures, ethnic backgrounds or from different countries live in close proximity to one another. There have also been hints throughout the course about what this might mean for the future of cities, but maybe, like me, you have been left wondering how you resolve these all too obvious problems that continually face us on our television screens through these images of riots and unrest ? Or, indeed, the everyday dilemmas that rich and poor, men and women, or people from different ethnic groups, living in the same place have to negotiate? What does all this mean for cities of the future and the people who live shoulder to shoulder with one another?

In considering this, James Donald, a cultural analyst, gives a timely caution:

> I take seriously a warning from the most practical and commonsensical of urban critics, Jane Jacobs: 'Designing a dream city is easy; rebuilding a living one takes imagination.' Those who fantasise about turning the city into an efficient machine, with all its component parts flawlessly engineered and geared, misrecognise the space of the city. They see it as a territory to be bounded, mapped and perfected. This is the overweening dream of Enlightenment rationality: to render the city transparent, *to get the city right*, and so to produce *the right citizens*. It is a dream which, in disavowing

them, is doomed to reproduce and repeat the anxieties, repressions, and censorships that provoke the dream. It wishes away the aggression, the conflict, and the paranoia that are also part of urban experience. The city is not a problem that can be solved. It is the eternal, *impossible question of how we strangers can live together*. Rebuilding a living city – a city which jumbles together multiple and conflicting differences – therefore requires less a utopian plan than a poetics of political imagination.

(Donald, 1997, pp.182; emphasis added)

The quote hints at the dilemma of trying to sanitize or view the city in some 'holistic' or over-arching way that ignores the tensions that exist as part of city life. Note that Donald suggests that those who aim for this utopian city try to 'get the city right' for 'the right citizens'. My immediate response to this was, who are the 'right citizens'? Do you have to have a particular skin colour, gender or political stance or just support the right football team?! Or perhaps we create the 'right people' as George Orwell did in *Nineteen Eighty-four*, where Big Brother is watching to ensure that people behave in a particular way. Crucially, though, Donald makes it clear that the differences are in fact part of what makes a city: it is a cosmopolitan place, and we should be asking a different and impossible question about how 'strangers can live together' in the space of cities. To see why this might be an impossible question, we need only look at some of the tensions that arise in cities around the world to realize the complexity of trying to resolve them: each group has strong arguments to back up their case for space, and each forms a part of that cityscape. These tensions make up everyday life within a city, as the example in Extract 2.1 shows. This talks about a community which has defined itself in terms of the space it occupies ('over the bridge') and by its religion (see also Meegan, 1995).

EXTRACT 2.1
Pat Ayers: 'Over the Bridge'

Athol Street is situated in the north end of Liverpool and runs down between Scotland Road and Great Howard Street. Although intersected by Vauxhall Road and the viaduct which carries the Liverpool to Southport railway line, it is the Leeds/Liverpool canal which provides the main divide and sets apart the area over the bridge from the top end – a division which endures both for those who still live there and in the memories of those who have left; if they said, 'Where do you live?' you said, 'Over the Bridge'.

… All the basic needs of family, work, education, shopping, leisure and health care, were provided in the immediate area so there was little need for people to travel outside the security of familiar neighbourhoods. On top of this there was an expectation that children born and reared Over the Bridge would stay there after they left school, went to work and married: 'You stayed in your own community … It was sacrilege to marry out of Over the Bridge.' …

…

'… We used to stand out by the railway bridge, in Athol Street and throw stones as they were going to Southport. You know, on the twelfth of July, they [the Orange Lodge] used to go to Southport, always and ever … And as the trains would be going past, of course they knew it was a Catholic area, they'd throw all the lemonade bottles and everything out through the train windows. Needless to say, at night-time, when they were coming back there'd be retaliations.'

…

'… They'd have King Billy on a big rope on the twelfth of July and string it across Athol Street. And as soon as the train'd get near, they'd set fire to it and then the bottles would come out.'

Source: Ayers, 1990, pp.2–4, 58

Notice how important this space is to the people who live there, and the tensions it generates with neighbouring communities. In such a small space within this city there are very real tensions that periodically erupt in localized unrest. This extract brought home to me the sheer magnitude of differences that inevitably exist within a city in terms of culture, ethnicity and so on, and how difficult it would be to create a city without such tensions. I could certainly see Donald's point about needing a political imagination!

In this part of the course, we will explore the tensions and ideas that arise from different groups living in such close proximity to each other, which you have looked at in different parts of the course. In this way, the dilemma that Donald identifies should become clearer: why striving for a utopian city is so problematic as different groups try to co-exist in the same space.

1.1   WHAT DO WE MEAN BY 'THE SOCIAL'?

However, before we go any further with this discussion we need to define what exactly we mean by the term 'social'. This presents an immediate problem for me because I could go back through this course identifying 'social implications' in every aspect of city life that has been examined! In which case the course essay would take the form of a book, which is definitely not the aim! Obviously, we need to be careful here to be clear about what you need to focus on. Throughout the course 'the social' has been used as an *umbrella* to include all dimensions of society, cultural and economic, as in the references to 'social processes'. For example, authors have considered aspects that have ranged from transport, crime and surveillance, to global dimensions and an ordering of the cityscape through planning and administration. All of these have significant implications for the social fabric of the city and as you work through this theme, it is important to recollect its breadth. However, for the purposes of this part of the course we shall be focusing on a much narrower, more tightly defined set of aspects of the social theme: these are shown in Figure 2.1. You might choose not to look at all of these aspects, but simply to focus on one or two of them. Concerns will centre on how the various aspects of social life identified in Figure 2.1 are lived out within the physical structures of cities.

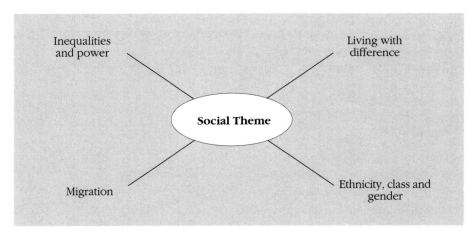

FIGURE 2.1   *The social theme*

1.2   THE COURSE ESSAY ON THE 'SOCIAL THEME'

The aim of this chapter is to provide you with the opportunity to develop key ideas and issues raised in the course materials within the context of a given theme, in this case particular social aspects of city life, through an examination of different forms of empirical information. Initially this will help you to decide which of the three themes you wish to choose for your course essay. If you choose to write a course essay on the social theme, then this chapter will guide you in how to set about writing it

Each of the course essay questions will not only ask about one of the themes, but also require a particular focus to your discussion based on course arguments (see the Course Essay Question Booklet). In the case of the social theme, you will be expected to consider a selection from the different aspects shown in Figure 2.1 in relation to the particular argument identified in the question. You will be required to demonstrate a familiarity with, as well as an understanding of, information contained in the course texts, audiocassettes and the TV series. There are additional readings provided at the end of this chapter which you may wish to draw on as well to enrich your essay.

In order to marshal the information effectively, you will need to think about how to make relevant use in your argument or discussion of the different forms of information that you have available. This is not as difficult as you may think. Stop and think for a minute about the various readings, newspaper cuttings, images, maps and graphs you have looked at during your study of the course.

These are all forms of empirical information: they provide information from a particular viewpoint, presented in different ways. In other words, throughout the course you have been developing the necessary skills to enable you to make use of the different materials in the course essay. This chapter will help you to develop these skills further.

This chapter has been organized to enable you to get the most from the 'social theme'. The next section re-examines the key course arguments and considers how they might apply to urban social issues, what questions they might prompt, what issues they require you to investigate, and so on. Following on from this, section 3 undertakes a selective review of the course with the social theme in mind. It should help you to begin drawing together the various aspects of this broad theme. It will not, however, do all the work, but simply start the process off. You will need to re-examine the course materials for yourself, to pull out the relevant points, and re-work them in a form you can use in your course essay. However, this section should give you some ideas and hints on what to look for.

This chapter also provides an additional body of information at the end of the chapter – extracts from articles and books, media cuttings, data – which we hope will be useful in providing extra resources to draw on in your course essay. The readings at the end of the chapter contain a wealth of empirical information upon several different large cities around the world. They will provide you with fresh material to add to the examples you have already encountered in other parts of the course. They have been carefully selected to give interesting perspectives on urban issues pertinent to this theme. You are encouraged to draw on this resource to develop and enrich your course essay.

Writing the course essay is the point in the course when you can bring in any relevant materials that you have collected yourself during the year. We hope you will include your own current newspaper cuttings, articles and other forms of material, as long as they are used in an *appropriate* and *course-informed* manner. This would make the work more interesting and help you to start to apply the conceptual ideas used in the course and the different aspects of the social theme to current affairs. However, as indicated in the Chapter 1, the use of outside sources is optional and a top-scoring essay need not contain any other additional material, provided it uses the course materials effectively. Inevitably, you will need to be *selective* in the materials that you use to illustrate your argument (see Chapter 1). But it is important that you select from a range of course components, including the TV programmes and audiocassettes as well as the course texts.

In this way, the course essay provides you with the opportunity to utilize the transferable skills that you have developed throughout the course and apply them to different and diverse materials. The temptation is to jump right into the readings at the end and get on with the business of drafting the course essay. However, the rest of this chapter is crucial to an understanding of the social theme, placing it in the context of the course material: a 'rushed job' will miss the point – and the marks!

2 *Key course arguments and 'the social'*

Each of the course essay questions will ask you to examine a theme from a particular focus. The focus will be based around three sets of course arguments. This will require you to re-work and connect earlier materials in new ways, as well as incorporating some of the new material provided in the three 'theme guides' in Chapters 2–4 of this book. In this section we will look at these broad course arguments and the social issues and questions they might prompt, while each of the subsections focus on one particular set of arguments.

2.1   THINKING SPATIALLY ABOUT SOCIAL ISSUES

Before we consider some of the key dilemmas that this argument might generate in relation to the aspects of the social theme that we are considering, let's take time to think about the types of issues you should be thinking about. You will have realized by now that the spatial configuration of the city can result either in the mixing of people or in their physical separation. In this way, the multitude of different groups of people experience city life in often contrasting or conflicting ways. As a result of this, people are connected to some parts of city life in varying degrees and not others and this will in turn affect their imagination of it. Thus, the ways in which people view the layout of the city and the important places within it are often very different.

ACTIVITY 2.1   Look at the photos below. They are taken from an exhibition of photographs of landmarks in Cape Town taken by young people aged ten to eighteen. Take a moment to look at the images. What do you see and what does it say about the young people themselves? Can you see why these images might provide an interesting insight into the social aspects of city life? ◆

(a)   A drawing of Cape Town on the walls of Ashley Court, Lavender Hill (Photo: Marwaan Manuel)

(b)   Kaapse Klopse finals, Green Point Stadium (Photo: Andrea Eden)

(c)   Angel in the Anglican Cemetery, Groote Schuur Hospital, Observatory (Photo: Jason Cope)

(d)   Waiting for the train, Wynberg Station (Photo: Yvette Kruger)

(e)   Changing booths, Muizenberg Beach (Photo: Jolene Martin)

FIGURE 2.2   *Photographs from* Cape Town: Landmarks of a New Generation, *organized by The Getty Conservation Institute. (All photographs courtesy of the J.Paul Getty Trust.)*

(f)   Behind Streets Community Service Project, Woodstock (Photo: Dominique Johnson)

(g)   Siphiwo stalking a dog at No. 42, NY 70, Nyanga (Photo: Percival Nkonzo)

What struck me was the diversity of pictures and the different definitions of the landmarks of that city. They offer a glimpse of the very different stories and imagery of a city that each person and each group experience. They also indicate the different interpretations of the space of the city and the importance attached to places within it. Have another look at the reading on communal places (**Bk 3 Reading 4C**). This reading enables us to develop this line of thinking a bit further. Look at the way in which particular communal structures in the city form the focus of each of the individual's maps. They centre on the familiar, or those buildings or places which have a particular meaning to them, such as the Ithna-Asheri mosque for Jamila, or the Catholic church for Francis. As the author, Richa Naga, observes, it shows us clearly that there is no single interpretation or experience of the city. But it also indicates the role that these communal buildings and residential areas indirectly play in intensifying racial segregation and stereotyping. Immediately this presents a social dilemma because the very communities that offer some stability and security to people, help to reinforce the lines of difference and the tensions between the various groups, as Extract 2.1 from 'Over the Bridge' showed.

ACTIVITY 2.2   Now read Extract 2.2 which is taken from *Pole to Pole* by Michael Palin. At this point in his journey Michael Palin has arrived in Istanbul and this is his brief commentary on what he, as a traveller, experiences of the city and its people. As you read, think about connections with the different aspects of the social theme. ◆

EXTRACT 2.2
Michael Palin: from *Pole to Pole*

Istanbul is a very noisy city, much of the noise from a huge construction programme. A companion to the famously crowded Galata Bridge across the Golden Horn is almost complete. A last massive section of its six-lane highway, waiting to be lowered into position, rears up at a right angle, a huge phallic symbol of regeneration. Sevim says the reconstruction is going on at such a pace that her husband, given a month's notice of redevelopment, went into work on Monday morning to find his shop gone. There are those with reservations about the pace of change. One is Altemur Kilic, a Turkish writer, diplomat and friend of Turgut Ozal, the President. He remembers Istanbul only 30 years ago as a city of 750,000 people, home to a flourishing number of foreign communities – Greek, Jewish, Armenian and what was known as Levantine, comprising Italians, English and French who had lived in Turkey all their lives. He himself went to the English-run Istanbul High School for Boys … Altemur played cricket, read the *Boy's Own Paper* and grew up in an Istanbul which was small enough to give him 'a sense of rather being somebody in a big city'. Now the city population has swelled to eight million and the real Istanbuliots, as he calls them, are very few.

As I step out of his elegant, unostentatious house on a small sloping street in Emirgan, I could be in the South of France, with the blue waters of the Bosporus catching the sunlight, people taking a drink or a coffee beneath the shade of ash and mimosa trees and the almost unbroken line of passing traffic.

Down by the Galata Bridge, close by the old spice markets, the pace of Istanbul life is at its most frenetic. Ferries are constantly loading and unloading providing a regular and copious passing trade for the street food sellers. Fishermen dart in, light up charcoal braziers and rocking crazily in the wash of the ferries sell their grilled catch then and there. You could have a street dinner every night of the week here and never eat the same menu twice … As a result of the climate, history and geographical position, Istanbul is the quintessential trading city. Russia and the Mediterranean and Europe and Asia meet here, and though a walk through the endless arcades of the old covered market gives an overwhelming sense of richness and variety, there is no better place to see trade in its rawest, purest form than the square outside the gates of the Beyazit II Mosque and the impressive Islamic-arched entrance of Istanbul University. Here an extraordinary dance of commerce goes on. Groups are constantly gathering, splitting and reforming. Eyes always on the move. These are furtive people on the very edge of the law, buying and selling in the spirit, if not the currency, of this great commercial city. There are Azerbaijanis, Iranians, Poles, Romanians, Ukrainians and Afghans. Most of them sell out of black plastic bags. I see Marlboro cigarettes traded for dollars and plastic train sets, cheap Eastern European trainers, an anorak, some metal ornaments – all attracting the crowds.

By the end of this hot, hard day the ministrations of a proper Turkish bath, a hammam, are irresistible.

The Cagaloglu Hammam, a splendid emporium of cleanliness, is this year celebrating 300 years in business, during which time it has cleaned amongst others, King Edward VII, Kaiser Wilhelm, Florence Nightingale and Tony Curtis. I can choose from a 'self-service bath' – the cheapest option, a 'scrubbed assisted bath', a 'Massage à la Turk – you'll feel years younger after this vigorous revitalizing treatment' or the 'Sultan Service', which promises, modestly, that 'you will feel reborn'. At 120,000 Turkish lira, about £17, rebirth seems a snip …

Source: Palin, 1992, pp.94–9

Notice the way in which the old is being removed from the cityscape to make way for the new developments. These developments in the spatial layout of the city are, however, apparently generating tensions among some of the urban populace, as one set of dominant rhythms is superseded by another. There is a hint that these developments are generating lines of inequality as some, like Sevim's husband, have their lives disrupted to make way for new enterprises.

However, we can see how the old rhythms nevertheless remain as part of the structure of the city but, like the Aztec pyramid in *La Plaza de las Tres Culturas* **(Bk 1 Ch. 3)**, or São Paulo's Anhangabaú valley **(Bk 1 Ch. 2)**, it reflects a former set of interconnections that existed within and between that city and other places. The writer whom Michael Palin talks to, Altemur Kilic, appears to come from an affluent household and his experiences of city life as a boy reflect many of the traits that characterized the élite members of society during the empire. These experiences are likely to be very different from those of Sevim and her husband, again highlighting the very different experiences individuals have of city life. Kilic's recollections of the 'old Istanbul' show that even then it was a meeting-place of different cultures and traditions; a trading hub at the centre of a very different set of interconnections. Notice his concerns over the rapidly increasing size of the city – a result, we are told, of huge influxes of migrants **(Bk 3 Ch. 2)**. The spatial configuration of the 'new Istanbul' juxtaposes old with new: the Cagaloglu Hammam baths and the Beyazit II Mosque close to the imposing new companion to the Galata Bridge that is being constructed. The square near the university displays the active mixing of different people that was shown in the illustration of the Bombay bazaar **(Bk 1 Ch. 3)**. It has a feeling of mixing rather than segregation; a blurring of social boundaries, in sharp contrast to the gated communities of the wealthy **(Bk 3 Ch. 3)** and the racially defined Asian areas of Kariakoo **(Bk 3 Ch. 4)**. These provide really good contrasting views of 'living with difference' and 'ethnicity', aspects of the social theme identified in Figure 2.1: they illustrate the complex ways in which different groups of people, defined along lines of 'race', class and wealth, and living in close proximity to one another, are able to co-exist.

However, the picture of Istanbul is much more complex than it might first appear to a traveller. Have another look at section 4.1 (in **Bk 3 Ch. 2**) where Gerry Mooney has a closer look at some of the social tensions that the juxtaposition of old and new have produced. Gerry points out that this modernizing of the cityscape has involved a re-ordering of space in an attempt to reimagine the city along the lines of a European city. Michael Palin's feelings about stepping out into somewhere in the South of France would clearly have produced a few smiles of satisfaction from the city planners! This re-ordering has meant the separation of areas into functional zones, a social distancing from the migrant *gecekondus* and the emergence of *Bahceshirs* or 'garden cities' as a retreat for the middle classes. Here the old, with its gendered yet unsegregated spaces, is giving way to new spaces that are producing inequalities and tensions along apparently new lines. We could be forgiven for using the saying 'in the good old days …'! Clearly, though, new connections have since been created that make a return to the old impossible to achieve.

As Extracts 2.1 and 2.2 and the readings from the chapters have illustrated, the spatial argument – thinking spatially about social issues – focuses on the multiplicity of city life and how the different stories are drawn into the space of the city through its wider interconnections with other places. However, crucially it helps to inform us about how these multiple stories co-exist within this space.

There are a number of key dilemmas or questions that we might think about when using the course arguments. One example might be the following:

ACTIVITY 2.3   How does the spatial layout of the city produce tensions between different groups of people living there?

Take a moment to jot down how you might tackle this question by breaking it into its component parts. Think about these specifically in relation to the four aspects that we are focusing on in this theme, shown earlier in Figure 2.1. You might find it useful to use a mind map to jot down any first thoughts. (Look back at Figure 1.1 for an example.) You could then put them into some kind of order afterwards. ◆

The first thing that struck me was how wide-ranging this question is and how much I could write as an answer. This is why it is not only useful but in fact very important to think about more specific questions that we would need to ask if we are to construct a succinct and measured account. Using a mind map helps because afterwards you can sift through all the ideas that you have jotted down and pick out those that are relevant to the question. I came up with a whole series of smaller questions that we might need to consider; you have probably found others. This is how I would begin:

- I would need to know what forms of tensions might be produced within city life. There have been a number that have run through the course: **Bk 1 Ch. 4** provides a helpful starting-point; the Course Guide gives a really good overview; I could watch the final **TV** programme again, or listen to the audiocassette, **AC** 3 Side A, which has a discussion of various aspects of the social theme.

- The next question that I feel would need to be addressed is how these different tensions are experienced by various groups of people, such as migrants, ethnic minorities, women. There are many examples in the course: for instance, migrants and ethnic groups in Sydney **(TV)**; overseas Chinese **(Bk 3 Ch. 7)**; or the experiences of the coloured community in Cape Town **(Bk 3 Ch. 4)**. There are also examples of women's experiences of city life **(Bk 3 Reading 5A; Bk 2 Reading 6B)**, whilst some overall ideas about different city stories are given in the **TV** programmes as a whole.

- This in turn leads me to consider the extent to which this affects the lived experiences of these different groups: for example, are some moving towards greater segregation thereby separating themselves from 'other' groups within the city – such as the *Bahceshirs* or 'garden cities' and the gated communities both in **Bk 3 Ch. 3** or the role of nimbyism **(Bk 3 Ch. 5)**, or is there an active mixing going on, as in the Bombay bazaar **(Bk 1 Ch. 3)**?

- I might also examine the ways in which inequalities between different groups of people are reinforced by the spatial configuration of the areas in which they live. Thinking specifically about differences between groups, I might focus on differences in the experiences of women and those of men (for example, **Bk 3 Ch. 3**) or perhaps minority ethnic groups (for example, the Algerians in Paris **(Bk 3 Ch. 1)**). Similarly, we could consider the experiences that migrants have of city life: for instance, we could look at the élite migrants in Amsterdam **(Bk 2 Reading 1A)** or the migrants in Mexico City **(TV)**.

- Equally, I might consider the way in which the layout of housing areas on peripheral estates (e.g. **Bk 3 Ch. 2**), access to particular shopping areas (e.g. **Bk 3 Ch. 4**) or the design of the transport systems **(Bk 2 Ch. 2)** affect the lived experiences of these different groups.

- Finally, I might think about the way in which divisions and segregation are constructed within a city to separate groups from each other (e.g. **Bk 3 Ch. 4 and Ch. 7**) and the ways in which these have reinforced lines of inequalities within cities for example in Mexico City **(TV)** or the women in suburban areas **(Bk 3 Reading 1D)**.

As you can see, the question is very broad-ranging and allows us to tap into a whole set of issues from across the course materials, including television programmes and the audiocassettes. Clearly, though, other questions will draw on different chapters from the course and provide more pertinent examples, so remember to consider the course materials before selecting your examples. However, it is important that you focus tightly on some, though not necessarily all, of the aspects of the social theme shown in Figure 2.1 and then select appropriate examples to help you to illustrate your points.

2.2   INTENSITY OF CITY LIFE

A second argument that we need to think about focuses on the intensity of city life and how this relates to the aspects of the social theme that we are considering. Once again it would be useful just to recap what we mean by the intensity of city life. **Book 1 Chapter 4** emphasizes the way in which the interactions and activities of the people in cities create an intensity of social relations within the city and between cities. This intensity in turn is reflected in the way in which the city is organized and in its physical character. It was shown that the openness of cities can be seen in their role as nodes within a wider set of social relations and this openness allows the flow of people, money and goods into and out of the city adding to the intensity of the activities between the city and other places – something that was termed *open intensities*. Think back to the quote by Donald at the start of this chapter. Can you see the problems that he has with those who try to engineer the city? The idea of viewing a city as a bounded territory clearly misses the point about the 'openness' of city life.

In addition to this open intensity, it has also been suggested that the interactions of people within cities produces and reproduces *felt intensities* as a result of the spatial proximity of these intense activities and their interactions within the city itself. This can produce a positive vibrancy and generate a new cultural richness; however, it can also result in exclusion and disconnection as groups fight for space and privacy or to become part of the dominant rhythms of city life.

ACTIVITY 2.4   Now look at Extract 2.3, which comprises short passages from *Beyond All Pity*, a diary of a young Brazilian woman, Carolina Maria de Jesus, living in a *favela* or squatter settlement in São Paulo during the 1950s and '60s. Although her diary was written over thirty years ago, the problems facing the *favelados*, or residents of the *favela*, have altered little; indeed the number of these squatter settlements is increasing.

While you read this extract, think about the implications of overcrowding and the intensity of interactions between different people living in the *favela* and how it might affect their experiences and views of city life. ◆

EXTRACT 2.3
Carolina Maria de Jesus: from *Beyond All Pity*

I classify São Paulo this way: The Governor's Palace is the living room. The mayor's office is the dining room and the city is the garden. And the *favela* is the back yard where they throw the garbage … *(p.42)*

Oh São Paulo! A queen that vainly shows her skyscrapers that are her crown of gold. All dressed up in velvet and silk but with cheap stockings underneath – the *favela*. *(p.51)*

The worst thing in the *favela* is that there are children here. All the children of the *favela* know what a woman's body looks like. Because when couples that are drunk fight, the woman, so as not to get a beating, runs naked into the street. When the fights start the *favelados* leave whatever they are doing to be present at the battle. *(p.55)*

More new people arrived in the *favela*. They are shabby and walk bent over with their eyes on the ground as if doing penance for their misfortune of living in an ugly place. A place where you can't plant one flower to breathe its perfume. To listen to the buzz of the bees or watch a hummingbird caressing the flower with his fragile beak. The only perfume that comes from the *favela* is from rotting mud, excrement, and whisky.

Today nobody is going to sleep because the *favelados* who don't work have started to dance. Cans, frying pans, pots – everything serves to accompany the off-key singing of these night bums. *(p.57)*

While I was dressing I heard the voice of Durvalino arguing with a strange drunk. Women started to appear. They never miss these things. They can stand for hours and hours just watching. They don't think of anything even if they left a pot on the stove. A fight for them is just as important as the bullfights in Madrid are for the Spanish. *(pp.92–3)*

When I go into the city I have the impression that I'm in paradise. I think it just wonderful to see all the women and children so well dressed. So different from the *favela*. The different coloured houses with their vases of flowers. These views enchant the eyes of the visitors to São Paulo who never know that the most famous city in South America is ill with ulcers – the *favelas*. *(p.93)*

> I left my bed at five in the morning to get water. I don't like to be with those women because at the tap they speak of everybody and everything. I feel so bad. If I could only lie down for a while! But I don't have anything for the children to eat. The only thing to do is to go out. I left João studying. I only got ten cruzeiros and found some metal. I found a wood drill and a school boy asked for it. I sold it to him. He gave me three cruzeiros for a cup of coffee. I went by the street market. I bought a sweet potato and a fish. When I got back to the *favela* it was noon. I heated food for João and cleaned up the shack. Later I sold some tin cans and got 40 cruzeiros. I came back to the *favela* and made supper. *(pp.98–9)*
>
> Here in this *favela* you see things that would make your hair stand on end. A *favela* is a strange city … The drunks who are hidden during the day come out at night to bother you. *(p.99)*
>
> Source: de Jesus, 1990

There were a number of points that occurred to me as I read these extracts. I was struck particularly by the way in which Carolina made contrasts with other areas of the city that she was not a part of – it gave me a sense of the disconnection that the residents of the *favela* were experiencing. They had their own set of rhythms that constituted their everyday lives, ones that were hidden or obscured by the dominant rhythms of city life that, for example, the visitors would see. We can see the parallels here with the discussion of the dominant economic rhythms in Tanzania **(Bk 2 Reading 6B)**. In a similar way to the shanty town dwellers in São Paulo, the women in Tanzanian cities have created informal activities producing new rhythms of everyday life beneath the dominant rhythm of structural readjustment. Another point that you will have spotted was the obvious lack of privacy resulting from the sheer concentration of people within the *favela,* which meant that people's lives overlapped; their activities necessarily interacted with one another at a very intimate level with little scope for choice. Also, the actual fabric of the shacks appear in themselves to prevent any separation from the *favela* or enable a withdrawal into self. Carolina, in her fight to feed her family and cope with ill-health, is clearly repulsed by this intrusion and yet is unable to escape from it all. As a result of this, her diary appears to be her way of escaping from the intensity of life in the *favela.*

The felt intensity of living in such close proximity that is reflected in Carolina's diary is in stark contrast with the gated communities described in the course books **(Bk 1 Ch. 2; Bk 3 Ch. 3)**. They have arisen in response to fears produced by the intensity of city living and are an attempt to *de-intensify* urban space by demarcating privatized spaces. Indeed, if you have another look at Extract 2.4 on São Paulo by Teresa Caldeira **(Bk 1 Ch. 2)**, this demonstrates clearly how the proximity of different groups of people, such as those living in the *favelas*, generate fear and concerns about crime and danger. It is these fears that lead groups to put up physical barriers demarcating privatized, exclusive spaces, spaces that accentuate the inequality of relations between different groups.

Those living in the apartments gazing out and down from their secure homes onto the favelas will have very different experiences of city life compared to people like Carolina living in the *favela*, whose gaze and walk is stopped by the secure walls of the gated communities.

The extract from Carolina's diary illustrates vividly the effects of the intensity of city life on one particular group of people within a city. However, it was clearly pointed out that the experiences of various groups of people in cities are very different, reflecting the inequalities that cross-cut and divide city life (see **Bk 1 Ch. 4**). Consider again the example of Benedita da Silva **(Bk 3 Reading 2A)**. There are clear lines of similarity between the experiences of the two women, but nevertheless some striking contrasts. Both live amidst poverty and grew up in areas that have been almost disconnected from the rest of city life, whilst their experiences of the city have also been coloured by their gender. However, whilst Carolina has a distanced view of the wealthier classes, Benedita has worked among them and 'cleaned the bottoms of several leading public figures' and now meets them on equal terms. What strikes me immediately, though, is the way in which Benedita's political role means that the shanty town where she lives is now connected to other places, including the President of France's personal office! For me, this offers a vivid illustration of the 'open intensities' at work in cities.

The extracts and readings in the chapters provide many other examples of how the intensity of city life relates to the different aspects of the social theme. Crucially, they indicate that, as cities grow, the activities of different groups living in them lead to an *intensification* of the social relations, thereby increasing the tensions that already exist within cities. Once again a number of issues arise when course arguments are applied. A possible course essay question would be:

ACTIVITY 2.5   In what ways do the different activities that occur in cities result in social conflict?

Once again, jot down what questions you would need to ask in order to address this question. Remember to select from the four aspects of this theme shown earlier in Figure 2.1. ◆

This question is very wide-ranging and there are many different ways of tackling it. Here is a set of questions that I might start off with, but clearly there are others just as valid. Crucially, this is a process of piecing together evidence from the rest of the course and, as such, it is important to develop a method of working that *you* feel happy with. In other words, this is just one way of tackling the course materials and it is not the definitive model!

So, this is the list I came up with:
- First, I would need to specify what groups I was talking about – in this case the focus would be on men and women of different social groups, minority ethnic groups and migrants.

- The next question might focus on the types of interactions that we are talking about: for example, the patterns of work, the travel patterns or the residential areas of the city.

- Then, do these patterns of interactions vary within the different groups of people with whom we are concerned – such as the racial patterning seen in Dar es Salaam **(Bk 3 Reading 4C)**?

- This leads on to thinking about power relations and inequalities: so, for example, which of these patterns of interaction within the city generate the greatest intensity and create the dominant rhythms of city life? We could think about the financiers in London, New York or Tokyo **(Bk 2 Ch. 6)**.

- Then there are the other, less obvious patterns of interaction that are obscured by the dominant ones but nevertheless form part of the rhythms of city life: as in the case of Filipina migrants **(Bk 1 Ch. 2),** or the women in the suburbs or the black residents of Harlem **(Bk 3 Ch. 1)**.

- Similarly, we might consider how these different patterns are juxtaposed to one another or even overlap yet remain apart from one another (see, for example, **Bk 1 Ch. 2**).

- It is important to consider the way in which the spatial patterns of the city affect these diverse groups, so we should ask whether the spatial configuration of the different areas of the city might help to shape the intensity of the interactions between different groups. For example, the restrictions on where certain groups can locate in the city may result in overcrowding in particular areas. In contrast, the need to avoid 'other' groups can in turn produce structures in the city's fabric that alters its physical layout, as with the *Bahceshirs* ('garden cities') in Istanbul **(Bk 3 Ch. 2)**.

2.3 URBAN TENSIONS

The third and final set of arguments we need to consider focuses on the urban tensions that cross-cut city life as different groups of people attempt to co-exist within the same space of cities. A useful starting-point would be to consider what we mean by urban tensions. Throughout the course you will have seen that the drawing-in of different groups into the space of cities can generate either new mixtures or new divisions. It is the sheer numbers of different people coming together and living close to one another within the space of cities that generates this potential mixing or division. Thus, the co-existence of different groups from a multitude of cultural and social spheres presents us with a whole set of tensions within the fabric of cities. You have encountered a number of these across the course: for example, community and difference, movement and settlement, sociability and anonymity, order and disorder. These tensions are highly ambiguous in their impact, affecting the lived experiences of people in very different ways and, as a result, have often been presented in the course as paradoxes.

For example, city life allows the creative mixing of different social groups, offering new opportunities for some people, while, for others, it instils a fear and a need to seek safety in a community. Think, for instance, of the segregated Chinese community in Vancouver **(Bk 3 Extract 4.1)**, or the fortified shopping malls and gated communities of many North American cities **(Bk 3 Ch. 3)**. Similarly, city life can offer the possibility of anonymity, of being a stranger, like Elise and Arezki in Paris as they avoid the police **(Bk 3 Extract 1.1 and Reading 1A)**; anonymity, moreover, can offer new opportunities or freedoms of expression, as for the women breaking away from the rigid social rules of Victorian Britain **(Bk 2 Ch. 3)**; while for others this anonymity is a source of extreme loneliness and isolation. We also saw how the shanty towns were viewed by city planners as disorderly areas for deviant social groups and therefore problematic, but in fact offered an orderly, responsive and self-organized community for the residents **(Bk 3 Ch. 2)**.

ACTIVITY 2.6   Before you go any further, have another look at the quote by Donald at the beginning of the chapter. We can see a bit more of the dilemma that Donald is hinting at – for every city-dweller the experience of city living is clearly very different and their needs will also vary considerably. In order to 'get the city right' we would be faced with the unanswerable question, 'for whom?'. ◆

In this section we shall have a look at community and difference as one example of urban tensions, but it is important not to neglect the other tensions when you begin to answer the course essay. In the Course Guide, Phil Pinch explains community and difference as 'a tension between the sociability of community life and feelings of anonymity amid the differences and sheer numbers of people in cities.' In addition, there is the argument that now that cities are home to many different groups of people, 'communities' seem to have become increasingly difficult to identify (see Chapter 1 of this volume). Indeed, as Linda McDowell observes **(Bk 2 Ch. 3)**, because the move to the city often brought with it greater social and spatial freedoms, some people came to live in the city specifically to escape from 'community'. For instance, we might think of the 'new' woman of the twentieth century for whom the city offered anonymity and a new set of opportunities for social interactions. In terms of the social theme, we can see how being a stranger and the anonymity associated with it allowed new lived experiences to be created along different lines of equality. In contrast, for other groups there appear to be pressures to construct or reconstruct community, as the example of New York's Little Italy shown in Figure 2.3 illustrates.

The tension between community and difference has been developed throughout the course. Indeed, you may recall that it was suggested that the rise of technology is leading to a 'deskilling' of workers which has resulted in an increasing need to derive a sense of self-identity, self-worth and stability from a community rather than the workplace **(Bk 2 Ch. 3)**. Maspero's accounts of people living in the Aulnay 3000 estate in Paris, where security and social networks have been established over time in the face of harsh employment conditions **(Bk 2 Extracts 3.1, 3.2 and 3.3)**, and the account of Benedita da

FIGURE 2.3 *In New York's Little Italy, residents recreate the celebration of the Feast of San Gennaro with market stalls bearing foods reminiscent of its Italian connections. However, the festival lasts eleven days – a world away from Naples where the tradition began and where it remains a one-day religious event.*

Silva's life in her shanty town **(Bk 3 Reading 2A)** are good examples of this. However, we can see from Iris Marion Young's arguments **(Bk 3 Ch. 4)** that although, for some, community creates a unity and self-identity, it is often based on opposition to 'other' groups. Thus, we can see that communities often represent (outwardly at least) relatively homogeneous groups based on the exclusion of others who are different. If you have another look at Extract 2.1, 'Over the Bridge', at the start of this chapter, you can see how the two communities have established themselves in direct opposition to one another along lines of social difference, defining their communities by what they are not. In terms of the social theme, these communities can be defined, for example, in terms of migrant groups like the Little Italy of New York, or perhaps of ethnicity, as in the example of areas of Cape Town **(Bk 3 Ch. 4)**, or simply by class and wealth, as the examples of São Paulo in the previous section showed.

However, although there is often an outward unity displayed by many communities, there are inevitable internal differences that can be heightened between groups within the community. Think, for example, of the young Asian women in Balsall Heath in Birmingham **(Bk 2 Ch. 3)**.

ACTIVITY 2.7   Have a look at Reading 2A supplied at the end of this chapter; these extracts from *New Ethnicities* (Back, 1996) comprise a series of interviews with residents living in and outside of Southgate, an area of London. Notice the very different 'voices' of the people. Their experiences of that place indicate the complexity of the idea of community. Even those living within Southgate have very different views and experiences of that community. ◆

In the course materials we have seen how communities within cities are often juxtaposed with one another and how this can generate tensions. Indeed, in some cases, whole communities are moved to remove any perceived threat or concern, as in the example of the coloured residents in a middle-class area (Mowbray) of Cape Town **(Bk 3 Ch. 4)** or the low-income area located next to the downtown area of Cairo **(Bk 3 Ch. 3)**. In other cases we have seen how more affluent communities erect physical barriers to protect their space in the form of gated communities.

Have another look at section 2.3 in **Bk 3 Ch. 6,** in particular at the descriptions of Mexico City and London. For me, the descriptions of these two cities illustrate the inequalities and very different lived experiences of various communities within cities. The example of Spitalfields in London highlights the very real tensions that exist between communities occupying the same space and the social power relations attached to those tensions. The example of Mexico City in addition shows the way in which the different social experiences of communities are also reflected in different environmental experiences of city life, illustrating the important overlap between the social and environmental themes. We can take this further, though, if we look again at the chapter on city politics. **Book 3 Reading 5A**, 'Streetwise', illustrates clearly that not only do people experience the same space in very different ways, but that these experiences are linked to different and highly unequal power relations. Furthermore, these power relations can be connected to the ethnicity of the individuals: the 'voices' in Southgate hinted at differences along these lines (Reading 2A at the end of this chapter). We could also draw in the difference of gendered experiences: for instance, think back to the example of women in the suburbs **(Bk 3 Reading 1D)**.

ACTIVITY 2.8   Linda McDowell argues that conflicts can arise because of different social groups with overlapping uses of the same public space and she gives the example of Tompkins Square Park in New York **(Bk 2 Ch. 3)**. Now look at Reading 2G from 'Tompkins Square Park and beyond' at the end of this chapter which develops this account. While you read it, think about the way in which the different communities are juxtaposed and the unequal power relations involved. ◆

What really caught my attention in this reading is the way in which a single group of people in the city – the homeless – are being 'driven' from a particular space in the city. We can see parallels here with the attitudes of the officials to the low-income groups in the extract on Cairo or the way in which the 'working girls' were forced out of the Balsall Heath community by a local group of men (both in **Bk 2 Ch. 3**). However, at the end of the reading on Tompkins Square Park I was struck by the fact that this group was joined by 'Jewish grandmothers'! It conjures up a vivid picture in my mind of the 'mixing-pot' of people living in cities, the ever-changing nature of communities and their blurred boundaries. The inequalities and power relations between and within communities are clearly not static but appear to be constantly shifting.

Once again there are a number of key dilemmas that we might consider with respect to urban tensions. One of these might be:

ACTIVITY 2.9   Why does the juxtaposition of some communities generate conflict while in other cases tmhere is tolerance and respect?

Take some time now to think about this question with respect to the social theme and jot down your ideas. Again, I shall use a series of smaller questions to do this, but you should develop whatever method you feel comfortable with. ◆

Once again, the question is very broad and although on the surface may appear simple, it opens up a whole set of ideas. For example,

- A starting-point might be to think about the different types of communities in cities. For example, there are the élite business communities in Mexico City and London **(Bk 3 Ch. 6)** or in Moscow, Singapore and Kuala Lumpur (see **TV**), the migrant communities such as the Syrian, German and Italian communities in Chicago **(Bk 1 Ch. 1)**, or the squatter settlements or *gecekondus* of Istanbul **(Bk 3 Ch. 2)**.

- The next question might focus on why some communities are intolerant of one another. Here we might think about fear, insecurity and the close proximity of 'other' groups. There are many examples of this throughout the course: for instance, the gated communities in US cities **(Bk 3 Ch. 3)** or in São Paulo or Istanbul **(Bk 2 Ch. 1 and Bk 3 Ch. 2)**.

- This might lead on to thinking about whether this intolerance is based on differences between the various groups of people living in these communities and, if so, in what ways. You may find the **TV** programme on Sydney useful for this.

- We could also consider whether these differences are based on unequal social power relations. For this we would need to look at the differences between the communities that are juxtaposed to one another in the city. We would also need to think about whether the differences between the communities have changed over time. For instance, we could look at the example of the Chinese community in Vancouver **(Bk 3 Ch. 4)**.

- Finally, we would need to consider whether some communities do manage to co-exist and how this might be the case. But we would need to be careful here to remember the dilemma raised in the quote by Donald – that different people experience city life in very different ways and what works for one group of communities will not necessarily work for others.

This section has tried to get you thinking about how course arguments can be used to explore urban social issues. Here we have looked at each argument in turn, but hopefully you will have noticed that they are in fact far from separate. Each has been presented in this way to help you to focus your initial thinking. However, it is possible you will need to draw in aspects of the other two arguments to develop an adequate answer.

3 Developing a strategy: pathways through the course material

Chapter 1 of this volume provides a clear strategy for developing your course essay: what this section will try to do is to make you think through the detail of this strategy by applying it to the social theme. You may find it useful at this point to have another look at the checklist laid out in section 4 of Chapter 1 before you go any further. This section will outline three main stages:

- *Stage 1:* Mapping key aspects of the theme
- *Stage 2:* Identifying key theoretical arguments
- *Stage 3:* Making cross-course links.

3.1   STAGE 1: MAPPING KEY ASPECTS OF THE THEME

To be able to address the question, we will need to review the earlier parts of the course, but this time drawing out the relevant arguments, materials and examples of each book that connect with the four aspects of the social theme that we shall be examining. However, before we can do this, the first stage is to think about the four social aspects in turn and make a map of what material each chapter might (broadly) provide. A good way of mapping this type of information is to produce a 'mind map' that indicates the type of material and the source. Figure 2.4 shows my attempt at doing this for some of the key points in Book 1, but you might also want to refer back to the notes on mind maps in Chapter 1 section 4.

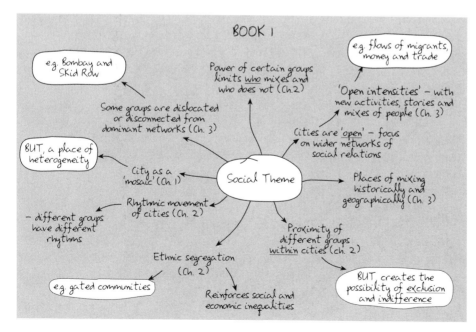

FIGURE 2.4
Mind-map for
Book 1

An alternative method that you could use if you find mind maps unhelpful is simply to list the key components in each chapter that are relevant to the theme. Box 2.1 shows my brief jottings of some – *but not all* – of the key issues in the first three chapters of Book 2. However, with either method it is important to restrict yourself to the key points, otherwise the list or the mind map will be huge!

BOX 2.1: Book 2

Chapter 1:
- Juxtaposition of different groups of people – produces tensions of insecurity, fear, crime
- Asymmetrical power relations exist between diverse groups
- Social distancing of groups through built environment – gated communities – produce new patterns of social segregation
- City is a place of hybrid meanings and identities – time-space extensibility

Chapter 2:
- Transport arteries producing divided communities – entrenchment of racial segregation
- Racial tensions – fear of walking the streets, gated communities
- Differential access to transport – affects the way groups view the city

Chapter 3:
- Anonymity and fear – social segregation – no mixing
- Innovation and excitement – creative, mixing, hybridity

ACTIVITY 2.10   Thinking about the different aspects of the social theme noted in Figure 2.1, you should repeat this process, drawing out the relevant arguments, materials and examples from each chapter for the rest of Book 2 and for Book 3, using either one of these methods. Alternatively, you may wish to try another method of mapping the information. The key is to use a form that *you* feel is going to be clear for you to use in later work. ◆

Having produced a list or map of the various chapters in the three books, you need to think about how to tackle the material contained within each. We saw earlier that the social theme, even narrowly defined for our purposes, is multi-dimensional in nature so that each of the different aspects conveys many stories each with its own spatial character. What this means in terms of the course essay is that it is not possible to answer a question adequately on the social theme using a single chapter. Rather, what you will need to do is develop a set of notes that looks across the chapters and which allows you to build up an integrated view of some of the aspects of the theme. The next sections will try to show you how to make these links across the chapters.

3.2   STAGE 2: IDENTIFYING KEY THEORETICAL ARGUMENTS

The next stage is to think about the theoretical arguments you might need to consider regarding the different aspects of the social theme. The key starting-point for thinking about this is Book 1 where there is the initial discussion of what a city is and the different worlds that compose cities.

ACTIVITY 2.11   Jot down very briefly what you think are the key arguments in each of the chapters in Book 1. Hint: you are only looking for a few key points and you should be able to identify these from the bullet points in the chapters.   ◆

Here are my thoughts on this.

In Chapter 1 of Book 1 we are presented with the city as a collection of images that have social significance. In addition to this, the notion of a 'geographic plexus' was introduced to highlight the way in which cities are composed of a series of networks ' ... through which flows, interchanges and interactions take place' (**Bk 1 Ch. 1** p.16). It can also be seen as a place of heterogeneity where different groups of people come together creating new forms of culture and social interactions with a multitude of different stories, often paradoxical in nature. In Chapter 2 we can add to this the different rhythms of city life that result from the activities of these different groups of people as they move about the city. Crucially, the chapter argues that ' ... cities bring all kinds of relationships into close proximity yet, by virtue of the juxtapositions produced, create the possibility for indifference and exclusion ...' (**Bk 1 Ch. 2** p.62). Indeed, the power of certain groups effectively limits the degree of mixing, thus the heterogeneity of the city observed in Chapter 1 is nevertheless characterized in parts of the city by forms of segregation and exclusion, as the examples of the residential enclaves and gated communities showed. Chapter 3 showed the way in which the different stories and histories are produced and reproduced as a result of a city's wider social interconnections, drawing flows of people into the 'open' city and adding to the intensity of activities within that place. However, different groups of people are connected by different networks to different places, whilst others are disconnected and these add to the divisions within a city, observed in Chapter 2. This point is extended in Chapter 4 by the observation that the spaces in the city are not only divided but include rhythms and interactions that are highly unequal.

Thus, the picture that we take away from Book 1 is that the different social relationships of a city cross-cut urban space with very different sets of rhythms, movements and the power relations that are attached to them, making some spaces and groups more dominant than others. It indicates that the lived experiences of city life for various groups of people will be marked by difference and diversity – a multiplicity of social stories – that sometimes overlap or are juxtaposed to one another.

Before we go any further, let's consider how these theoretical points might be applied to an understanding of city life.

ACTIVITY 2.12   Now read the two extracts reproduced below from Jonathan Raban's *Soft City*. As you read them, think about how these extracts relate to the different theoretical points about the city that we considered for Book 1.

What is your response to Raban's statement that, 'The city as we imagine it, the soft city of illusion, myth, aspiration, nightmare, is as real, maybe more real than the hard city one can locate on maps in statistics ...' (Raban, 1974/1998, p.4)?

How do the extracts relate to arguments about the city ' ... as an assemblage of seemingly contradictory social relationships' (**Bk 1 Ch. 1** p.50)? ◆

EXTRACT 2.4
Jonathan Raban: from *Soft City*

A

In October 1972 when the evenings had begun to darken early in London, a nineteen-year-old boy stepped out of Nash house on the Mall, Decimus Burton's splendidly laid-out approach to Buckingham Palace. The boy had been watching a movie at the Institute for Contemporary Arts, was bored, and wanted a cigarette. Just outside the ICA is a wide flight of steps, scantily lit and shaded by trees. The boy came out here for his smoke. It was a warm, Indian-summery night, and the Mall was buzzing with strolling couples and tourists out after dinner from their hotels. When the movie ended, the crowd emerging from the ICA mistook the boy's body for a zonked junkie or a pavement drunk. It's the sort of thing you see often enough in Piccadilly; here it was misplaced, an incongruous touch of squalor on this much swept and tended triumphal avenue.

The boy will live, but he will be permanently paralysed. Two men he said, came at him from the side of the steps: one gagged him with his hand, the other got his arm round his neck and severed his spinal cord with a $2\frac{1}{2}$ inch blade of a penknife. The whole encounter had a ghastly surgical precision. Nothing was stolen; the men were total strangers ... We have so separated ourselves, person from person and group from group, in the city, that we have made hatred a dreadfully easy emotion.

...

B

In the city, we are barraged with images of the people we might become. Identity is presented as plastic, a matter of possessions and appearances; and a very large proportion of the urban landscape is taken up by slogans, advertisements, flatly photographed images of folk heroes – the man who turned into a sophisticated dandy overnight by drinking a particular brand of vodka, the girl who transformed herself into a latter-day Mata Hari with a squirt of cheap scent ... For the new arrival, this disordered abundance is the city's most evident and alarming quality. There are so many people he might become, and a suit of clothes, a make of car, a brand of cigarettes, will go some way towards turning him into a personage even before he has discovered who that personage is … the adept city-dweller is engaged in the constant manipulation of these stylistic quantities [of the different commodities], continuously relating his self-presentation to his audience through the medium of such expressive objects.

Source: Raban, 1974, pp.4–6, 59–62

There is quite a lot we can draw out from these extracts. For example, Steve Pile argues that urban life offers a whole set of paradoxes, an ambivalence or set of tensions that run through urban living **(Bk 1 Ch. 1)**. He observes that, 'there is something paradoxical here about the individual's relationship with city life: it is both liberating and stifling; both stimulating and deadening' (p.44). In the first of the two extracts we can see the mixture of excitement and danger that the city offers juxtaposed – the crowds out for their stroll and those leaving the movie compared to the very graphic description of the boy, a victim of the dangers of the anonymity that city life brings. But we can see that these experiences overlap, for the boy was initially part of the former group out to have a good time in the hub of city night life. In contrast, the second extract shows the potential of city life – the effect of the heterogeneity of the city – the ability to adopt your own identity. It highlights how the new forms of social interaction and other forms of culture are produced and reproduced as people interact with others or react to other groups around them.

3.3   STAGE 3: MAKING CROSS-COURSE LINKS

What the last section started to do was to make theoretical links between the various points raised in the different chapters in Book 1. This section is intended to show you how to make cross-course links between chapters based on aspects of the social theme. This is an important exercise because a crucial part of the course essay is for you to demonstrate that you can draw out the key course arguments and apply them, in this case to the social theme. In order to do this effectively it is useful to be systematic in your initial trawl through the course, working through each book in turn, identifying key arguments and making cross-course links. Here we will try to work through this process using the first three chapters of Book 2. So, first of all, we need to have a good look at each of these early Book 2 chapters in turn and identify the key social aspects that are developed in each.

Book 2 Chapter 1

In Chapter 1, Amin and Graham observe that, 'Streets, parks, squares, shopping areas, cafés and restaurants are often places of connection where different relational webs meet and overlap – mixtures of migrants, itinerants and locals, as well as different social and ethnic cultures' (section 3.1, p.16). However, these juxtapositions of difference, they argue, produce variegation or diversity in city life and often they create tensions such as a fear of crime or feelings of insecurity which can reproduce themselves in physical forms of exclusionary development.

Look, for example, at the extract on 'Fortress America' by David Dillon (**Bk 1 Extract 1.1**) and that on São Paulo by Teresa Caldeira (**Bk 1 Extract 1.2**). These extracts indicate that these groups are establishing social distancing yet remain in spatial proximity to the poorer groups within the cities. (Remember the parallel points that Steve Pile makes about groups on Chicago's Gold Coast (**Bk 1 Ch. 1**).) These developments, we are told, are producing and reproducing new patterns of social segregation which draw upon the tensions of fear and excitement that at one and the same time attract groups to cities, but within the gated fortresses of exclusive forms of the built environment. However, a key point from the perspective of the social theme is that these new patterns are also generating new social forms along new lines of *inequality*. Furthermore, they suggest that this 'mixing' is occurring to groups all over the city as they interact or react with one another.

We are also told that the effects of spatial proximity can produce hubs of vitality in some parts of the city, but areas of disadvantage in others – the unequal social relations mentioned in **Bk 1 Ch. 4**. The extracts from the article by Denis Cosgrove, on the financial traders and the prostitutes, indicate the way in which different social groups are juxtaposed and that the spaces that they occupy overlap within cities (**Bk 1 Extract 1.5**).

Another key point made is that the city is composed of multiple time–spaces, so that not only do different groups overlap and interact with one another, but at different times of day and night the groups change and the interactions and frictions derived from them change.

ACTIVITY 2.13   Have another look at the quote from Donald at the beginning of this chapter. Can you see the point that he makes about the dangers of viewing the city in some holistic way that ignores the tensions that exist in city life? ◆

Donald suggests that, instead of this, cities need to be seen as places of multiple and conflicting differences. Furthermore, as Amin and Graham suggest, these differences are not static but change during the course of the day.

Finally, Chapter 1 also indicates that the city is actively engaged in constructing social and cultural identities which are hybrid, multi-dimensional, ambiguous and fluid, but again emphasizing that these constructions often involve highly unequal power relations tying different groups together within cities.

Book 2 Chapter 2

Now have another look at Chapter 2 by Hamilton and Hoyle. They suggest that the routes that transport arteries take produce divided communities. This extends the points made in **Book 1 Chapters 3 and 4** that different groups of people are connected in highly unequal ways by different networks to different places. Indeed, the transport networks not only physically divide different communities but can further entrench social segregation often along racial lines. If we then consider the role of differential access that occurs within a city, we can see how these divided communities are in fact cross-cut by other lines of division *within* them. This can be a particular problem for women, the elderly or the unemployed who may have limited access to private forms of transport, notably the car. For these groups the city represents a different, often dangerous, place as they tackle the different forms of public transport. This is of particular interest as we are thinking about the social theme because these groups need not be confined to the peripheral housing estates and squatter settlements, but can be part of the households that reside in the gated communities considered earlier. In this way people *within* communities differentiated by, for instance, their gender or age can have very different lived experiences even though they occupy similar residential spaces.

Book 2 Chapter 3

In Chapter 3 on movement and settlement, Linda McDowell looks at the diversity of areas within cities. She argues that the re-ordering of social and spatial relationships as cities expanded has created new divisions between the public workplace and the private space of the home, allowing people from different backgrounds and experiences to mix freely. This portrays a much more positive image of life in the city, with mixing that generates a cultural vibrancy as diversity produces innovation and excitement, a very similar image to that portrayed in Extract 2.4(B) in the previous section. For some groups, such as women, elderly or disabled people, these new divisions provide greater freedom and new experiences of life as old traditions mix with new ways, creating changes in people's lived experiences and new forms of identity – the heterogeneity of city life that Steve Pile refers to (**Bk 1 Ch. 1**). In this way the city provides anonymity and new opportunities for different groups, but particularly for women seeking to move beyond the social boundaries of suburban or rural lifestyles.

McDowell also observes the effects of globalization on cities, with the flows of migrants for reasons ranging from the economic, to natural disasters, such as flood or famine, and to persecution of some form. It is this diversity of migration that has created the variegation of urban population that Amin and Graham examine in Chapter 1. Yet we can see that this variegation is characterized at its extreme by two very different flows of people: those in the most well-paid jobs and those in the least well-paid jobs.

ACTIVITY 2.13   Think about the connections between Chapters 1, 2 and 3. In what ways do the migrant flows that McDowell observes add to our understanding of the different aspects of the social theme? ◆

For me, these two migration flows can be related to the asymmetrical power relations and fear of urban unrest observed in Chapter 1 and the issues of racial tensions, divided communities and access to transport in Chapter 2. In addition to this, McDowell suggests that the increasing job insecurity and unemployment resulting from economic restructuring in cities means that a person's identity may be related more to his/her home life than work. This raises concerns over practices of exclusion and intolerance: see Sennett's comments on this (**Bk 2 Ch. 3** pp.101–04).

ACTIVITY 2.14   Now re-read Extracts 3.1–3.3 in Book 2, which recount Maspero's travels to the suburbs of Paris and his encounters with the people there. As you re-read them, think about the following issues and how these extracts might add to our understanding of aspects of the social theme:

- Who lives in these areas?
- The role of transport in the development of separate cultural spaces
- The internal diversity of views of its inhabitants and also the planners
- The role of fear and insecurity in social segregation along ethnic lines. ◆

I was particularly struck by the links between the Maspero extracts and the transport chapter **(Bk 2 Ch. 2)**: not only are these people struggling economically, trying to find suitable work, but they are located on the periphery of the city away from the economic activities of the core. These people could be by-passed by rich Parisians; they were effectively disconnected and thereby excluded from the other parts of Paris as a result of the lack of efficient transport. Thinking about the social theme, it suggests that there is an inequality of power relations between the residents in this peripheral part of Paris and other groups, which is shaped by the physical structure of the city itself. This area has developed a level of cultural identity in response to this separation, although there are also indications that there are multiple identities *within* the area, alluded to by Akim's father. Groups differentiated perhaps by gender or ethnicity may have very different lived experiences within the same spaces of the city.

The following quote from Iris Marion Young has already been cited by McDowell **(Bk 2 Ch. 3** p.128). Notice the parallels between this quote and the one by James Donald at the start of this chapter:

> The ideal of community privileges unity over difference, immediacy over mediation, sympathy over recognition of the limits of one's understanding of others from their point of view. Community is an understandable dream, expressing a desire for selves that are transparent to one another, relationships of mutual identification, social closeness and comfort. The dream is understandable, but politically problematic, I argue, because those motivated by it will tend to suppress their differences among themselves or implicitly to exclude from their political group persons with whom they do not identify. The vision of small, face-to-face, decentralized units this ideal promotes, moreover, is an unrealistic version for transformative politics in mass urban society.
>
> (Young, 1990a, p.300)

Here, Young clarifies the problem of 'how [we] strangers can live together' within communities in a city. She identifies the difficulties of multiple and conflicting differences co-existing and the way in which attempts at such co-existence can in itself be externally divisive, even if there is some consensus within the community. From this we can see how these communities can create the possibility of exclusion and indifference (observed in **Bk 1 Ch. 2**) and can produce the new forms of social division that Amin and Graham talk about **(Bk 2 Ch. 1)**. They can be seen in the examples of the gated communities of Los Angeles, but also the ethnic communities of Aulnay in Paris or in Balsall Heath in Birmingham. All create new spaces that in doing so become exclusionary spaces for 'other' groups within the city who are defined by what they are not.

◆　　◆　　◆

What I have tried to do in this section is to draw out some of the links between these three chapters, but there are many more. Take some time now to go through the chapters again and see what other connections you can find.

Now think about the remaining chapters in Book 2 and also Books 1 and 3. Look at each of the chapters in turn and consider the ways in which different aspects of the social theme are developed through each. Remember, some of the chapters will contain much more on this theme than others.

And last, but not least, turn to the resource materials provided at the end of this chapter to find additional material relevant to your proposed course essay.

I hope this chapter has brought you to a point where you are confident to draw from across the whole range of materials available and to select and use relevant parts in a way which will serve the aims of your course essay.

References

Amdur, L., Baus, J., Cho, P., Conley, D., Duncombe, S., Joseph, H., Kessler, D., Parker, J., Song, H. and Zukin, S. (1995) 'The bubbling cauldron: global and local interactions in New York City restaurants' in Smith, M. P. (ed.) *After Modernism: Global Restructuring and the Changing Boundaries of City Life*, pp.105–32, Comparative Urban and Communtiy Research Vol. 4, London, Transaction Publishers.

Ayers, P. (1990) *The Liverpool Docklands: Life and Work in Athol Street*, University of Liverpool, Dockland History Project.

Back, L. (1996) *New Ethnicities and Urban Culture: Racisms and Multiculture in Young Lives*, London, UCL Press.

Baudrillard, J. (1988) *America*, London, Verso.

Bergen, M. (1997) 'Children in the city: an interview with the Mayor of Rio', *The Urban Age*, vol.5, no.1, p.23.

Dimenstein, G. (1991) *Brazil: War on Children*, London, Latin American Bureau.

Donald, J. (1997) 'This, here, now: imagining the modern city' in Westwood, S. and Williams, J. (eds) *Imagining Cities: Scripts, Signs, Memory,* pp.181–201, London, Routledge.

Gilbert, A. and Ferguson, J. (1994) *The Latin American City*, London, Latin American Bureau.

Gray, P. (1996) 'Renewal in a divided city', *Housing Review,* vol.45, no.3, July–August, pp.72–3.

Helmore, K. (1997) 'Out of the tunnel of urban childhood: helping the children of the urban poor emerge into a brighter future', *The Urban Age*, vol.5, no.1, pp.5–7.

Hopkins, R. (1997) 'City of the child-catchers', *Observer*, Review section, 23 February.

Housing Agenda (1997) 'Poverty has a woman's face', November, pp.9–10.

Jesus, C. M. de (1990) *Beyond All Pity*, trans. by David St. Clair, London, Earthscan (originally published as *Quarto de Despejo*, Lisbon, Livraria Francisco Alves, 1960).

Marks, K. (1998) 'Asian youth cynical about city policing', *The Independent*, 21 October, p.9.

Meegan, R. (1995) 'Local worlds' in Allen, J. and Massey, D. (eds) *Geographical Worlds*, Oxford, Oxford University Press/The Open University (D215 Book 1).

Merry, S. Engle (1981) *Urban Danger: Life in a Neighbourhood of Strangers*, Philadelphia, PA, Temple University Press.

Orwell, G. (1949/1989) *Nineteen Eighty-four*, Harmondsworth, Penguin in association with Secker & Warburg (first published 1949 by Secker & Warburg).

Pacione, M. (1997) *Britain's Cities: Geographies of Division in Urban Britain*, London, Routledge.

Palin, M. (1992) *Pole to Pole*, London, BBC Publications.

Smith, N. (1996) 'Tompkins Square Park and beyond' in King, A.D. (ed.) *Re-Presenting the City: Ethnicity, Capital and Culture in the 21st Century Metropolis*, London, Macmillan.

Resource materials for the social theme

As indicated in section 1, here are some additional resources provided for you in writing your course essay on the social theme. You will find that they are grouped by topic.

1 ARTICLES ON ETHNICITY

Reading 2A consists of extracts from qualitative interviews with people living in or near Southgate in London. It is an area that has signicant proportions of ethnic minority residents, from the Caribbean in particular. The author suggests that it is seen by those living in adjacent council estates as a 'no-go' area where there is a lot of crime. However, this is not a view held by the residents themselves.

Reading 2B offers a good example of inequalities of groups within cities.

READING 2A
Les Back: from *New Ethnicities and Urban Culture: Racisms and Multiculture in Young Lives*

Well, everybody says that [streets crime and mugging is prevalent], and I've got a friend who has been mugged three times, but I've walked through the estate and I've been coming home late at night and nothing ever happened to me … I think that certain sections of the community talk about it as being a big problem – that is mostly middle-aged white people who read the Daily Mail, you know.

… The only trouble that does happen on the estate is between rival black factions and that isn't much … I mean there are several families of white crooks, I think most of them are locked up now, but people don't think about that – they think, 'Ooh, a black area, there must be a lot of muggings.' But there has been very little aggression in the pub between whites and blacks and certainly the few times there have been police raids [on the pub] white people have been just as angry about it as black people, who were largely the people being arrested and put up against the wall. There were black and white people saying 'What the bloody 'ell do you think you are doing?' *(Debbie, 35-year-old white woman)*

Racial problems are not so much on Southgate. When I was livin' on the other side of the borough then there was racial arguments … My brother lived in that area and he had to be moved out because we had National Front sprayed on our door. I mean we had a fear, we were literally frightened to go home because we didn't know what was happening, we didn't know if there was going to be somebody waiting for us. We were burgled by the NF, they poured ink all over the carpet – it was a cream carpet and they poured red ink all over the house sort a thing. I mean that is basically why we moved out. I don't find much of the racial problems now because I think the area is too dominantly black. I mean out of the 74 houses in my block, 15 to 20 people are white, the rest are all black. I think I know of two Asian families living in the block. The Asian families, they don't come out of their house. *(Erwin, black, Jamaican parents)*

Funnily enough over the years it has grown into a family thing, white, black, all races. I see myself as Southgate to tell you the truth. And I know so many things, well I know things I shouldn't know. It just doesn't seem to matter any more down here, maybe in a different area, but down here everyone is integrated and mixed. I don't even think of colour, the way we integrate and mix and I know everyone. I could talk the most cockney you'd think that I was a white man standing the other side, or I could talk Jamaican and you wouldn't understand a word that I said, you know what I mean, so I fit in both worlds. I fit in perfect. There is no racist stuff, I want nothing to do with colour. *(Michael, 24, Jamaican parentage)*

Well, it just doesn't seem to matter what colour you are any more. People have learned to live together – maybe there are a few of the older ones – but this is a community area right now, it doesn't matter where you come from. *(Tony, 18, black, Jamaican parents)*

Southgate? Well, it is no more than a ghetto. In fact, they call it The Ghetto. Now the place is probably 60 per cent black, but in about five or ten years it'll end up somewhere near 80–90 per cent. Everybody who lives there wants to get out. People are getting up to their eyes in debt to get off the estate. I lived there for three years. The bloke next door was a complete animal. He had dreadlocks and everything. I am not racialist, but the man lived like an animal. I am not kidding – his house was full of cockroaches. The council had to fumigate the place several times.

[Later in the same interview]

I can see the estate turning into a black ghetto. Didn't you see it on the telly the other night? Postmen getting mugged. They are mugging the postmen to get at the giros, do you believe that? How low can you get? I am not racist, but mugging is a black problem. You look at the amount of muggings and most of them are black. I am not saying that whites don't get involved in crime, but that's mainly break-ins. What riles me is that people just won't do anything. I know

it sounds racist but it ain't right. *(Phillip, 25, with French and English parentage)*

It's very prejudiced – here it is unbelievable right, but the point is that it is undercover now … like when I was younger it was out in the open, you knew who was racist and I liked it better then. Yes, because people don't want to be called racist now because it is something to be ashamed of. *(Debbie, 19, white, German and Italian parents)*

Source: Back, 1996, pp.108–9, 105–6, 111–112, 116, 121

READING 2B

ASIAN YOUTH CYNICAL ABOUT CITY POLICING

BY KATHY MARKS

MOHAMMED, 19, is hopping mad. 'I'm on a 10pm curfew for breaching my bail conditions, right?' he says. 'So the police come round my house at 10 to check that I'm in. Then they come again at midnight, 1am, 3am, ringing the doorbell over and over, waking my little sister, upsetting my mum. They're just taking the piss, man.'

Mohammed and his three friends are slouched outside Nasim Food Store in Manningham, an inner-city area of Bradford scarred by poverty and neglect.

Three years ago, Manningham was thrust into the national spotlight when Asian youths clashed with police during two nights of rioting. Today, the Stephen Lawrence inquiry visits Bradford as part of its tour of the regions, seeking insights on the policing of minority communities.

Among those giving evidence to the one-day hearing will be Lloyd Clarke, Deputy Chief Constable of West Yorkshire, who has acknowledged institutional racism exists within the force.

The riots in summer 1995

were a severe jolt to Bradford, which had always prided itself on relatively good race relations. These were the first violent confrontations between police and Britain's traditionally peaceful Asian community. Images of young Muslim men hurling fire bombs and smashing shop windows were unparalleled.

Since then, West Yorkshire Police have implemented a series of initiatives aimed at improving community relations. The city is awash with multi-agency panels and partnerships, with consultation groups, youth forums and cultural awareness programmes.

Inspector Martin Baines, appointed to the newly created post of community and race relations officer for Bradford, says criticism of police made by an independent commission of inquiry into the riots was valid. The inquiry report concluded that officers lacked understanding of the mainly Pakistani community, and that they treated residents 'with hostility and contempt'.

'A lot has changed since the

disturbances,' Insp. Baines says. 'People have started to work together to build bridges and to make Bradford a safer place.'

But here, as in other parts of the country, there is a yawning gap between policy and practice. Asian youths claim they are targeted by police because of their colour and families complain that police fail to take reports of racial harassment seriously.

These are grave charges in a city where minority ethnic residents make up nearly 20 per cent of the population and suffer a high level of racially motivated crime – 213 incidents were reported to police in the year ending last March.

Ishtiaq Ahmed, the highly respected director of the Bradford Race Equality Council, says many officers on the beat still demonstrate 'canteen culture' attitudes. 'They use insulting language, they are dismissive of victims of crime', he says. 'And there is a tendency to regard all young Asian men as druggies and layabouts.'

Mohammed Amran, a youth justice worker, agrees. 'It's

the senior managers who work hard to build links with the community,' he says. 'They disappear at 5pm, leaving the grassroots bobbies in charge, and I have not seen any change at the grass roots.' Some of the initiatives have been notable successes, though. A scheme setting up centres to report racial harassment has led to a 25 per cent increase in the reporting rate. A campaign to recruit police officers from ethnic minorities attracted 100 applications.

But Manningham has other problems. Young Asians suffer from educational underachievement and unemployment of up to 60 per cent.

The youths loitering outside Nasim Food Store say the area is also notorious for drugs. 'You can get anything round here,' boasts Danny, 16, in his flat Yorkshire accent, waving at a gleaming BMW, driven by two dealers. He adds: 'It's Diwali (the Hindu festival of light), so guess what I'm going to do tonight? I'm going to buy me some blow, get mashed and go to sleep, same as any other day'.

Source: *The Independent*, Wednesday 21 October 1998, p.9

2   ARTICLES ON MIGRANTS

Reading 2C is based on an ethnographic study of the migrant labour force in a sample of restaurants in New York. Reading 2D consists of extracts taken from an ethnographic examination of residents' perceptions of danger in a North American city, and give a good example of community and difference within the same space in a city.

READING 2C
Louis Amdur *et al.*: 'The bubbling cauldron: global and local interactions in New York City restaurants'

The restaurant industry, including hotels, is the largest employer in the US service economy. With rapid turnover, low wages, and low-skill kitchen jobs it attracts immigrant workers who participate in an ethnic division of labor reflecting both global and local patterns of change. In the largest US cities, especially New York, the restaurant work force is also recruited from arts producers, who are drawn to centers of the service economy and markets for their creative work. Ethnographic study and interviews at four restaurants in New York City show that restaurants play a significant role in reproducing the international labor markets and 'artistic mode of production' typical of a global city. At the same time, restaurants' internal hierarchies reproduce the ethnic and social divisions of labor typical of the larger society as well as the economic polarization of the city as a whole. Global and local forces equally shape cuisine, labor recruitment, entrepreneurial mobility, and clienteles suggesting that the study of transnational space should focus on both economy and culture in changing urban institutions. This study also questions a number of macroeconomic assumptions about immigrant labor markets and transnational capital flows.

   The development of the restaurant industry in New York is inextricable from global processes of change. Not only does it respond to the general growth of services, especially high-level business services, in a global city but it also reflects interregional capital shifts and a steady supply, since the immigration laws of 1965 and 1986, of 'new' immigrants. Restaurants generate a large number of low-wage and 'dead-end' jobs that are often filled by immigrants who lack English language skills and US educational credentials (Bailey, 1985). These factors, and the restaurant industry's traditional barriers to unionization, make this a pliable labor force. Restaurant jobs in turn support the structural inequality described as polarization, which divides haves from have-nots in the urban economy by work, wages, and prospects for advancement. Whether it is truly industrialization for export in sending countries that encourages immigration (Sassen, 1988) or a variety of internal economic and political processes that push out a relatively skilled part of the population, restaurants in receiving countries (and the hotel and travel industry more generally) represent an employer of first and last resort. Significantly, restaurants are among the fastest growing sectors of the service economy in the United States as well as in New York City.

…

Restaurants as cultural and economic institutions

… Restaurant staff – especially waiters – who have direct contact with customers present themselves along with the menu. They may be seen as potential employees or as trendsetters by culture industry executives. The way they talk and dress provides a large part of the restaurant's ambience. Waiters thus not only provide a backdrop for business meetings, they also contribute to the production, circulation, and consumption of symbols. A restaurant's style, especially in Manhattan, is both implicitly and explicitly negotiated by waitstaff and management. The accents and appearance of waiters affirm distinctions between restaurants as surely as menu, price, and location.

   Waitstaff are not the only source of a restaurant's role in facilitating the accumulation of cultural capital. Restaurants indicate social class and other distinctions. Being seen in a particular restaurant, or with a certain person, or occupying a 'good' table are all indicators of power and status in a city or an industry. By the same token, customers establish a restaurant's relative status. A restaurant that attracts social elites, celebrities, or industry leaders in any field gains luster. Restaurant design also contributes to the production of a city's visual style. Architects and interior designers, restaurant consultants, and restaurant industry magazines diffuse global trends that are adapted to local styles. Owners are amenable to submitting their own vision to these agents' mediation and even hire publicists to further the presentation of a specific image. Restauranteurs often appear as a cultural synthesis of the artist, the entrepreneur, and the social organizer. The restaurant itself is both theater and performance. It serves and helps constitute the Artistic Mode of Production.

In a curious way, restaurants also synthesize the global and the local. They receive culinary styles of preparation and trends from other parts of the country and the world and institutionalize them in their menus. Yet, they also adapt strange food to local tastes and eating patterns. Moreover, they form agglomerations by restaurant type, which then become neighborhood institutions (Little Italy, Chinatown). In New York restaurant cuisine, the local reterritorializes the global.

Restaurants similarly bring together a global and local laborforce and clientele. The industry's labor market mobilizes immigrants and natives whose networks – both cultural and economic – influence a restaurant's style. The division of labor along ethnic and national lines generally parallels the division into 'front' and 'back' regions with higher or lower social status, with the exception of high-status chefs. Moreover, a restaurant's status is influenced by the cultural style, economic level, and ethnicity of global and local clienteles. While some restaurants serve the tourist trade, others are appropriated as meeting places of an international business class or for maintaining ethnic contacts. In other words, in a global city, restaurants bring together global and local markets of both employees and clientele.

New York restaurants

The restaurant industry, one of the fastest growing industries in the United States, employs over 5 million people nationwide, including 130,000 at more than 5,000 restaurants in New York City (US Department of Labor, 1989). During the 1980s, the New York restaurant industry alone added 20,000 jobs. Over 33% of the workforce in New York City restaurants are immigrants, not including increasing numbers of undocumented immigrants (Winnick, 1990) …

…

Looking at the type of jobs employees do and their educational attainment confirms a degree of polarization in the restaurant between those who work in the 'front' – i.e., the dining room/bar area – and those who work in the 'back' – i.e., the kitchen. Out of 19 'front' respondents in our sample, 12 are immigrants, 3 are US migrant artists or actors, and one is an immigrant dancer from Western Europe. The majority of those who work in the 'front' and who come in contact with customers hold college degrees or are in college now, while no one who works in the 'back' has any college education. Out of 13 waitstaff, four have a bachelors degree, one has an acting degree, and three have some college education. Only five have no higher education. Out of 3 bartenders, one has a bachelor's degree, one has an engineering degree, and one has no college education. Out of 3 busboys [i.e. assistant waitstaff], one has a bachelor's degree, one went to bartending school, and one has no college or restaurant education …

…

… While job applicants who have cultural capital (approximated by English-language skills and middle-class background) find their way to jobs in the front of the restaurant or at the top of the kitchen hierarchy, it is possible for others to work their way up from entry-level positions. Ultimate career goals, however, differ. For cultural producers, restaurants are always a temporary job, even though other interviews we have done with waiters indicate that they generally continue working in the restaurant industry for many years. For immigrants, restaurants offer both entry-level jobs and access to entrepreneurial opportunities. As they perfect their language skills and become knowledgeable about the industry, restaurants provide their own ladder for internal promotions. Yet, waitstaff and kitchen staff all depend on their personal relations with the chef and owner. They lack health insurance, cannot anticipate promotions, and earn less than the minimum wage.

References

Bailey, T. (1985) 'A case study of immigrants in the restaurant industry', *Industrial Relations*, vol.24, no.1 (Spring), pp.205–21.

Sassen, S. (1988) *The Mobility of Labor and Capital: A Study in International Investment and Labor Flow*, Cambridge, Cambridge University Press.

US Department of Labor; Bureau of Labor Statistics (1989) *Employment Hours and Earnings, States and Areas, 1972–1987*, Vol. III, Minnesota-New York (March) Bulletin 2320.

Winnick, L. (1990) *New People in Old Neighborhoods*, New York, Russell Sage Foundation.

Source: Amdur *et al.*, 1995, pp.105–6, 109–10, 116, 120

READING 2D
Sally Engle Merry: from *Urban Danger: Life in a Neighborhood of Strangers*

Chapter 2 The setting

Dover Square is a neighbourhood of contrasts …

…

The diversity of an entire city is compressed into a small neighborhood.

Dover Square is located in the center of a major North-eastern city at the juncture of a Chinese and a white ethnic neighborhood. This is an aging port city, and many parts of the central city reflect decades of use by one immigrant group after another. The city has traditionally served as a first stop for a wide variety of immigrants, particularly the British, Irish, Italian, Syrians, Portuguese, Chinese, and Puerto Ricans, as well as black migrants from the rural South. The mix of ethnic and racial groups in Dover Square and the adjacent neighborhood, to which I have given the fictitious name James Hill, is unusual in this city of tight, closed ethnic neighborhoods, intense ethnic politics, and strong ethnic loyalties. Even after generations in the United States, many individuals in this city still identify themselves primarily in terms of their ethnicity …

Chapter 4 A neighborhood of strangers

Dover Square is a neighborhood in which residents continually encounter strangers. People who do not live in the development often use the laundromat or supermarket, park their cars in the courtyards and walk to their jobs downtown, or simply pass through the area. They are passersby, appearing in the [housing] project only fleetingly but never participating in its social life … They are people who appear only for a moment, and then disappear never to return again.

Another kind of stranger inhabits Dover Square as well. This is the person who has lived next door or down the street as a neighbor for five or ten years, but who is still not known as an individual with a name or personal history. These people share public spaces, walkways, stores, and the laundromat with one another, yet remain anonymous. They continue to view one another only as members of social categories … These are the people who are in a social system, but not of it. They may stay for a long time, but are potential wanderers, people who never give up their freedom to leave. In general, members of one ethnic group in Dover Square view members of other ethnic

groups as this kind of stranger. Although well over half the families have lived together for ten years, they inhabit separate social worlds. Within each ethnic group are clusters of friends and kinsmen and paths of freely flowing communication, but between the groups the boundaries are sharp and social contacts rare. Because the groups are evenly dispersed throughout the project, people who live next door to each other remain strangers. They use the same stores and laundromat and traverse the same walkways, but their paths cross without touching.

Dover Square is not a community, in the sense of a cohesive local social unit to which residents feel identification and belonging …

…

The social boundaries between ethnic groups persist because each group is encapsulated within a network of social relationships and set of institutions linked to nearby black, white, Chinese, and Hispanic communities (see Mayer, 1961). The majority of families in the project regularly visit kinsmen, friends, churches, and social organizations in their nearby ethnic community. Jobs, friends, marriage partners, social services, and recreational opportunities are all primarily available within these communities. Consequently, relations with co-ethnics carry an expectation of continuity that is not characteristic of relations with neighbors in Dover Square. Neighbors are only temporary associates, here today but gone whenever they move away, while people in the same ethnic group are connected by enduring ties. The denser mesh of personal ties and group affiliations within ethnic groups means that Dover Square residents are far more accountable to their fellow ethnics than they are to their neighbors of different ethnicity.

The Chinese community

The pattern of encapsulation is most extreme for the Chinese residents. Because well over half of the adults speak little or no English, they are dependent on connections to Chinatown for access to jobs that do not require the ability to speak English. Chinatown provides opportunities for Chinese-language social services, recreational activities, religious services, and familiar foods. But even the younger generation, those born in America who speak excellent English, maintain close ties to the Chinese community in Chinatown and in Dover Square.

Chinatowns are traditionally cohesive, insular ethnic communities, a pattern of isolation developed in response to the pressures of American society, the immigration situation, and the 'sojourner' pattern of immigration. Discriminatory US legislation impeded Chinese immigration, while the hostile reaction of

American society created encapsulated communities. The mob violence in California during the 1870s and 1880s drove immigrants out of agricultural, labor, mining, and railroad work into ghettos in large cities where they could protect themselves, and legislation passed by some states restricted Chinese access to some jobs, marriage to white women, and full legal rights in court. For the immigrant, security lay in maintaining close ties with kinsmen in Chinatown and in China, not in absorption into American society (Lee, 1960; Sung, 1967; Nee and Nee, 1974).

...

... [T]he Chinese community is knitted together by several kinds of social relationships. Although different categories of Chinese live in the project, extended networks frequently cut across the divisions. Communication about reputations and identities flows freely through the extended social networks of the Chinese community. Further, all Chinese residents are connected to and more or less dependent upon the institutions of Chinatown for jobs, social services, and important social relationships. Relations with these institutions are enduring even if individuals move from one neighborhood to another. The result is that Chinese residents are encapsulated in Chinatown's social and institutional structure, which inhibits their freedom to flaunt public opinion or desert the community.

The black community

The black population of Dover Square can be roughly divided into three groups: the respectable families who work for a living and value a cohesive family life, marital stability, and steady work; the hustler families who are generally poorer and struggle to survive through legal and illegal means; and the street youths, young people who regularly socialize together and live by crime and hustling.

Those who like to think of themselves as respectable make up about three-fourths of all the black families. Generally, they are supported by a male head of house who works, and they condemn their neighbors who hustle rather than work. They strive to keep their children away from the street youths who lounge conspicuously in the playground, but are not always successful. For many of these families, the church is a central focus of social life. But, because they attend a wide variety of churches in James Hill and Winslow, the neighboring black community, rather than one local church, their common interest has not made them a cohesive social group. Smaller networks of friends make up subdivisions within the group, and there are about ten respectable families who are completely socially isolated.

The other families, which I have labeled hustlers because that is the term they use for the variety of quasi-legal and illegal strategies they adopt to make a living, constitute one-quarter of the black families. They are generally poorer than the respectable families. Some of the parents did illegal things in the past, while a few are currently engaged in gambling, prostitution, or fencing stolen goods. Those heads of household who work generally hold uncertain, unreliable, and low-paying jobs, often in custodial, food, or domestic services. Others earn a marginal existence through welfare payments supplemented by other forms of hustling, a pattern among very poor families ... Although they rarely form close friendships with the youths who hang out in the playground, the hustler families are, if not necessarily approving, at least friendly and sympathetic toward them. They tend to look the other way when their children commit crimes. Most of the street youths come from hustler families.

Both the respectable and hustler categories include families that live on welfare and are headed by women. Some women who raise their children on welfare are able to maintain a position in the respectable social circle and keep their children away from the street group. Others find themselves unable to counteract the attractions the street has for their children ...

...

The street group, between twenty and thirty young blacks aged fourteen to twenty-five, are convinced that there are more pleasant and profitable ways of life than the drudgery of a steady job. They support themselves through a variety of activities such as pimping, prostitution, drug pushing, selling marijuana, gambling, burglary, purse snatching, pocket picking, and robbery. Occasionally, one of them will take a job, but only as an interim arrangement, not as a permanent commitment ...

They constitute a dense, interconnected social network of individuals who have grown up together, have fallen in love with each other, sired one another's children, and become one another's mortal enemies ... The group's boundary is fuzzy: at the periphery are people who join and leave at different times. Residents of public housing projects in James Hill and Winslow residents occasionally join the Dover Square group. Not everyone in the group is black: two whites, two Chinese and two Hispanics more or less regularly hang out with them.

...

The black population of Dover Square is knitted together by a web of kin ties and friendships formed before they moved into the project ...

...

Thus, black families in Dover Square belong to social networks that extend to James Hill and to Winslow, and they participate in the institutions of these two communities.

The white community

The white population is more diverse and less interrelated than either the blacks or the Chinese. About fifteen families, more than one-third of the white families in the project, are Syrian-Lebanese who have moved from James Hill. They maintain close ties with their friends and kinsmen in James Hill ... The rest of the families are a potpourri of white ethnics: eight Irish, three Italian, one Greek, one Jewish, one Australian and ten other families. When it first opened, the project attracted a group of more educated, middle-class whites who were active in community organizing efforts, but with the waning of the inner-city esprit de corps of the 1960s, all have moved out.

The white families are a shrinking minority ...

Unlike the blacks and the Chinese, few kinship ties unite the white families, nor do their grown children settle in the project ... The failure to settle adult children in the project underscores whites' intentions not to remain, as well as the greater availability of good housing for whites elsewhere in the city ... The few white youths in the project socialize either with the street group of with friends outside the project. Many of the whites who moved in from James Hill, about half of the white families, maintain pre-existing social ties from that neighborhood and return for its recreational and social activities, but the other half are from neighborhoods all over the city and suburbs. They brought no kin or friends with them and now retain connections with a wide variety of neighborhoods all over the city. Many have children living the the suburbs or in other cities.

Thus, the white community is less interconnected than either the Chinese or the black community. Most whites feel they are a beleaguered and isolated minority ...

Relations between ethnic groups

Social boundaries between the ethnic groups are sharp and persistent. No common institutional affiliations cross-cut these lines except for the Catholic Church, which draws together a few respectable black families and some whites, and the tenants' association, which similarly incorporates a few activist whites, blacks and Chinese. Otherwise, friendships or shared group affiliations are rare. The major exception is the street group, which has as multi-ethnic composition and is characterized by intimate social ties. Even though two-thirds of the children in the project attended the same elementary school before the onset of school busing, they rarely formed lasting friendships there ...

...

Thus, because of the social structure of the neighborhood, individuals are encapsulated within networks or ongoing social relationships with members of their own ethnic and class groups, not with their neighbors. Shared membership in corporate groups, kin networks, job situations, and community organizations creates an expectation of future interaction with ethnic groups ... There is, however, no similar expectation of continuity in social relationships with neighbors of different ethnic groups. Even for families who have lived next door to one another for ten years, there is still no anticipation that after they move out, their relationship will continue. This expectation of termination discourages investment of time and energy in the creation of a relationship and reinforces boundaries between social networks. People are reluctant to initiate contacts with others who are culturally different and not connected to their social network in any enduring way. This reluctance prevents the creation of crosscutting ties and impedes the flow of information about reputations, about those individuals who are trustworthy and those who are not. Thus, it increases the prevalence of relations between strangers within the project.

Crime and social boundaries

In many ways, the social structure of Dover Square itself contributes to the high crime rate. Crime occurs because of the conjunction of two factors: poverty and anonymity. The former establishes the incentive to steal, the latter creates opportunities to steal successfully. Low income, unemployment, and racial discrimination drive individuals to crime as a strategy for avoiding physical discomforts, hunger, and social isolation that comes from not having the money for socializing with friends. It is poverty that drives people to weigh their own survival and that of their family against the loss that may be incurred by a stranger; it is poverty that pressures people to choose family over loyalty to abstract norms of fairness ...

Anonymity, caused by the heterogeneous ethnic composition of the project, facilitates predation as a mode of survival by allowing criminals to rob their neighbors with minimal fear of apprehension. Many Dover Square residents observed that, in general, criminals prefer not to work close to home, where they can be too easily identified by their neighbors. But in Dover Square, where neighbors are often strangers, a resident can rob or burglarize families close to him without fear of identification. This means he can commit crimes in his home territory, one which to him is relatively safe, predictable, and familiar, while appearing to his victims as if he were a stranger from a distant area. He can rob the same people whose daily habits and material possessions are easily visible to him.

References

Lee, R.H. (1960) *The Chinese in the United States of America*, London, Oxford University Press.

Mayer, P. (1961) *Townsmen or Tribesmen: Conservatism and the Process of Urbanization in a South African City*, Cape Town, Oxford University Press (2nd edn, 1971).

Nee, V. and Nee, B. de Bary (1974) *Longtime Californ': A Documentary Study of an American Chinatown*, Boston, Houghton Mifflin Company, Sentry Edition.

Sung, B.L. (1967) *Mountain of Gold: The Story of the Chinese in America*, New York, Macmillan.

Source: Merry, 1981, pp.31–2, 93–4, 96–7, 108–10, 115–18, 121–3

3 ARTICLES ON 'OTHER' LINES OF INEQUALITY OR DIVISION

Reading 2E provides another interesting 'take' on the disadvantages that women face, in this case in cities in Britain. Reading 2F gives an example of segregation based on social differences, in this case religion, and provides a useful link to Book 3 Chapter 4. Reading 2G tells the next episode in the story of Tompkins Square Park that was introduced in Book 2 Chapter 3.

READING 2E
'Poverty has a woman's face'

Kathy Stansfield reviews a discussion paper by Oxfam which outlines a multi-level strategy to incorporate gender issues into its work.

Single mothers are frequently in the spotlight, and rarely in a sympathetic way. Usually they are victims of politicians' or editors' venom, accused of jumping the housing queue, not looking after their children properly and reluctant to go out to work. Rarely are the recalcitrant fathers even mentioned.

When attention turns to unemployed young men, the issue is one of the need for employment, loss of self-esteem and the safeguarding or restoring of their traditional role in society as breadwinners. There is fear of male exclusion as an emerging trend, with the potential violence and involvement in crime this implies.

…

Too often politicians cite the family as the seat of all virtue, with the roles of traditional, nurturing, dependent mother and breadwinning father clearly identified. Research which could be construed (inaccurately) as implying that children of working mothers are less bright was gleefully seized on by the media. And when high-profile women give up their stressful jobs to look after their families, it is seen as indicative not of preference but of failure to compete in a man's world.

These are all gender stereotypes. There are many others which limit thinking in policy formulation and understanding of support networks. The most important are those affecting poorer women who do not have the choices of their richer sisters. For urban regeneration to succeed, a gender dimension needs to be brought to bear in research and policy. The need is to strengthen the community and allow choice for all about their lifestyles.

The report points out that 'patterns of disadvantage are different, both socially and spatially, as a result of gender inequalities'. The problem is that where this is not recognised by those seeking to intervene, structural inequalities for women may be reinforced rather than alleviated.

Women tend to suffer most because they are seen to have little economic role (though it is increasing) and to be financially dependent on men; their child-rearing, caring, home-making activities tend to be less visible, being unpaid and more time-consuming than men's earning roles. Yet they form the warp and weft of communities, usually being the ones to take on work in community groups, and with informal support networks with other women.

…

The author stresses that the gender dimension is 'very important in analysing and addressing poverty'. There is much research which shows that men's and women's experiences of poverty are different, and worse for women. If gender is not taken into account in the design of training programmes, for example, inevitably they tend only to benefit men.

Yet the household is the basic unit of analysis in most cases, which means that the gender dimension can be overlooked and mistakes made. As the report says, 'Unless women's poverty, and their positive coping strategies, are well understood, urban regeneration policies and programmes will not meet their real needs.'

Reference

May, N. (1997) *Challenging Assumptions: Gender Consideration in Urban Regeneration in the United Kingdom*, a discussion paper by Oxfam for the Joseph Rowntree Foundation.

Source: *Housing Agenda*, 1997, pp. 9–10

READING 2F
Paddy Gray: 'Renewal in a divided city'

Like most cities Belfast has undergone dramatic change. This includes significant population loss, inner city decline, changing employment patterns and deep rooted and concentrated deprivation. Policies of the 1960s and 1970s were based on the principle of population dispersal, encouraging people to move out of the city.

The Housing Executive, from its formation in 1971, concentrated its efforts on the physical fabric of dwellings, and through a combination of large scale redevelopment and refurbishment of the city's inner stock it managed to transform living conditions, mainly in working class areas. The net result, however, has been the break up of communities and the dispersal of the indigenous inner city population. Whilst the more affluent moved to the suburban areas, the Executive concentrated on improving the conditions of the poorer households, with very little infrastructure to lure the essential ingredients to create a sustainable population. A successful city needs to stop haemorrhaging, and the answer now being tried in other major cities is to reurbanise the population. This can only be a success with full community participation, which is needed to help recreate the necessary infrastructure to attract the population back.

The problems of Belfast have been further exacerbated by the period of conflict which has produced a highly segregated population in the city, particularly in public housing. The development of overspill estates and the suburbanization of industry had slightly modified residential segregation. But as sectarian conflict escalated between 1970 and 1972 this tendency was sharply reversed. Catholics crowded back into West Belfast, and generally the population of Belfast moved to areas where they felt safe. There was, therefore, a high pressure for housing in certain parts of the city, whilst elsewhere the picture was one of dereliction. In blunt terms, 'Catholic' Belfast was bursting at the seams, whilst large tracts of 'Protestant' Belfast were empty and desolate.

This demographic picture of Belfast was much more apparent in the public sector estates. Some commentators estimate that over 60,000 people moved within a four year period, the largest population movement since the second world war in Western Europe. Today, Belfast is sill a highly segregated city, although segregation in the owner occupied sector is generally less pronounced. In fact, 70% of the population of Belfast lives in segregated areas, representing the highest degree of division ever in the city …

…

… In the… Housing Policy Review, published in December 1995, the government announced that the Northern Ireland Housing Executive will retain its role as the single comprehensive housing authority, but in terms of the management and provision of social housing, a more diverse framework will be encouraged to increase choice and encourage new providers.

The community must be an integral part of this process. Communities consist of a range of different people: they need homes which are affordable to them; they require shops, schools, health facilities, leisure facilities, they need jobs which are accessible and will actually provide financial benefits; and they need to feel part of the decision-making which affects their lives.

All of this requires an approach which looks at need at a very localised level, in a way which maximises local resources, and in a way which requires a range of organisations working together to link services.

Source: Gray, 1996, pp.72–3

READING 2G
Neil Smith: 'Tompkins Square Park and beyond'

Shortly after 5.00 a.m. on 3 June 1991, 350 police officers dressed in full riot gear moved into Tompkins Square Park in New York City's Lower East Side, woke more than 200 sleeping residents, and evicted them. Remaining clothes, tents, shanties, other structures and private belongings were bulldozed into several waiting sanitation trucks, and seven protestors were arrested. The 10.5 acre park was then cordoned off with an eight-foot high chain link fence, and most of the 350 officers were left to patrol its perimeter. Access was allowed to only two parts of the park: to the playgrounds, children and their guardians were allowed to pass the police guard; and to the dog run, dogs and their owners were permitted to pass.

Tompkins Square Park became a national symbol … of the struggle against gentrification and homelessness on 6 August 1988 when a force of 400 police, ostensibly attempting to re-enforce a nineteenth century curfew in the park, initiated a police riot against homeless residents, protestors, punks and other park users. As a result of that riot, 121 complaints against the police were filed with the Civilian Review Board, but none resulted in a civil conviction. For the next three years, until the final eviction in June 1991, the park became a focal point of resistance in the city, drawing in homeless people and squatters, some housing and anti-gentrification activists, as well as local anarchists. As many as 100 structures were erected in the park at any one time, and nearly 300 people slept there on its busiest nights; squatters took over as many as 50 buildings in the neighborhood, housing as many as a thousand people. Meanwhile the city's homeless population swelled to between 70 000 and 100 000.

Only gingerly at first did the police return to the 'liberated zone' of the park, then more brazenly with three attempted 'sweeps' of Tompkins Square and a series of pitched battles between December 1989 and May 1991. Many of these battles occurred around May Day or Memorial Day celebrations, organized around such demands as 'Housing is a Human Right' and slogans like 'Gentrification is Genocide' and 'Eat the Elite', as well as the original 1988 slogan: 'Whose park is it, it's our fucking park'.

'This park *is* a park … It is *not* a place to live', explained Mayor David Dinkins, heralding the park's final closure in June 1991 (Kifner, 1991). Dinkins, a Liberal Democratic and sometime member of Democratic Socialists of America, was elected with strong support from New York City's housing and anti-homelessness movement, but quickly sanctioned the first evictions of homeless people from the park in December 1989 only weeks after his election, initiating a four-year corrosion of Dinkins' connections with the mass support that had elected him. As the *Village Voice* noted of the evictions, for 'the homeless residents, many of them now scattered in abandoned lots around the park, the closing of the park was just one more betrayal for an administration they thought would stand up for the rights of the poor' (Ferguson, 1991a). In finally closing the park, Dinkins borrowed a script not from housing or homeless advocates but from the editorial pages of the *New York Times*, which quoted the Webster's dictionary definition of 'park' then judged that Tompkins Square was no park at all: 'A park is not a shantytown. It is not a campground, a homeless shelter, a shooting gallery for drug addicts or a political problem. Unless it is Tompkins Square Park in Manhattan's East Village'. Homeless residents of the park, according to the *Times*, had 'stolen it from the public' and the park would have to be 'reclaimed'. Just three days before the closure, the newspaper inveighed against further partial solutions, preferring instead a 'clean sweep' as 'the wiser course though riskier politically'. There were , it seems, 'some legitimately homeless people' who 'live in the park', and therefore 'misplaced sympathy abounds' (*New York Times*, 1991). In an interview for National Public Radio, Parks Commissioner Betsy Gotbaum borrowed from the same script, adding her own racial coding of the urban frontier: 'It was filled with tents, even a teepee at one point … It was really disgusting'.

…

… It is worth quoting at length from an eyewitness report by Sarah Ferguson of just one incident, which offers a visceral portrait of the agency behind the revanchist city:

> Since the police takeover 3 June, there have been nightly gatherings on the steps of St. Brigid's Church on Avenue B [on the southeast side of the park], a focal point of community resistance. On Friday, a dozen parents with their children gathered among the punks and anarchists and tried to march against the line of riot police blocking their way, chanting 'Open the park!' When they were forced back onto the sidewalks, some 800 residents took to the streets, banging on drums and garbage can lids, and leading the police cordon [protecting the park] that dutifully followed them from Loisaida through the West Village and back through the projects off Avenue D – what locals call the nightly 'walk the pig' routine.

They were confronted on the steps of St. Brigid's

by at least 100 cops, who beamed blinding high-intensity lights into the crowd. The protesters remained peaceful until two undercover cops shoved their way into the church entrance on Avenue B, claiming they wanted to inspect the roof for bottle throwers. One parishioner, Maria Tornin, was struck in the face and knocked against the stairs by one of the cops, and Father Pat Maloney of Lazaru Community was shoved against the wall. Backed by his parishioners, St. Brigid's Father Kuhn pushed the undercover cops out the door.

'When the law ends, tyranny begins, and these guys are tyrants', shouted Father Maloney, leading an angry mob to the paddy wagon where the undercovers had fled …

Last Saturday, as bulldozers rumbled past the ripped-up benches and shattered chess tables [in the cordoned-off park], a second demonstration of over 1000 Lower East Side residents linked arms around the park. As the church bells of St. Brigid's rang out, dreadlocked anarchists in combat boots and nose rings held hands with Jewish grandmothers in print dresses and plastic pearls in a peaceful show of unity not seen since the 1988 police riot.

(Ferguson, 1991b, p. 24)

References

Kifner, J. (1991) 'New York closes park to homeless', *New York Times*, 4 June.

Ferguson, S. (1991a) 'Should Tompkins Square be like Gramercy?', *Village Voice*, 11 June, p.20.

Ferguson, S. (1991b) 'The Park is gone', *Village Voice*, 18 June.

New York Times (1991) 'Make Tompkins Square a park again', *New York Times*, 31 May.

Source: Smith, 1996, pp.96–8

4   ARTICLES ON STREET CHILDREN IN CITIES

Reading 2H provides a really good overview of the problems facing street children. Readings 2I and 2J offer interesting insights into how city administrators view the concerns about street children and also the responses of police officers acting without restraint. Reading 2K gives the 'voices' of some of the children that have to survive on the streets of Brazil's cities and provides a good contrast to the responses by the state.

READING 2H
Kristin Helmore: 'Out of the tunnel of urban childhood'

ANTANANARIVO. This threadbare, faded capital of Madagascar sits precariously on 12 steep, verdant hills. Below one of these hills, in the center of town, a tunnel was dug decades ago. Today, the tunnel futilely attempts to organize the snarls of smoking traffic that wind endlessly through the city's narrow, cobbled streets.

Just inside the tunnel, on the sidewalk thick with pedestrians, three or four babies sit by themselves. The babies are old enough to sit up unassisted, but not old enough to walk or – apparently – strong enough to crawl. Their mothers, knowing they will stay put, park them in the tunnel near the curbside, with an empty tin can in front of them, to beg from drivers inching their way along or from pedestrians who often jostle the infants as they hurry by. The babies are naked and very dirty, their noses perpetually running. They sit in filth and they cry much of the time. As is typical in developing countries, there is no emission control for vehicles in Madagascar, and heavy soot-black exhaust fumes make up the air the babies breathe all day long.

These babies in their tunnel are very real, yet they are also a telling metaphor for the condition of children in cities throughout the world. For the very poor, who constitute about one-third of the population of large cities in the developing world, an urban childhood is often a dark and frightening passageway leading to an uncertain future. At the end of it, to be sure, there is the promise of choices and opportunities that a rural environment cannot provide. But mere survival for children in the dark tunnel of

urban poverty is problematic – and the promise of a better life is not always fulfilled.

Living conditions

Every day, more and more families arrive in the cities of the developing world from stagnant, impoverished rural villages, and it is mainly for the benefit of their children that they come. 'As bad as life is for urban children in the slums of the city, their chances of survival and their choices in life are much more restricted if they stay in the rural areas,' says Janice E. Perlman, president of Mega-Cities, a nonprofit organization based in New York that transfers innovative solutions to urban problems from one megacity to another.

According to the United Nations, there will be 23 megacities with populations greater than 10 million by the beginning of the next century – 18 of them in the developing world. These cities, and smaller ones like Antananarivo, are increasingly overcrowded. Adequate housing, infrastructure, and services cannot keep pace either with birth rates or with escalating levels of urban migration.

In industrialized countries, many cities are friendly, safe, nurturing places for children to grow up in – at least, for middle- and upper-class children. Dr Perlman cites Paris and Tokyo as having the best daycare systems in the world – even though, in Tokyo, social services are not available to the growing community of low-income foreign workers. But even in rich countries, children of the poor often live in developing country conditions: inadequate housing, malnutrition, poor health care, substandard schooling, lack of daycare, vulnerability to violence and drug abuse are just some of the perils they face. And among middle-class urban families with two working parents, children are often neglected, as the responsibilities of child-rearing are increasingly passed on to institutions such as schools, and to the cities themselves.

Meanwhile, in the fast-growing cities of the developing world, more and more millions of children are growing up in slums, squatter settlements, or shantytowns. In 1990, a report from the International Labor Organization (ILO) estimated that more than 50 per cent of the populations of Bombay and Lagos lived in slums or shantytowns; in Cairo, where thousands of families actually live in a huge cemetery, the figure was 84 per cent. The populations of these cities are also young.

The families of the babies in the Antananarivo tunnel live in black plastic tents on the sloping ground next to the tunnel's mouth. They have no sanitation, no electricity – indeed, no flooring and no windows. Their homes are cramped, hot, dark, and airless. The mothers use charcoal for cooking, and the children often contract respiratory ailments from the smoke. In winter, the families have no heat.

Under slum conditions like these, psychological pressures can be devastating. Having left behind the traditional structures and support networks of the village, recent arrivals experience a sense of alienation and depression in crowded, impersonal, fast-paced cities. Unskilled jobs are hard to come by, and men who cannot find work to support their families often turn to alcohol for solace, taking out their frustrations in violence toward their wives and children. Many are absent for long periods, searching for work. Others simply leave – to find a new woman and beget more children.

An increasingly large proportion of urban families is headed by a woman, with little or no education, who bears sole responsibility for her children's well-being. Food is more expensive in cities than in rural areas, and mothers must be highly creative, energetic, and courageous just to make ends meet. Those who are desperate enough may come to see their children – even six-month-old babies – as potential earners of income to help feed the family. As early as they can, many women send their children out into the streets to beg or work. And, in fact, many children seek the streets of their own accord. Home life in the slums is often so tense and turbulent many children find it less stressful to fend for themselves.

…

… For many children in the cities of developing countries, the world of work starts almost as soon as they can walk, hold a hammer, or roll a cigarette. Like the laboring children in the industrial cities of 19th century Europe and America, hundreds of millions of children are working today in cities throughout the developing world.

Take Shadab, for example. He lives in the fast-growing city of Aligarh southeast of New Delhi in northern India …

In the sweltering heat and ear-splitting noise of a small factory, nine-year-old Shadab grinds pieces of metal on a high-speed grinding wheel. Since he was six, he has worked 12 hours a day, six days a week. He earns the equivalent of US$0.17 per day, which he proudly gives to his mother to help feed the family. His father is dead, and as the oldest child, he is the principal breadwinner.

Source: Helmore, 1997, pp.5–7

READING 2I

City of the child-catchers

They do like their tourists here. But to keep the streets neat and tidy for them, hungry children are carted off in nightly raids. Still want to go to Madagascar?

In the capital of Madagascar, Antananarivo, many thousands of children live on the streets. Madagascar is, by many estimates, the poorest country in the world and the capital sees the extremes of its poverty. The children, some barely old enough to walk, survive in gangs of 30 or more. Some sleep in skips or in road tunnels; most scavenge for food among the city's rubbish. The gangs take the place of the family. The children in a particular gang look out for each other and subsist by doing small, menial jobs in the market place, by begging, stealing or by prostitution.

The Madagascan government, ever keen to encourage tourism to the island, has recently come up with a solution to the growing population of children on its capital's streets. It has set up a special police department. The department, led by a woman, Madame la Commissaire Livah Radelina, organises nightly raids known as 'rafles' during which children sleeping rough are collected in wagons. Some of the children are then sent to private detention centres. The rest – those suspected of criminal activity, of 'delinquency' or 'theft' – are sent to prison. There are no trials, and their sentences often run for three or four years.

Source: *Observer*, Review section, 23 February 1997, p.1

READING 2J
Margaret Bergen: 'Children in the city: an interview with the Mayor of Rio de Janeiro'

Brazil, and Rio de Janeiro in particular, has come under attack for its handling of the problem of street children. The mayor of Rio, Luis Pablo Conde, discusses street kids and the city's municipal solutions.

Interviewer:

In July 1993, off-duty policemen opened fire on children sleeping in front of Candelaria church, killing eight. Why do you think this happened, and could it happen again?

Conde:

Society looks on street children as potentially dangerous, lawbreakers. Sometimes they are, because of the harsh struggle for survival on the streets. The truth, however, is that these children are vulnerable. They suffer violence, are exploited, and are often forced into crime. The Candelaria incident happened because of the general view of street children and teenagers, and the policemen's feeling that they could act with impunity.

I don't think anything like that will ever happen again. The municipality's education specialists are out on the streets trying to persuade the children to give up that life. The policemen involved in the Candelaria affair are in prison – some with sentences lasting over 100 years – and that should certainly deter others.*

Interviewer:

How could the view of these kids as dangerous criminals be changed so that they would be seen as children in great need?

Conde:

Such views won't be changed quickly, because they have become entrenched over a number of years. In large cities, people live in fear and see everything as a threat. Violence is an everyday occurrence. Buildings are constructed to be inward-looking, so as to offer safety and some defense, and houses are becoming refuges. However, in poorer areas there is no chance of isolating and protecting oneself. A shanty offers no tranquility – and even less protection. When kids take to the streets, it's because they don't think they're any worse off on the streets than in the place where they lived before, with its tiny shanties, open sewers, and violence.

My office is attempting to integrate these poorer communities into the city, turning them into urban development areas, providing sanitation facilities and equal, democratic access to services.

I believe that the first step in changing the view that the poor – whether in the slums or on the streets – are potential criminals is to deinstitutionalize inequality. It is also important to ensure that organizations within society participate more fully and effectively in the formulation and implementation of social policy, as is happening in Rio de Janeiro.

Note: *As reported in the 20 June 1997 *Washington Post*, one of the policemen originally sentenced to 261 years was acquitted of the murders in a new trial, and his sentence was reduced to 18 years for a single count of attempted murder.

Source: Bergen, 1997, p.23

READING 2K
Gilberto Dimenstein: from
Brazil: War on Children

Voices from the Passage House

'When my mother died, it was like losing everything I had. It was then that I went on the streets, but I didn't expect to be treated so violently by everybody, including by the other women on the street.

'My family's got a house and a bit of land, but I've been living on the streets since I was seven, the year after my mother died. I worked as a servant in a family house, but then a friend told me to come to the city.

'I got by in the city, picking up men, though I had to put up with them hitting me. What really makes me angry is the way that these machos beat you up all the time. It makes you want to kill them, that's why I don't live with a guy. I just sell my body to them from time to time.

'The street's got nothing for anybody. I live on the street but I suffer a lot. I play about, I have a bit of a laugh, but no-one ever knows what I'm really thinking and I keep wondering to myself why there's no love in life. Sometimes the police force us to steal. You can be sitting there, minding your own business and they come and start kicking you, beating you up, just because you're on the street. I never stole anything. I'm just on the streets because that's where I live.' *(Katia)*

'It's our destiny. The sign of the street girl is to love the bandit. Nothing can change this. We are going where we can. We are on the street. We are already dead.'*(13 year old)*

'I know that the street has nothing to give, only beatings. That's why I sniff glue, I don't feel anything. I steal and get beaten up, I cut myself, but this has nothing to do with me.' *(14 year old)*

'If I look at you a lot, you are going to know a lot about me. Because of this I prefer not to look.' *(16 year old)*

'How can I speak about my life, when they beat me up so that I won't speak?' *(18 year old)*

'If I talk about these things, will I go mad? I never used to talk. I don't know how. I am black and poor.' *(17 year old)*

Source of quotes: *SOS Meninas,* Ana Vasconcelos and *Proceedings of First Meeting of Street Girls*, Recife, June 1989, organized by Ana Vasconcelos and the Passage House.

Voices from the street

'We sniff glue because we need to. We steal – watches, necklaces. We don't have anywhere to eat, we don't have anywhere to sleep, we don't have anywhere to stay – that's why we steal. I steal, I walk around, I sniff glue, and then I can't do anything. I haven't got a Dad – he died seven years ago. I have eight brothers and sisters and can't really stay at home, so I live on the street. That's how I lead my life.

'I'd like all of us to be able to work, so we all could be healthy and have a house to live in. We should all have our rights, we should have our hope and our family alive. We shouldn't need this death squad to kill people, we shouldn't need to rob or steal anything.'

'I started living on the street when I was seven years old, when I lost my mother and couldn't survive. Me and my brother were hungry and then a friend of mine took me to the street. When I got to the Brasagiaria I became a prostitute. Then I started to steal because as a prostitute I couldn't support my family. When I was thieving the men came to arrest me, they beat me up and did a lot of things. They put me in jail where I had to eat bread and water and spent three days in isolation, before I was taken to the FEBEM (Foundation for Child Welfare) and beaten up again. I used to spend one or two months in prison and then I would escape to the street again. I used to take drugs and start stealing again, and then get arrested and beaten up. Always stealing and getting beaten up. When I got fed up with being beaten I went back to being a prostitute, but then the bastards slapped me around if I didn't want to have sex with them. If I was to tell that to the policemen they would just put me in jail and beat me up again.

'It hurts to be beaten by other people because they are not our parents and never brought us up. They don't know why we are on the streets and they never even try to find out. They just beat us up because they think we are thieves and bad people. They speak badly of us, but they should know that even thieves need some love and care, and be conscious of the way we live.'

'I was 13 years old when I went to live on the streets because my mother didn't have the means to support me. She used to go out to sell fish and leave me in the house all day, and I used to spend the whole day very very hungry. Then I made a lot of friends and went out stealing. They'd nick things and I'd be the lookout. Then we went home and divided up the stuff and sold it. So I learned to steal and used to do it all the time – I was never afraid. I used to look one way and then the other and if I didn't see anyone I would take whatever was in front of me. The first time I was arrested everyone ran away except me, and the lads left the bag of stuff right next to me. When I got to the police station they opened the bag and found clothes, watches, necklaces, whisky and they started calling me names, such as a whisky bootlegger. They took me to a room and slapped me and kept on asking who did I sell it to and I kept telling them that I didn't know.

'They got a ladder and handcuffed my hands and legs to it, and they put a stick between my hands and legs and turned me upside down and hung me from the ladder. They got hold of a rubber hose and started hitting me and asking who I sold my stuff to and I kept telling them I didn't know. They spent more than half an hour just beating me up but I still didn't tell them. When they saw that my eyes were rolling they took me down and put me in the cell. The next day the man I used to sell the stuff to went to the station and paid them to let me out.'

Source of quotes: *World in Action*

Source: Dimenstein, 1991, pp.36–7, 22–3

5   GENERAL ARTICLES AND TABLES

Reading 2L gives a vivid description of city life from an on-looker's eyes.

READING 2L
Jean Baudrillard: 'New York'

More sirens here, day and night. The cars are faster, the advertisements more aggressive. This is wall-to-wall prostitution. And total electric light too. And the game – all games – gets more intense. It's always like this when you're getting near the centre of the world. But the people smile. Actually they smile more and more, though never to other people, always to themselves.

The terrifying diversity of faces, their strangeness, strained as they all are into unbelievable expressions. The masks old age or death conferred in archaic cultures are worn here by youngsters of twenty or twelve. But this reflects the city as a whole. The beauty other cities only acquired over centuries has been achieved by New York in fifty years.

Plumes of smoke, reminiscent of girls wringing out their hair after bathing. Afro or pre-Raphaelite hairstyles. Run-of-the-mill, multiracial. City of Pharaohs, all obelisks and needles. The blocks around Central Park are like flying buttresses, lending the huge park the appearance of a hanging garden.

It isn't clouds that are fleecy here, but brains. Clouds float over the city like cerebral hemispheres driven by the wind. The people have cirrus clouds in their heads or coming out of their eyes, like the spongy vapours that rise from earth cracked by hot rains. Sexual solitude of clouds in the sky; linguistic solitude of men on the earth.

The number of people here who think alone, sing alone, and eat and talk alone in the streets is mind-boggling. And yet they don't add up. Quite the reverse. They subtract from each other and their resemblance to one another is uncertain.

Yet there is a certain solitude like no other – that of the man preparing his meal in public on a wall, or on the hood of his car, or along a fence, alone. You see that all the time here. It is the saddest sight in the world. Sadder than destitution, sadder than the beggar is the man who eats alone in public. Nothing more contradicts the laws of man or beast, for animals always do each other the honour of sharing or disputing each other's food. He who eats alone is dead (but not he who drinks alone. Why is this?).

Why do people live in New York? There is no relationship between them. Except for an inner electricity which results from the simple fact of their being crowded together. A magical sensation of contiguity and attraction for an artificial centrality. This is what makes it a self-attracting universe, which there is no reason to leave. There is no human reason to be here, except for the sheer ecstasy of being crowded together.

…

In New York there is this double miracle: each of the great buildings and each of the ethnic groups dominates or has dominated the city – after its own fashion. Here crowdedness lends sparkle to each of the ingredients in the mix whereas elsewhere it tends to cancel out differences. In Montreal, all the same elements are present – ethnic groups, buildings, and space on the grand American scale – but the sparkle and violence of American cities are missing.

Clouds spoil our European skies. Compared with the immense skies of America and their thick clouds, our little fleecy skies and little fleecy clouds resemble our fleecy thoughts, which are never thoughts of wide open spaces … In Paris, the sky never takes off. It doesn't soar above us. It remains caught up in the backdrop of sickly buildings, all living in each other's shade, as though it were a little piece of private property. It is not, as here in the great capital New York, the vertiginous glass facade reflecting each building to the others. Europe has never been a continent. You can see that by its skies. As soon as you set foot in America, you feel the presence of an entire continent – space there is the very form of thought.

By contrast with the American 'downtown areas' and their blocks of skyscrapers, la Défense has forfeited the architectural benefits of verticality and excess by squeezing its high-rise blocks into an Italian-style setting, into a closed theatre bounded by a ring-road. It is very much a garden *à la française:* a bunch of buildings with a ribbon around it. All this has closed off the possibility that these monsters might engender others to infinity, that they might battle it out within a space rendered dramatic by their very competition (New York, Chicago, Houston, Seattle, Toronto). It is in such a space that the pure architectural object is born, an object beyond the control of architects, which roundly repudiates the city and its uses, repudiates the interests of the collectivity and individuals and persists in its own madness. That object has no equivalent, except perhaps the arrogance of the cities of the Renaissance.

…

They say the streets are alive in Europe, but dead in America. They are wrong. Nothing could be more intense, electrifying, turbulent, and vital than the streets of New York. They are filled with crowds, bustle, and advertisements, each by turns aggressive or casual. There are millions of people in the streets, wandering, carefree, violent, as if they had nothing better to do – and doubtless they have nothing else to do – than produce the permanent scenario of the city. There is music everywhere, the activity is intense, relatively violent, and silent (it is not the agitated, theatrical activity you find in Italy). The streets and avenues never empty, but the neat, spacious geometry of the city is far removed from the thronging intimacy of the narrow streets of Europe.

In Europe, the street only lives in sudden surges, in historic moments of revolution and barricades. At other times people move along briskly, no one really hangs around (no one wanders any more). It is the same with European cars. No one actually lives in them; there isn't enough space. The cities, too, do not have enough space, or rather that space is deemed public and bears all the marks of the public arena, which forbids you to cross it or wander around it as though it were a desert or some indifferent area.

The American street has not, perhaps, known these historic moments, but it is always turbulent, lively, kinetic, and cinematic, like the country itself, where the specifically historical and political stage counts for little, but where change, whether spurred by technology, racial differences, or the media, assumes virulent forms: its violence is the very violence of the way of life.

Such is the whirl of the city, so great its centrifugal force, that it would take superhuman strength to envisage living as a couple and sharing someone else's life in New York. Only tribes, gangs, mafia families, secret societies, and perverse communities can survive, not couples. This is the anti-Ark. In the first Ark, the animals came in two by two to save the species from the great flood. Here in this fabulous Ark, each one comes in alone – it's up to him or her each evening to find the last survivors for the last party.

Source: Baudrillard, 1988, pp. 14–15, 16–17, 18–19

READING 2M
'Planes of division'

TABLE 1 *Area of residence and anxiety about crime (percentages)*

	Feeling unsafe out at night	Feeling unsafe at home	Very worried about burglary	Very worried about mugging
Risk of crime in ACORN* area:				
High	41	15	26	23
Medium	39	13	24	23
Low	28	9	15	15
Area:				
Inner city	43	15	27	25
Non-inner city	30	10	17	16
Signs of disorder in area:				
More of a problem	41	15	25	23
Less of a problem	27	8	15	15
All British Crime Survey	32	11	19	18

Note: * ACORN classification assigns respondents' homes to neighbourhood groups according to demographic, employment and housing characteristics of the immediate area.

Data from: Mirrlees-Black, C. and Maung, N.A. (1994) *Fear of Crime: Findings from the 1992 British Crime Survey*, London, Home Office Research and Statistics Department, Research Findings No. 9.

Source: Pacione, 1997, Table 10.5, p.252

TABLE 2 *'Before' and 'after' crime statistics for areas covered by CCTV in Birmingham and Airdrie*

(a) Birmingham	Before CCTV (3 months to 3/91)	After CCTV (3 months to 9/91)
Woundings	46	27
Robberies	79	55
Thefts from a person	89	63
Indecency	8	3
Damage	62	80
(b) Airdrie	**Before CCTV (12 months to 8/92**	**After CCTV (12 months to 8/93)**
Car break-ins	480	20
Theft of cars	185	13
Serious assaults	39	22
Vandalism	207	36
Break-ins to commercial premises	263	15

Data from: Birmingham City Centre Development Group (1992) *City Watch*, Birmingham, Birmingham City Centre Development Group; Wills, J. (1993) 'Candid cameras', *Local Government Chronicle*, 17 September.

Source: Pacione, 1997, Table 10.7, p.258

TABLE 3   *The growth of self-help housing in selected Latin American cities*

City	Year	City population (000)	Population in squatter settlements	Percentage of city population in squatter settlements
Rio de Janeiro	1947	2,050	400	20
	1957	2,940	650	22
	1961	3,326	900	27
	1970	4,252	1,276	30
Mexico City	1952	2,372	330	14
	1966	3,287	1,500	46
	1970	7,314	3,438	47
	1976	11,312	5,656	50
	1990	15,783	9,470	60
Lima	1956	1,397	112	8
	1961	1,846	347	17
	1969	3,303	805	24
	1981	4,608	1,455	32
	1991	4,805	1,778	37
Buenos Aires	1956	6,054	109	2
	1970	8,353	434	5
	1980	9,766	957	10
Caracas	1961	1,330	280	21
	1964	1,590	556	35
	1971	2,200	867	39
	1985	2,742	1,673	61

Data from: Gilbert, A. (1990) *Latin America*, Routledge, p.66, based on a variety of primary and secondary sources, supplemented by Azuela, A. (1989) *La Cuidad, La Propiedad Privada y El Derecho*, El Colegio de México, p.41; Webb, R. and Fernández, G. (1991) *Péru en Números 1991*, Cuánto S.A.

Source: Gilbert and Ferguson, 1994, Table 5.1, p.82

READING 2N
'Facts and figures'

- Globally, one out of every three people is a child under the age of 15. In some countries, the proportion is even higher. In many parts of Africa and the Middle East, children account for half the population. Even in industralized countries, between one-fifth and one-quarter of the population are children.

- In seven of the developing world's largest cities, approximately 30 per cent of the population is under 15 – that's some 30 million children in these cities alone.

- Almost half of the developing world's population of children under the age of five live in absolute poverty. In Latin America and the Caribbean, children under the age of 18 make up 41 per cent of the total population; 42 per cent of these children live below the poverty line.

- Since 1990, around 60 million children died before their fifth birthday; 42 million of these were killed by diarrhoea, pneumonia, measles, malaria, or malnutrition.

- In Africa's 'mega-villages' – agglomerations of up to 500,000 people – infant mortality has shot up from 70 per 1,000 in the late 1970s to 90 per 1,000 in the early 1990s.

- In 1993, diarrhoea and acute respiratory infections caused more than 7 million deaths among children under age five in developing countries; this represents 58 per cent of all deaths in this age group.

- Working children in Brazil contribute between 20 and 40 per cent of the family income. In Bangalore, India, children contributed 19 percent of the family income. In Egypt, boys employed in factories and workshops contributed one-quarter of family income. In Haiti, 130,000 children between the ages of 5 and 18 are employed as 'domestic servants' – a condition not far removed from slavery.

- An estimated 250,000 children under 18 – some as young as 7 – are presently serving around the world in government armed forces or armed opposition groups. Children took part actively in 33 armed conflicts in 1995–96.

- In the United States, a gun takes the life of a child every 92 minutes – the equivalent of a classroom of children every two days. Since 1979, more US children (60,008) have died from gunfire than American soldiers died during the Vietnam and Gulf wars and US engagements in Haiti, Somalia, and Bosnia combined.

- Every school day in [the US], 1,644 Hispanic public school students are suspended, and 773 Hispanic babies are born into poverty; 4,404 black public school students are suspended, and 805 black babies are born into poverty; and 6,674 white public school students are suspended, and 1,611 white babies are born into poverty.

Data from: CDF Facts, Save The Children Fund, International Labour Organization, Macro International, Population Council.

Source: *The Urban Age*, vol. 5, no. 1, 1997, p.8

CHAPTER 3
Exploring economies of cities

by Mark Hart

1 *Introduction*

To me one of the most distressing aspects of city life in the late 1990s is the juxtaposition of individuals and communities experiencing poverty and severe social problems, such as crime and drug abuse, alongside those experiencing unprecedented levels of affluence. The story is much the same from continent to continent, irrespective of the political, economic or cultural context that prevails (see **Bk 1 Ch. 3**). Whether experiencing economic growth or decline, all cities are witnessing the symptoms of growing social exclusion: unemployment, male joblessness, feminization of an increasingly casualized workforce, widening gaps in income levels, increasing gaps in educational and skill levels, deteriorating health and life expectancies for the poorest members of society. In short, the quality of life for large numbers of the urban population, whether workers or not, has been seriously undermined. Further, these symptoms tend to be concentrated in the areas of cities dominated by immigrant and minority ethnic communities.

As we have seen in Book 2, challenges of competition from a global economy are at the centre of the reshaping – or fragmentation – of the social and spatial geography of cities. Sometimes when one considers the process of economic globalization, the only people that seem to matter are the highly educated professionals. It is only they who have the capacity to connect with the key elements of economic globalization – the information economy supported by associated technologies. Transmission, according to Sassen (1998), is the important feature of globalization, much more so than the physical infrastructure, and as a consequence the information economy and those who can exploit or work within it assume a privileged and powerful position in the labour market.

Yet the lives of the essential 'extras' in global cities – the disadvantaged workers (such as immigrants, people of colour, women) are caught up in the new transnational economic geography, whether as 'factory workers in export processing zones or cleaners in Wall Street' (Sassen, 1998), and their reality is clearly different. They are bound to a particular city, unlike corporate capital and those who control it, and as a consequence must accept the economic consequences that prevail. Sassen (1998) talks about these parallel but connected worlds in terms of the lower and upper circuits of globalization (as you will see in Reading 3B below). The only connection between them is the city itself, which in her analysis operates as the site for a localized expression of the global economy.

This point was illustrated very well by discussions in the late 1990s surrounding the future location of Europe's capital markets after the introduction of a single currency. The issue provided a perfect example of the competitive arena in which cities now find themselves operating. The debate at that time provoked such headlines as *'London under threat'*, but the threat was seen by many commentators simply in terms of London's *position* as Europe's largest financial centre, and indeed – in terms of international business – the world's. The likely implications of a move to Frankfurt for the urban population of London, whether in work or not, did not even enter the debate. It was all about London keeping its competitive position as the world's leading financial centre.

So how do we connect these seemingly detached 'economic' events to the lives of people in cities? Hopefully, the following activity will help kick-start your thinking in that respect as it introduces you to different ways of seeing the relationships between the economic dimension and cities.

ACTIVITY 3.1   Look at the following four statements:

1   Cities and their vast concentrations of people, it seems, are an economic necessity, even if they exhibit some of the most extreme forms of social division.

2   Cities have become more competitive and entrepreneurial in an era of intensifying globalization of manufacturing, trade and finance.

3   An understanding of the connections between cities and economic prosperity has become vital as the scale of economic exclusion and social polarization has increased.

4   We may not like the way cities have developed but we have come to accept that urbanization and the resultant impacts go hand in hand with economic development.

Quite a thought-provoking set of statements about the economies of cities! Do you agree with these sentiments? Are you convinced by the in-built assumptions about the primacy of the economic processes? If not, think about what alternatives there are about how we view cities.

Further, think about the phrase 'economic necessity' in the first statement – an economic necessity for whom exactly? – the range of individuals and communities that live in cities or the various 'actors' on the stage of the global economy?

And, finally, jot down some of the course ideas that might help you structure a response to some of these statements and questions. The list does not have to be exhaustive at this stage – but how many can you identify? ◆

Well, how did you get on with that last question about using course ideas? Hopefully, you will have found, like me, that the course has equipped you with the necessary conceptual framework to engage with the challenges posed by these statements. We need to *think spatially* in order to grasp how the economies of cities work through their range of connections to other parts of the world. The notion of *open intensities* is important here, too, in that it helps you to think about how economic processes impact upon the nature and pace of social relations within and between cities. At the same time there are also clear *tensions* in cities that have been produced by the economic realm – the huge inequalities and differences that you can see within all cities. I will stop there, but you can see already how our economic city stories are beginning to be informed by course arguments and ideas. I will return to these course arguments in greater detail in section 3.

The impact of broader economic processes upon our various experiences of city life is neatly captured by the following quote from Sassen (1998): 'The de-nationalising of urban space and the formation of new claims by transnational actors, raise the question: whose city is it?' (p.125 in Reading 3B below).

This question of *'Whose city is it?'* is an important one and may help shape your own thinking of how to make sense of the many overlapping and contradictory economic city stories that have emerged throughout the course.

In this chapter I want to get you to think more systematically about the nature and impact of the economies of cities and show you how to connect the economic dimension with course arguments. However, what you will be presented with is my own particular path through the course materials thinking about urban economic change. My approach will be to examine the *world of work* within and between cities with a particular emphasis on the issue of access to work for various groups within the urban population. The choice of topic serves to illustrate how course arguments can be applied to economic issues. We will see how understanding the world of work can be helped by using our spatial imaginations to make sense of interconnections, and competition, between cities, and the tensions and intensities that this 'openness' creates. More on this later.

So, the objective is clear. By the time you get to the end of this chapter you should be much more confident about what the course has to say about the economic dimension to urban change and also about how to respond to the sort of question you might be asked to tackle for your course essay.

1.1   WHAT DO WE MEAN BY THE 'ECONOMIC' IN THE CONTEXT OF CITIES?

Although the course has not been constructed from an explicit economic standpoint, in many places it is clear that underpinning many of the ideas and arguments that you have encountered in the three course books, the television programmes and audiocassettes is a set of questions concerning economic issues. In other places, the economic theme needs to be more carefully teased out. To enable you to engage more effectively with course ideas and to develop your own skills of analysis and critique, you are being asked to draw out these economic issues which were touched on by the various contributors to the course. For example, looking at the final section of **Bk 1 Ch. 3,** you are confronted with some powerful imagery which to me sums up the economic challenge facing cities – the immense scale of the *dis*connected or 'structurally irrelevant people' living within cities. How does one begin to devise appropriate responses to these problems? Doreen Massey, of course, was not just talking about the exclusion of these groups in economic terms. However, what you now have the opportunity to do in this chapter is to probe more deeply into the economic basis to the question by using course thinking and ideas to provide a framework for your inquiry.

At the outset, therefore, it might be useful to spend some time setting out what we mean by the 'economic' in the context of cities and how you will be asked to use it in the course essay. At a very basic level we are talking about the nature of the economic base of cities and how that has changed over time. But remember that cities are open and we need to think about the economic base of cities in terms of what goes on between cities, and between cities and the wider world. This economic base can be defined in many different ways but in simple terms it can refer to the economic activity that we find there – the range of businesses and organizations and the spectrum of employment opportunities and incomes that they provide. However, that is clearly only a partial understanding of what can be considered to be the economic base of cities and indeed such traditional definitions fall into the trap of focusing solely on the more positive side of the city economy – the businesses, the jobs and the wealth generated as a result.

There is another side to the economic base, which, as you will have gathered from my introductory comments, reflects the inability of certain groups to gain access to the jobs and incomes on offer in the city. These groups must also be considered part of the economic base in that, although detached from the jobs and the businesses, they live in the city, are part of its character, and engage in a range of consumption activities from purchasing basic goods and services to use of forms of city infrastructure such as transport and housing. These disadvantaged groups are also part of the city economy in many other ways, for example, in terms of their contribution to the image of a city as it seeks to position itself in the global market-place. Large numbers of the urban population who are dependent on welfare regimes and social programmes are seen by some (can you think of who these people or groups might be?) to be diverting public and private sector investment away from more prestigious and profitable projects.

So we need to define 'economic' in as wide a sense as possible if we are to successfully understand the way in which the economies of cities function and contribute to a sense of what cities are.

There is also the need to think about the way in which the economies of cities are connected to many different economic circuits at the national and global levels. But how might this be done? In an effort to conceptualize this more effectively, let us go back to an earlier course reading and pick up on some of Michael Porter's ideas which you came across in Book 2 **(Bk 2 Reading 7B)**. There, Porter's views on the nature of territorial competitive advantage were applied to the problem of the inner cities. In essence, Porter saw the resolution of the inner-city problem as a process of merely identifying the inner city's true competitive advantages in economic terms.

ACTIVITY 3.2   Go back now and re-read the article by Michael Porter on 'The competitive advantage of the inner city' (**Bk 2** pp.312–19) and pick out the range of competitive advantages that are put forward for the inner cities. Further, try to assess their usefulness to appropriate policy responses to revitalize the inner cities. ◆

The sort of factors that Porter identifies *could* serve to define for you what is meant by the 'economic' in terms of the economies of cities. Your list should have included some of the following factors: strategic location; land; capital; infrastructure; operating costs; local market demand; integration with regional clusters (such as the proximity to internationally competitive firms and sectors) and human resources. The clear impression that Porter leaves you with is that neo-liberal conventions driving the private sector and wealth creation is how we should think about the economies of cities. The overriding importance, from Porter's perspective, is the ability of cities to prosper on the strength of developing their competitive position internationally. The problem, as Thrift points out, is the primacy given to economic forces and what it misses in terms of an understanding of urban life. Jenny Robinson **(Bk 3 Ch. 4)** agrees with Thrift's concern and provides a useful discussion on the way we need to think about the urban property market as a social creation that moves beyond 'the workings of the anonymous capitalist market'. We therefore need to develop a broader view of what exactly we mean by the term 'economic' in the context of cities.

Individual cities have followed many different economic trajectories over time and we need to understand the dynamics of that process. Leading on from this, we need to think about the implications of the *economic performance* of cities, which is marked by considerable unevenness, for those that live there. Also, at any one time different groups can view the economic trajectories of a particular city in different ways; the *City Stories* TV series provided further evidence of that. One also has to bear in mind that the 'successful' economic performance of a city does not necessarily mean that it is a 'good city' to live in. Economic changes associated with the global operations of the financial institutions can have very real effects on the incomes of urban residents. One obvious example of these implications concerns the employment system and may include a direct loss of jobs, a considerable increase in part-time female employment (particularly among married women), increased instability of working schedules leading to longer and more unsocial hours, decreased full-time employment for young people and females, and increased numbers of individuals in precarious and low-paid employment. These new forms of work have a particularly negative effect in cities characterized either by deindustrialization or by a weak, dependent, less-developed industrial history such as those in southern Europe and the eastern part of Germany. The end-result is exclusion from adequate employment and – depending upon the nature of the support system – can produce a variety of outcomes. These range from the 'work-poor' households in the conurbations of the UK to the impoverished households hard hit by long-term youth unemployment in cities of southern Italy and Spain, or the growing numbers in every large city of young adult, homeless drop-outs. A crucial issue here is the extent to which it is possible for those excluded from secure formal employment to rely on informal work as compensation – and indeed survival.

Another way of thinking about the economic is to focus on the three specific and interrelated economic processes of *trade*, *capital* and *labour* and reflect upon their implications for connections between cities and city life. As an illustration you might look back at Steve Pile's chapter in Book 1 which explores the making and development of Chicago (**Bk 1 Ch. 1** section 2). The narrative on Chicago is underpinned by the way in which these processes have operated over time. For instance, you may recall how Chicago developed as a trading centre for agricultural and other products, and how capital investment in a railway network, centred on Chicago, allowed the city to extend its regional influence. You may also remember how Chicago's growth was integrally linked with flows of diverse migrant groups in search of work and opportunity.

The processes of trade, capital and labour can, then, help to structure your thinking about the economies of cities. For example, we can look at the way in which cities are connected through trading links (exports/imports in a traditional sense, but more importantly the exchanges taking place within and between enterprises operating in and through networks of cities), and capital flows and the implications that this might have for individuals within the labour market. Further, we need to consider the way in which trade, capital and labour are themselves subject to structural adjustments as a result of the actions of the World Bank or the International Monetary Fund (IMF). You will have already come across examples of the way in which such adjustments have impacted upon the lives of city populations. This point is clearly illustrated by the discussion of the impacts of structural adjustment policies by Michael Pryke **(Bk 2 Ch. 6)** which talks about the way in which life has changed dramatically for women in three cities (Harare and Dar es Salaam in Africa and Bogotá in Latin America). We will pick this up again in the next section of this chapter.

Finally, in studying cities using a spatial perspective, you came across a number of interrelated ideas and concepts that have a direct bearing on the economies of cities (see sections 3 and 4 of this chapter). These include such things as commodity and capital flows, points of exchange, migration, as well as less tangible, though equally important, concepts like creativity which is an important process in the renewal and success of city economies. A useful way of organizing these ideas is to think about the economic as operating at different scales, from the level of say financial markets and institutions right down to the level of individuals or communities. Tracing the economic theme through the course materials can inform in new and different ways how we define or think about cities, their precise roles in wider networks of interconnection and how the resultant internal 'disorders' impact upon the individual and their search for economic independence.

Before moving on, let me try to pull together for you the range of definitions or ways of thinking about the economic theme that we have managed to explore so far. Figure 3.1 might help you.

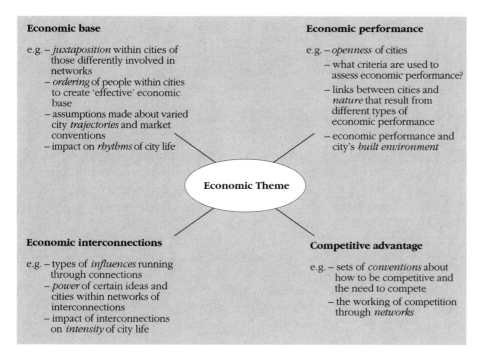

Economic base

e.g. – *juxtaposition* within cities of
those differently involved in
networks
– *ordering* of people within cities
to create 'effective' economic
base
– assumptions made about varied
city *trajectories* and market
conventions
– impact on *rhythms* of city life

Economic performance

e.g. – *openness* of cities
– what criteria are used to
assess economic performance?
– links between cities and
nature that result from
different types of
economic performance
– economic performance and
city's *built environment*

Economic Theme

Economic interconnections

e.g. – types of *influences* running
through connections
– *power* of certain ideas and
cities within networks of
interconnections
– impact of interconnections
on *intensity* of city life

Competitive advantage

e.g. – sets of *conventions* about
how to be competitive and
the need to compete
– the working of competition
through *networks*

FIGURE 3.1   *Aspects of the economic theme*

For me an understanding of the economies of cities must include more than a
perspective based on the private sector and wealth creation. It must touch upon
the lives of those outside the powerful economic circuits (or geometries) which
link together and are the basis of power of major cities **(Bk 2 Ch. 5)**. We cannot
think of the economy as divorced from the other aspects of urban life. So, to
repeat my earlier point, we need to define *economic* in as wide a sense as
possible if we are to successfully understand the way in which the diverse
economies of cities function and contribute to a sense of what cities are. That
means a clear connection to the worlds of the excluded or *dis*connected. An
examination of the world of work is an illustration of how that can be achieved.
Throughout the course there are many examples of these *dis*connections. The
ones that spring to mind immediately are the discussion of divided cities
(Bk 3 Ch. 4), the many Harlems **(Bk 3 Ch. 1)** and the focus on the urban
underclass in western cities and the population of Third World shanty towns
(Bk 3 Ch. 2), but there are many others!

Hopefully, from the above short discussion, you should be more at ease with
what is meant by the economic in the context of the course and also with the
sort of issues that are associated with it. The task now is to help you construct a
clear framework with which you can tackle the economic question as your
course essay.

2 *Developing a perspective on the economies of cities*

2.1   INTRODUCTION

The aim of this section is to demonstrate in more detail how you can use course thinking and ideas to shape your understanding of the economies of cities. I do this primarily with the use of a worked example using a reading by Nigel Harris. The broad theme of the article relates to the implications for city economies of the move away from protectionist policy stances by governments at the international level.

ACTIVITY 3.3   Take some time now to read 'Cities in a global economy: structural change and policy reactions' by Nigel Harris, which you will find reproduced as Reading 3A at the end of the chapter.

As you read this article I want you to concentrate on the following two issues:

●   There are nine key implications of the macro-economic reform for cities listed in the article. Take some time to organize them into a few key impacts by using the type of thinking you have encountered in the course. For example, when Harris talks about the expansion and increased importance of manufactured exports within the economies of cities as a result of the liberalization of protectionist regimes, we can think immediately about the course ideas of interconnections and openness. These notions will help to focus your understanding of the effects on cities of liberalization and, more importantly, through a spatial lens.

●   Explore again the section on the implications of reform for cities: think now about the ability of the emerging macro-economic policy agenda set out in the article to actually respond to or change the nature of urban life for the most disadvantaged groups of city populations. Try to divide these outcomes into positive and negative impacts. ◆

Harris (1997) is in no doubt at all about the implications of the processes of trade, capital and labour, and in general talks in terms of *globalization* as the end-result. Developing the focus on cities he argues that,

> … cities are the most dynamic centres of economic change in national economies. Changes in the world economy thus are likely to have their most radical effects in restructuring the urban economy and in refashioning old settlement patterns.

(Harris, 1997, p.1696)

Why are cities viewed in this fashion? This surely has to do with the notion of *intensity*. It is in cities that we find a multiplicity of economic interconnections coming together to produce effects that are not found elsewhere because of their density and interaction. Further, you will remember that many of the issues raised by Harris have emerged quite strongly in earlier parts of the course and particularly in the chapters by Michael Pryke **(Bk 2 Ch. 6)** and Nigel Thrift **(Bk 2 Ch. 7)**. Thrift argued that 'global economic change is increasingly the preserve of cities involved in often cut-throat competition with one another, in part as a result of [neo-liberalism]' (p.305), a point which Pryke explores in some detail. However, in Reading 3A what you saw was the author using the processes of trade, capital and labour to help 'kick off' *his* story of the importance of urban development in contributing to long-term economic growth. Harris's focus in the article is to demonstrate the effects on cities of the liberalization of a protectionist regime (what he terms macro-economic reform) and to discuss the various reactions that emerged in the 1990s. By contrast the course has provided you with a conceptual framework to understand cities that actually is more meaningful than the single discipline perspective of economics that Harris brings to the debate. By this stage of the course the issues raised by Harris should be familiar, but they can now be used to further develop your grasp of course ideas.

Let us look a little closer at the macro-economic reform package discussed by Harris and begin to connect it to the course debates. What the reform speaks to me of is a process of the *transnationalization* of the state and the ascendancy of neo-liberalism (Lovering, 1995). In other words we can see this transnationalization of relations as further evidence of the interconnections and the 'open intensities' of city life – the active centres, nodes or hubs of dynamic connections according to Castells **(Bk 2 Ch. 5** section 3.2). Neo-liberalism is a concept that should already be familiar to you from your study of Book 2. The policy orthodoxies that drive macro-economic reform are remarkably international in nature. It appears that international organizations, such as the International Monetary Fund (IMF), World Bank, GATT etc., and NGOs (non-governmental organizations) have become key sources of policy and authority alongside, and sometimes out of the reach of, national states. Re-visit Activity 7.1 **(Bk 2 Ch. 7** p.274) to remind yourself of the list of organizations governing the global economy you identified as influencing what goes on in cities. An international scale of governance is not responsible to any formal polity and it 'governs' with relative impunity (Lovering, 1995). So, the prospects for cities and their populations within this emerging international regulatory order remain a matter of much debate (see **Bk 3 Ch. 7** for a discussion on the emerging frameworks for the effective management of cities). The following quote underlines this point:

> One of the truly distinctive features of the world economy in the last decade of this century, especially when compared with mid-century, is that capitalism is now 'global but leaderless' (Glyn and Sutcliffe, 1992).

There is no transnational authority able to develop and administer a framework conducive to the generalization of national growth strategies. There is no coherent global or regional force able to impose or induce a new set of 'regimes of accumulation' oriented towards long-term industrial investment … The international regulatory space which is sustained by the new *'nebuleuse'* is oriented to economic priorities other than the growth of output and employment. It is concerned above all with financial goals, especially the reduction of imbalances amongst the leading countries and the restoration of stability (Singh, 1992).

(Lovering, 1995, pp. 122–3)

The connection between the economic and the political is further highlighted by the statement that, '… the globalization of the economy and its associated patterns of urbanization … rest on a complex web of interdependent and quite stealthy processes that are, collectively, of fundamental importance to the political economy of contemporary societies' (Knox, 1995, p.3).

This view is given further emphasis by Flanagan (1993) who raised important questions about the way in which city administrations in the United States responded to the restructuring of the international economy: see Extract 3.1 below. There was a concern that responses that served business interests did not necessarily serve the interests of the urban population in general and the most disadvantaged members of that population in particular. Such sentiments clearly echo the earlier criticism of Porter's approach to revitalizing the inner cities.

EXTRACT 3.1
W.G. Flanagan: 'Economic restructuring and the new urban reality'

Cities have always been the creatures of the expanding world, reflecting the political and economic conditions that characterize that world … The period of restructuring and adaptation since World War II is the era of immediate relevance to an understanding of the current phase of urban adjustment.

'Restructuring', as the term is used here, refers to widespread economic changes with profound sociological consequences … The most prominent features of restructuring include the relocation of industrial investments, the internationalization of markets, the transnationalization of corporate competition, the withdrawal of capital from manufacture in favor of diversified investment, the continued movement in manufacturing industries to capital-intensive production, the shift for a large section of the labor force from industrial to service employment, and the active competition among agents of local economic growth for mobile investment capital …

…

The restructuring of employment goes beyond the redistribution of work opportunities within and between metropolitan regions. It further includes the internationalization of labor markets, the division of domestic labor markets into the well-paid primary and poorly paid secondary (largely immigrant worker) sectors, technological (labor-saving) changes in industrial production, and the transformation from a manufacturing to a service-based economy …

The globalization of labor markets that puts First World and poor Third World workers in direct competition for many of the same jobs easily translates into the accusation that the former are 'unproductive' and 'spoiled'. The mobility of the employment-creating capital of the multinational firm follows the easy solution: jobs are moved 'off-shore' to the cheaper labor supply …

…

In sum, economic restructuring has not been kind to industrial workers. Yet … the decline in industry has not fallen evenly across the shoulders of all elements of the working class. Some regions, such as those favored by the location of cutting-edge electronic industries or oil exploration and refining have boomed while others … have declined. But, restructuring is a dynamic process, and as such it produces no final end product. Cities different in their origins and place in the international economy … move back and forth, out of the shadows of economic decline and into the light of growth or recovery …

In the mounting conservative mood of the 1970s and 1980s, … government continued to look to the market and to count on growth to remedy any shortcomings of the market-based society.

…

The official economic optimism that characterised the politics of the 1980s, and the persistence and deepening of social problems, eventually led … to … criticisms of the idea that the workings of the market automatically promoted the general social welfare. Many workers in those older cities of the United States that were experiencing recovery found that they were priced out of their housing by rising costs. The restructuring of local employment found many members of the working class commuting long distances to work because the local housing markets were inflated by affluent newcomers employed in the new corporate office towers …

…

Critics believe that the faith that governments place in the capacity of the market to correct the problems of the city is misplaced. The problems, instead, are market-induced …

…

The point that is conveyed most clearly in the foregoing account of restructuring is that locally manifested change is not local in origin. In other words, the big story of the city is bigger than the city itself.

Source: Flanagan, 1993, pp.74–5, 78, 79–80, 81, 83

ACTIVITY 3.4   Look again at the last sentence of Extract 3.1 that refers to the 'big story' of the city. How might you construct that big story? Jot down a few thoughts on how course ideas might be used to underpin Flanagan's discussion. ◆

As I read Extract 3.1 the course arguments of order/disorder, community/difference and movement/settlement came to mind as key elements of that 'big story'. I also found myself moving across all three course books to flesh out the narrative. For example, the idea of movement/settlement, together with community/difference, provides a framework within which we can begin to understand the position of migrant workers in urban labour markets and their locations in the suburbs: the *Roissy Express* extracts in **Bk 2 Extracts 3.1–3.3** and **Bk 1 Extracts 2.2 and 2.5** illustrate this very well. Looking at how McDowell and Allen use this journey demonstrates very clearly the way in which economic tensions interact with social issues. Also this 'big story' impacts very forcibly on the lives of the *dis*connected in cities. However, this 'big story' needs a theoretical framework that enables you to hold the various elements together. The next subsection will address this issue.

2.2   ENGAGING WITH COURSE ARGUMENTS

Returning to the Harris quote at the beginning of the previous subsection you will remember that he is arguing that there is a continual reshaping and redefining of urban space for the many different groups who live and work there. To what extent do you agree with this view? Further, how would you actually go about the task of collecting together the necessary materials that would enable you to assess its validity? Well, the simple reassuring message is that, by this stage of the course, you have already worked through most of the relevant material that would allow you to respond to these questions. Although the course does not give primacy to an economic perspective, the many economic aspects of city life have been explored in some detail throughout the course, albeit in a rather uneven way. And even where the 'economic' doesn't at first sight seem important and is not dealt with explicitly, as soon as one looks more deeply at urban tensions and stories the significance of the economic dimension becomes clear. Even chapters focusing on issues such as order and disorder or transport can be connected to the economic realm.

The purpose of the course essay is to get you to work through the course material again, this time with slightly different questions in mind – about the economic issues confronting cities. In addition, it will help develop your own skills of analysis and interpretation by demonstrating how one can use the conceptual framework of the course to construct your own understanding of cities and city life. This framework is based on three key threads that should now be familiar to you:

- **thinking spatially** about the way in which cities develop and operate
- exploring the series of **tensions** about the way in which cities work
- exploring city **intensities** and their impacts.

Although separated out here, it is important to remember the point made in the Course Guide, Audiocassette 1 Side B and throughout Book 1 – that thinking spatially actively informs our explorations and understanding of tensions and intensities.

Look again at the proposition made by Harris in the quote I used at the start of this section. Can you see how these three key threads help organize your thoughts on the issues raised? Here are some examples, but there are many others.

First, *thinking spatially* encourages you to engage more effectively with the range of factors and processes associated with the reshaping and redefining of urban space. Harris provided an example of how the economic processes of trade, capital and labour were useful in thinking about the economy of cities, but you need to go further and use your grasp of the spatial to construct your own narrative of how the processes of economic structural change impact upon the internal and external shape of urban space. The following quotations illustrate very well how effective thinking spatially can be, as we are able to begin to connect cities to the wider processes of economic globalization (similar sentiments, you will remember, were also advanced in **Bk 2 Chs 6 and 7**):

> Behind all these '*meanings*' of globalization is a simple underlying idea, which can be called de-localization: the uprooting of activities and relationships of local origins and cultures. It means the displacement of activities that until recently were local into networks of relationships whose reach is distant or world-wide.
>
> (Gray, 1998, p. 57)

> Globalization can … be defined as the intensification of world-wide social relations which link distant realities in such a way that local happenings are shaped by events occurring many miles away and vice versa.
>
> (Giddens, 1990, p.64)

Second, the phrase 'redefining of urban space' begs the question 'Who is involved in the redefinition and for whom?' Is it an agenda that involves only those who live and *work* there, or does it involve those who live there but have no formal employment? In raising this question we immediately confront one of the most important *tensions* which exist in cities – the benefits of the market against the costs for certain individuals and groups. Pryke **(Bk 2 Ch. 6)** sums this up very well:

> … as the neo-liberal framework seeks to transform cities and their various spaces into investment opportunities, city life and daily routines all seem set to experience the impact of initial transformation and subsequent unsettling as flows of investment move through them.
>
> (Pryke, 1999, p.258)

The following quote by Lovering (1995) provides further evidence of the *tensions* which exist as a result of the impact of economic restructuring on the lives of individuals in UK cities. As you read it, think about how these impacts might be linked to some of the 'tensions' you have already met in the course – such as community/difference, movement/settlement and order/disorder.

> While the burden of economic restructuring is disproportionately passed to the cities, city dwellers are disproportionately blamed for the consequences. The vilification of unmarried mothers, and the criminalization of unemployed young males and ethnic minorities, target social groups which are disproportionately found in the cities. Lone parents account for up to four times as many households in northern cities as in the rural South, and ethnic minorities are largely confined to urban areas. The deligitimization of the urban poor in the name of the values of the more supposedly 'normal' groups who live in the suburbs is an old and dishonourable theme. The political disenfranchisement of the urban poor in the past decade has been more pronounced in the USA than in Britain, but in this as in many other respects, the USA holds up a picture which shows something of the future for European cities, so long as currently fashionable policy orthodoxies prevail.
>
> (Lovering, 1995, p.122)

Extract 3.2, again by Flanagan (1993), provides a Third World cities' perspective. It shows how relations between cities are varied and uneven, and that economic globalization does not produce the same effects in all cities.

EXTRACT 3.2
W.G. Flanagan: 'Third World cities and the world system'

It is widely recognized that Third World cities are not replications of cities in the economically advanced economies, either with regard to their origins or present circumstances. Discussions of economic change … that assume such parallels lose sight of the important historical, political, and economic differences that underlie urban change and growth in Third World regions, in contrast to the circumstances that produced and have modified cities in Europe and the United States. Among the reasons … are the lingering effects of colonialism, the international division of labor expressed in terms of the nature of exports and imports, and the enormous difference in population size that separate the experiences of currently rapidly urbanizing nations from those of the industrial revolution in its various phases.

However, … it is a mistake to cut off and isolate the discussion of Third World urbanization … The organization of space throughout the world is the physical manifestation of international relations of political and economic forces. It is appropriate to view the Third World cities as different, but their study cannot be separate from the study of cities in general.

…

The dimensions of urban growth in the Third World make it more dramatic than the growth of cities during any other era ... Urbanization in the poorer regions of the world is not typically driven by the expanding need for industrial workers, even though the displacement of industrial jobs from the First to the Third World is having a major impact on urban workforces in the more advanced (sending) economies ... [T]he urban populations of every Third World city suffer high rates of unemployment and underemployment. The industrial roots of Third World urban growth are more remote to today's most rapidly growing urban populations than during the industrial revolution, as the poorest economies continue to rely heavily on the export of agricultural products and raw materials ... Yet, expanding foreign debt, lack of effective domestic and regional markets, and limited levels of popular participation in economic growth cast doubt on any prognosis of a second industrial revolution for the Third World. The different international context of Third World urbanization sets it apart from the circumstances under which the cities of the industrialized West grew and prospered. Third World economies and the populations of Third World cities are considered to be at a disadvantage within the single web of economic expansion, competition, and change that links the world regions together.

Source: Flanagan, 1993, pp.108–10

What is important is that, whilst cities in general have a multiplicity of international economic relations or flows all of which have been conditioned by important historical and political events, for Third World cities these flows are conditioned by a particular history. Currently, the ability of 'cities of the South' to operate 'underneath' a dominant economic rhythm, that dictates structural adjustment policies, is an important question that is considered in some detail by Michael Pryke **(Bk 2 Ch. 6)**.

As we think spatially about cities, we need to work with a multiplicity of relations and their histories. But, that does not simply mean listing the various factors that connect cities, or come together in cities. Course arguments can help you here as they encourage you to recognize how the different strengths and connections come together in such a way as to produce an *intense* set of interactions. This intensity and the creativity that comes from it has the potential to make cities powerful and influential, as Michael Pryke suggests in **Bk 2 Ch. 6**.

Applying course ideas like this to Third World cities enables you to question more effectively the feasibility of these cities becoming 'successful' or 'powerful' in economic terms (see **Bk 2 Reading 5A**). Such thinking clearly has a bearing upon appropriate strategies to deal with uncontrolled urban growth in these 'cities of the South'. Participation in the successful economic networks does not necessarily guarantee sustainable futures. Why not? The answer lies in the nature of the multiplicity of relations and their particular histories. As Flanagan (1993) argues in Extract 3.2 there '... are the lingering effects of colonialism, the international division of labour ...'. You might find it useful to quickly skim-read **Bk 3 Ch. 6** to remind yourself of the debate on sustainability.

The concept of *transnationalization* of the state, and how it forces us to think spatially (the dynamic connections that Castells talked about in **Bk 2 Ch. 5**) is of importance here as we seek to understand the way in which neo-liberalism has set the agenda for the cities of the developing world. By way of illustration let us consider the effects of market reform in Mexico. As Gray (1998) argues:

> The absurdity of neo-liberal reform in Mexico arises partly from the fact that around half the population constitutes an excluded underclass. Increases in wealth that have arisen from market reforms have not trickled down even to the middle classes, still less into the underworld of the poor …

> Where the Mexican state will go in the wake of neo-liberalism cannot be known. A return to the economic nationalism of the past is not on the cards. In Mexico, perhaps more clearly than anywhere else, free market policies have manifestly failed; but they have left the society which they desolated with few positive options.

> (Gray, 1998, pp. 50, 53)

Another example would be to look at the impact of economic liberalism on the process of urbanization in China **(Bk 3 Ch. 6)**. The disturbing aspect of the move towards neo-liberalism has been the concentration on economic policies that are designed to *enable* the market to work effectively – the removal of barriers to the flows of capital for example. The financial crisis that was triggered in Mexico on 20 December 1994 (see Gray, 1998) and affected the Asian economies of the late 1990s served to highlight the perilous and fragile nature of that approach (see **Bk 2 Reading 8A** by Patralekha Chatterjee on 'A new economic reality on Asian city streets'). Consequently, the focus is on process rather than economic and social goals as the following quote from the World Bank on urban policy in the Third World illustrates. Policy should give priority to 'improving the level and consumption of investment, reinforcing the institutional capacity for operation and maintenance, seeking opportunities for greater private sector involvement' (IBRD/World Bank, 1991, p.3). The plight of the urban poor is to be addressed through polices that seek to improve their productive contribution rather than through attempts at redistribution or to involve them more fully in the development process. With the overriding concentration in the urban management agenda on competition between cities to attract and retain mobile assets the economic crisis of cities remains fundamentally untouched. A socially inclusive economic agenda, although recognized by many commentators as the way forward, still remains elusive in practical terms.

Finally, the *intensity* of city life, through the notion of *open intensities*, provides a means of understanding the ways in which changes in the world economy can impact upon individual cities (the rhythm of neo-liberalism perhaps). You can see from this discussion how these three threads are important tools of analysis.

It should be clear from the above discussion that the course essay is both a mechanism for allowing you to *review* the course while at the same time encouraging you to move forward and *apply* that knowledge to a perspective on cities and city life which has not been explicitly explored in the course. We can take this a little further now by providing examples of more precise questions such as

'What are the economic implications of the interconnectedness of cities upon the individual or household and how does this vary from city to city and between groups within the same city?'

or, further,

'How are the economic rhythms of the city connected to, or determined by, the network of powerful cities in the world?'

Such questions can be used in the construction of a spatial narrative and in the identification of the resultant dilemmas and tensions. The emphasis will be to build upon existing arguments and examples from the course to explore the economic dimension to urban issues.

3 Course arguments and the economies of cities

3.1 INTRODUCTION

You have now been introduced to what we mean by an economic perspective on cities and, in doing so, I have begun to point out to you where in the course material you can find the key course ideas, concepts and examples that will help you to understand the range of urban economic issues. In this section I want to expand on the three sets of course arguments that will provide the vehicle for your response to the course essay question posed under the economic theme. I intend to do this by using examples that focus on the ways in which *economic independence* in cities can be achieved. Why is this an important issue? To me it represents how individuals and groups can begin to take control of their own economic affairs in an interdependent world. Central to this issue will be an awareness of how the interconnections, juxtapositions, openness and intensities that constitute cities will impose themselves on any explanatory framework that you might seek to develop.

Before that, however, it is necessary to remind yourself of some of the 'big' questions confronting the economies of cities that you encountered as you worked your way through the course. To me, they include:

- How are the lives of individuals in cities affected by dominant economic rhythms?

- What are the long-term results of the uneven outcomes of the competition between cities?

- What is the future for the urban poor or the 'disconnected' in global cities?

- Whose city is it, anyway, in terms of the variety of economic claims that are made upon urban space?

Central to these questions is the issue of the polarization of urban society between the 'haves' and 'have-nots', a split that should more accurately be described as that occurring between 'work-rich' and 'work-poor' individuals, households and communities. The poor and non-poor, in many instances, do not live as neighbours. As Borooah and Hart state with reference to UK cities:

> … there are several areas where most of the residents are poor and unemployed. The difficulty of securing employment is compounded by the fact that employment opportunities are usually located some distance away from such areas. Moreover, as the concentration of poverty in these areas increases, these areas come to be seen as undesirable places in which to live. Thus, anybody who can leave, does leave … With this migration, the social buffers – in the form of mainstream values – that surround and protect

such areas erode over time and ultimately collapse. Neighbourhoods that have no role models and that have few legitimate employment opportunities will result in their residents possessing only a weak attachment to the labour market. Such persons will aimlessly drift in and out of low-wage, low-skilled employment and, indeed, may turn to illegal activities for income thus further weakening their ties to, and respect for, the legitimate labour market.

(Borooah and Hart, 1995, p.436)

The chapters by Linda McDowell **(Bk 2 Ch. 3)**, Steve Pile **(Bk 3 Ch. 1)** and Gerry Mooney **(Bk 3 Ch. 2)** – to take only three examples – develop many of the issues raised in this quote. When you have time, look back at those chapters and remind yourself of the examples and evidence that they use to demonstrate the impacts of population movements (migration), detached neighbourhoods and undesirable places in the wide range of cities they focused upon. You might like to collect and organize your own material on undesirable places and think about an economic dimension to them.

As a consequence of the weakening ties or disconnection from the formal labour market, urban ghettos possessing all the frightening characteristics of crime, drugs, poverty and unemployment are developing throughout cities. One of the outcomes of these developments is the formalization of ghettos in terms of 'gated communities' and 'building walls' (see **Bk 3 Ch. 3**). It is this depressing trend that prompted me to focus on the world of work as an organizing theme of this chapter.

Finally, whilst the questions and issues raised above dominate many of the debates on the economy of cities, the task for you is to be able to engage with those debates in a meaningful and structured fashion. Consider how McDowell, Pile and Mooney set up their discussions and arguments. What were their organizing frameworks? The *Crossing Paris* project had a clear rationale for Maspero, but we have used that example in a variety of contexts in the course to illustrate the importance of applying course thinking to an understanding of Paris in particular, and cities in general.

The remainder of this section will demonstrate how you can use the key course arguments and ideas. It is course thinking which will enable you to successfully construct your course essay on the economic theme.

3.2   THINKING SPATIALLY ABOUT URBAN ECONOMIES

One of the most important messages of the course has been to show you how much more you can understand of city life by adopting a spatial perspective. When we talk about the pattern of spatial polarization within the city, based on – for the purposes of this chapter – the ability of individuals to gain income from property and occupation, we can only make sense of this through the wider interconnections the city has with other places. Jenny Robinson develops this point very well in her discussion of the economies of differentiation (**Bk 3 Ch. 4** section 2.2). There is a clear interplay between the spatial configuration of the city itself and these interconnections (see also **Bk 3 Ch. 1** which discusses the many Harlems). Another example we can think about is the position of immigrants within France in the post-colonial period. It is, quite simply, impossible to make sense of the scale of ghettoization in French cities (Paris, Lyons and Marseille) without reference to France's colonial past and the aftermath of the Algerian war. This, of course, leads us into the wider issues of migration and citizenship and how they have found expression in the contemporary political, social, economic and cultural life of France and its cities. You will have already come across these issues in the readings about a transect of Paris on the *Roissy Express* (**Bk 1 Extracts 2.2 and 2.5; Bk 2 Extracts 3.1–3.3**). In those extracts you will have read graphic descriptions of life in the suburbs of Paris and how one can make sense of it in terms of a particular focus on movement and settlement. At one level there is the shift from the centre to the suburbs and, on another, the plight of the communities in the suburbs speaks of

> … the changing relations between metropolitan centres and peripheral cities constructed through imperialism or economic exploitation, but their current immobility is a consequence of economic and social changes, especially in the nature of work available in western cities …

(McDowell, 1999, p.117)

Further, the patterns of migration and integration of migrants that, on the one hand, have created the diversity and energy of multi-ethnic cities have also fed directly into the discrimination and inequalities evident in French cities. It is these patterns that help us see cities more clearly as spatial phenomena – at one level increasing the pressures for greater social polarization within cities linked to diverse wider connections.

In addition, as Massey argues (in **Bk 1 Ch. 4**), spatial configurations have repercussions. For example, the city can be thought of as bringing together flows of people and money and, arising out of this, a variety of new associations and interactions develop which produce particular effects. An interesting case is Storper's and Salais' observations on the fashion industry in Paris (**Bk 2 Extract 5.1**).

From an economic perspective let's now explore in more detail what some of these repercussions might be. First, we return to someone whose ideas you have already been introduced to – the work of Saskia Sassen.

ACTIVITY 3.5   Now turn to Reading 3B, 'Whose city is it? Globalization and the formation of new claims' by Saskia Sassen. What is the role that Sassen assigns to immigration in the development of the global economy?

Try to think about the sorts of repercussions that emerge as a result of a growing presence of immigrants in the urban workforce – where will this lead? You may find it useful to refer to **Bk 2 Ch. 3** as it looks at issues of urban migration and movement; it will provide you with a clear understanding of these issues as well as serving to connect them with economic questions. ◆

The final section of the Sassen reading, which addresses the issue of the formation of claims on the city, begins to answer that last question. It also provides a neat link back to the earlier point about the position of immigrants in French cities, and how certain communities and groups have begun to exert themselves in their search for economic independence.

ACTIVITY 3.6   You should now read the article by Sophie Body-Gendrot, 'Pioneering Moslem women in France' – Reading 3C – which documents the economic actions of young women of Moslem origin in French cities and provides you with a graphic picture of the repercussions of 'planned' social segregation. Steve Pile's opening chapter in Book 3 provides some useful contextual material for this article.

What I want you to do is to think spatially about this case study using discussions in the course books (hint: a useful starting-point would be to go back and look at Massey's concluding chapter to Book 1). What are the key aspects of this spatiality that you identified? ◆

My own response to the last question would be to see the dominant spatial configuration as being one of juxtaposition as a result of a clash of two worlds (or cultures) with an interconnected (not separate) history within cities already in economic crisis – the notion of cities as *sites of proximity and co-presence* sums this up quite well (see **Bk 2 Ch. 1**). Further, as McDowell argues, the current immobility of migrant groups in French cities is a consequence of the changing nature of work that has impacted upon the economies of those cities.

I raised the question of repercussions above and we now pick this up in greater detail as we move on to explore the two remaining sets of course arguments concerning *tensions* and *intensities*.

3.3   ECONOMIC TENSIONS IN CITIES

Using the same two readings, we can now explore the second key thread of the course from an economic perspective – the *tensions* that exist as a consequence of the interconnections and juxtapositions between social and ethnic groups and their participation/non-participation in the formal world of work. There is an economic dimension to the production of differences between urban spaces which then feed into the variety of tensions that can be observed. We can go further and argue that these differences between urban spaces have emerged out of the configuration of connections and disconnections within and between cities **(Bk 3 Ch. 1).**

ACTIVITY 3.7   Return to Readings 3B and 3C by Sassen and Body-Gendrot and this time jot down some of the tensions that they document. How do these tensions relate to those that run through the course? You will notice that Sassen refers to the work of Body-Gendrot in the final arguments of her article (see note 7) – for what purpose?

Again, reflect on where these tensions will lead. You might consider the implications at a range of levels: within the Moslem community itself as young women exert themselves in new ways; the competing claims on the city; transnational economic arrangements.

Remember to keep the focus on the economic as you do this, for example the way in which economic forces have produced many of the tensions that we can identify in cities. ◆

What is clear from the Sassen article, and Body-Gendrot provides a perfect illustration of it, is that within the context of the progressive deregulation of national economies, the *transnationalization* of the state and the rise of neo-liberalism, there is a struggle taking place within the city. That struggle, which has been produced to a large extent by a variety of economic relations over time, can best be understood when we begin to apply the course ideas on tensions. Why is that? Simply because, by using a geographical imagination that draws on such notions as community and difference, movement and settlement, and order and disorder, we can understand the numerous ways in which, as Massey argued **(Bk 1 Ch. 4),** the 'spaces and places of our urban world' are created. The primarily economic tensions presented in the Sassen and Body-Gendrot readings are specifically spatial and they, therefore, contribute to the economic mosaic that cities represent.

What strikes me about that struggle is the diversity of interests that are represented. The starkest illustration of these is competing claims between the representatives of international business on the one hand and the large population of low-income immigrant and minority ethnic groups on the other. How can all these competing claims be satisfactorily resolved? The example of young immigrant Moslem women in France demonstrates that by engaging in entrepreneurial activities, they may start to gain the respect of the wider urban population and the business sector in particular. The substitution of autonomy for dependence is the key to those changing attitudes.

A final tension drawn from these two articles that I want you to think about is that provoked by the question – how do we construct appropriate forms of urban governance and economic policies which will respond to this diversity of interests? Reflect back on the arguments presented by Nigel Thrift **(Bk 2 Ch. 7)**. You could also use Reading 3A by Harris to help develop your views on this issue. For Thrift, though, there may be ways in which the vision of a neo-liberal ascendancy over cities can be qualified. Do you remember what his three qualifications were? What is of importance is that Thrift engages with a specifically spatial analysis as he questions the seeming dominance of neo-liberal conventions. Reading 3C by Body-Gendrot provides another example of the attempts being made by those disconnected from wealth and power to construct their own economic networks.

3.4   EXPLORING CITY INTENSITIES: THE 'MIXING' OF ECONOMIC PROCESSES AND OUTCOMES

The final set of course arguments can be developed by referring once again to the two readings by Sassen and Body-Gendrot. This time the emphasis in the discussion will be on the *intensity* or *open intensity* of the relationships that exist in the economies of cities. The existence of the many economic worlds of the city, and their coming together (juxtaposition), captures that essence of a city's open intensity. Allen **(Bk 1 Ch. 2)** captures this intensity very well when he talks about 'the comings and goings of city life'.

Further, Massey **(Bk 1 Ch. 4)** sums up well the value of this approach when she relates the notion of open intensity to an attempt to grasp these multiplicities – within and beyond the city – and in some way hold them in unison. Well, how might we go about that task from the perspective of the economic theme?

ACTIVITY 3.8   Return to Reading 3B and think about the number of economic worlds, or stories, that you can identify within Sassen's sense of the city. Think about how cities connect in different ways with other cities and what binds these economic worlds together. Look again at the Body-Gendrot article for some clues here. Is it related to the nature of the city itself or is it an outcome of economic globalization? The centrality of place, as Sassen argues, is perhaps the key here. ◆

The concept of *open intensities*, when applied to the economies of cities, allows you to talk about the variety of firms, workers and work cultures that can be found there and how they connect the city to the wider network of global cities and the international economy. It is that sense of the city space itself which allows you to observe a vast array of economic relationships both within and beyond the city. The examples of these economic intensities and their spilling over into other aspects of urban life are numerous and can be seen everywhere: spatial imagination is required to piece them all together. Further, it is these intensities which provide the specificity of cities. The individuality, and indeed understanding, of Marseille as a city is wrapped up in a particular history. Traditional images include that of a great trading city and of an urban area made up of many village centres. Recent images include problems of unemployment and ethnic tension related to immigration from North Africa. The nature and scale of the economic intensities to be found there (such as the daily migrant flows to and from North Africa; the commercial infrastructure supporting two separate cultural worlds; and the move into self-employment by certain groups of Moslem women) reflect the city's particular role in France's colonial past. However, towards the end of the 1990s, Marseille began adopting the language of an entrepreneurial city and with the *Euro-Mediterranée* project of urban renewal is attempting to position itself as a key centre in the Mediterranean Basin for trade, services and telecommunications.

The *City Stories* TV series will also provide you with very powerful images of the layering of economic activity in other cities that will allow you to grasp and work with this notion of intensity. The analyses of Singapore, Kuala Lumpur and Moscow each provide illustrations of the intensity of interactions by introducing you to the multiplicity of networks in the city: for example, the impact of the juxtaposition of different networks in the case of Singapore and Kuala Lumpur, and how these networks undergo quite remarkable shifts in quite short time-spans; the connection of Moscow into the networks of the capitalist worlds; and the impact of neo-liberalism upon Mexico City. Further, the notion of intensity allows us to conceptualize the city in more relevant ways and permits us to engage more accurately with the question 'Whose city is it?'.

3.5   SUMMARY

Hopefully, what you have seen in this section is that applying course arguments to the economic theme was vital in order to understand two things. First, the readings by Sassen and Body-Gendrot were given an added dimension by using course thinking to engage with the authors' arguments. This is an important point with respect to the material you will include in your own resource file. Although these readings were new to you, I have connected them to a variety of chapters across the three course books in order that you can go back and explore course arguments and ideas in more detail. Second, the discussion of the world of work (formal or informal) within the economies of cities, and the ability of individuals to connect to it, has been located within the theoretical perspective of the course.

By using the same readings to engage with the three sets of course arguments I have illustrated, you will also have realized that it can be very difficult to talk separately about tensions and intensities and that both these concepts need to be thought through spatially. The existence of open intensities can create sets of tensions which, in turn, contribute to the character of the intensities. To illustrate this point, consider Sassen's discussion of the tensions created by the struggle to re-claim the city. These tensions have been shaped by the multiplicity of economies and work cultures that are found within the city. However, the repercussions of these tensions may well begin to change the very nature of the *economic intensities* – that depends on the nature of the policy response.

So, the task of constructing your course essay on the economic theme should be starting to become much clearer. However, before letting you loose I want to take you through a series of practical steps that you might find helpful in guiding your thinking on the course essay.

4 *Developing a strategy: the economic dimension to urban pathways*

4.1   INTRODUCTION

Chapter 1 of this book sets out in general terms a strategy for your course essay. Before reading any further, go back and read the short section 4 in Chapter 1. Building on that general advice what I want to do in this final section is to take you through three essential steps in the completion of your course essay on the economic theme. They are:

● *Stage 1:* Identifying the economic in the course

● *Stage 2:* Identifying key theoretical arguments

● *Stage 3:* Making cross-course links

The first step in the construction of your course essay is to go through the books, TV and audiocassettes picking out economic issues and problems and developing your own spatial understanding of the material. Also, you will need to select from these materials in diverse ways to draw out and illustrate some of the key economic issues affecting cities. How might this be done? This section illustrates *some* ways in which you can do this and raises some guiding questions for you to think about. Once this has been done, your task will be to apply course-wide arguments and perspectives to the economic theme.

4.2   STAGE 1: IDENTIFYING THE ECONOMIC IN THE COURSE

Where in the course can we begin to extract material on the economic theme? You will have already seen in this chapter the way in which I have connected the discussion on the economies of cities to various chapters in the three course books. This was deliberately selective but hopefully you will have gained sufficient examples to illustrate the vast array of potential material on the economic theme. As suggested in Chapter 1 of this volume, you might like to think about employing the useful tool of 'mind maps' to set out the type of material you want to use and the source. However, a simple list of the key elements in each chapter that are relevant to the theme will also suffice. Below I set out brief thoughts on some of the key issues relevant to the economic theme in Book 1 to get you started.

Book 1 Chapter 1

From the very first section we begin to see that many of the images of the city are dependent upon the notion of the economic power of that city and the way in which certain groups are connected to or disconnected from that power. The following quote from the chapter sums that up quite well: 'New York is born on the stormy seas of money; the city is built on the circulation and use of capital' (Pile, 1999, pp.7–8).

Later, in section 3, we see Pile talking about the intensity of city life and one aspect of that is the heterogeneity of cities. The discussion develops with the argument that 'the social stratification of cities becomes increasingly difficult to determine because people are continually straddling and crossing social hierarchies. People's statuses change, from context to context, and over time' (Pile, 1999, p.47). Although not addressed in the chapter, such a statement immediately raises questions about the economic dimension of *'What cities are'*. For example, you may want to think about the *'city as a work-place'* and how that connects with the discussion of the volatility and intensity of social interactions.

Book 1 Chapter 2

Moving on to 'Worlds within cities', we can continue this focus on the city as a work-place. What we need to think about here is the development of a sense of the economic worlds within cities and the ways in which particular groups are excluded from those worlds. How do these cross-cut the city landscape and what are the effects? Allen provides some very powerful imagery on this from the portrayal of city rhythms at the start of the chapter through to the detailed picture of the nature of city life. In the final section of the chapter the notion of *'indifferent worlds and detached lifestyles'* emerges, which to me is a very depressing narrative to confront. There isn't space to develop the point now but you might like to think about the ways in which these effects can be managed. From an economic point of view the objective is surely to develop the economic independence of individuals, families and communities within the city. How can that be done? How might these responses differ from city to city? As we saw in the Body-Gendrot article (Reading 3C), the response needs to be more fully contextualized using a spatial imagination.

Book 1 Chapter 3

Doreen Massey's chapter, 'Cities in the world', explores the ways in which the economic worlds *within* cities are connected to a global economic realm which itself is acted out through a network of city relationships. This point is picked up in the discussion in section 3 of the chapter when the concept of economic globalization is introduced – a concept you have already met at the start of this chapter. What is particularly useful in this discussion is the way in which Massey makes connections between three sets of ideas: the divisions within the city (see

Extract 3.1 on 'One space, two worlds: on Bombay', which echoes the ideas explored by Allen in his discussion of 'indifferent worlds and detached lifestyles' in section 4.2 of **Ch. 2**); the sets of interconnections between world cities, and the process of economic globalization. If you go back to the discussion in Section 2 of Chapter 3, you will note that these three strands were central to the way I went about constructing a perspective on the economies of cities.

Book 1 Chapter 4

The final chapter fulfils an important review function for Book 1 as well as pushing you further to think about the way we can conceptualize cities. The framework presented by Massey is one that will be important for you as you seek to structure your thoughts on the economies of cities. For example, what you see emerging from the discussion is a sense that we must keep sight of cities as spatial phenomena and understand the economic tensions and paradoxes that emerge.

So, without really getting into the detail, we have been re-examining the nature of *City Worlds,* only this time placing the economic dimension to the fore.

We can engage in a similar exercise with Book 2. For each chapter I will simply set out some ideas and issues relevant to the economic theme: see Box 3.1. You will then have the task of fleshing out the detail and adding your own thoughts. If I was asked to identify a central message for the economic theme from Book 2 it would be:

●   the openness of city economies and their place within the wider networks of economic connections (i.e. flows of money, goods and services and people).

ACTIVITY 3.9   Now try this for yourself using Chapter 7 by Nigel Thrift, 'Cities and economic change: global governance?'. List up to four general areas in this chapter where economic ideas/issues come to the fore. ◆

By now you should be getting a clear picture of where to find the economic material. To complete the task let me set out some of the ways the economic theme connects with Book 3. Perhaps you feel that the material in this book does not seem relevant to any discussion of the economies of cities. I disagree. What we see in Book 3 are some very detailed and informative examples of the outcomes from the range of economic processes at work within and between cities. In Box 3.2 you will find some pointers to Book 3 material of relevance to the economic theme. Again the list is far from complete and is there simply to get you started.

ACTIVITY 3.10   It's important that you make full use of book readings as well as the chapters themselves. With this in mind, choose any reading from Books 1–3 and jot down some of the ways in which it connects to the economic theme. ◆

BOX 3.1: Book 2

Chapter 1
- heterogeneity of city economies
- impact of the global economy upon the economies of particular cities
- global production networks, or chains of activity
- global relations and the intensification of contact between places

Chapter 2
- transport and the making of urban economies
- differing incomes and differing access to transport
- economic consequences of transport congestion and pollution

Chapter 3
- urban migration and movement
- migrants and low paid work in 'servicing' occupations
- the changing economic base of cities
- marginalized migrants in forgotten suburbs?

Chapter 4
- conservation versus economic development
- urban land use and structural adjustment

Chapter 5
- economic power and powerful global cities
- city networking
- economically powerful networks connecting cities as sites of power
- economic well being of marginal groups in powerful/less powerful cities

Chapter 6
- dominant economic rhythms
- neoliberalism
- macroeconomic adjustments (e.g. Stabilization, Structural Adjustment and Export-led Growth policies) and the lives of particular groups of people within cities
- uneven economic outcomes within and between cities

BOX 3.2: Book 3

Chapter 1
- internal differentiation of urban space
- impact of Harlem's economic disconnection from the rest of New York
- disconnected suburbs? – Tupperware products and networks

Chapter 2
- economic change can complicate views of order and disorder (cf. Istanbul)
- images and realities of disorder can hinder the capacity of cities to re-shape their economic futures
- tensions created by negative city images juxtaposed with the notion of an 'economically successful city'

Chapter 3
- replacing public spaces with privatized ones
- impact of shopping malls
- the use of gated communities to protect luxury lifestyles and secure property values

Chapter 4
- economies of differentiation
- impact of segregation on work

Chapter 5
- city 'marketing'
- private-public partnerships
- urban social movements – re-connecting the socially and economically marginalized or disconnected to city life

Chapter 6
- economic factors and processes and the notion of the unsustainable city
- sustainability and continued economic growth in cities?
- tensions between private business costs and the wider social costs
- the economic, environmental and the social realms interconnected

Chapter 7
- attempts to plan urban development in its diverse forms
- proactive development strategies and growth coalitions
- city management in a turbulent global market place

4.3   STAGE 2: IDENTIFYING KEY THEORETICAL ARGUMENTS

As already noted in section 3, an understanding of the economies of cities is greatly enhanced by adopting spatial thinking. Phil Pinch (in the Course Guide) and Doreen Massey **(Bk 1 Ch. 4)** provide some useful discussion of the value of that approach. Therefore, as you begin to put your course essay together, this is something that you need to carry forward in your mind. From the point of view of the economic theme there are a number of ways in which you can harness that spatial thinking.

A useful starting-point is the importance of viewing economic issues in cities in a wider context. All three course books provide a variety of material on that issue, but let me point you towards just one example. It is John Allen's discussion of power in the context of global cities, and the question of whether 'networks themselves "generate" cities as sites of power through their interconnections or whether cities "run" the networks through their concentration of resources and expertise' **(Bk 2 Ch. 5** p.202). To me this captures very well the way that cities may be conceptualized as a 'specifically spatial phenomenon, as a region of particularly dense networks of interaction' **(Bk 1 Ch. 4** p.160). Some elements or flows associated with these networks are transnational investment, migration, movement of goods and services and telecommunications.

Alongside these global networks, *within* cities there is a juxtaposition of different power networks which may create tensions or opportunities. The example of Kuala Lumpur demonstrates that the meeting of western-dominated economic networks with Islamic networks has produced mutually beneficial effects for the financial and economic base of the city. Allen **(Bk 2 Ch. 5)** argues that the trajectory of Kuala Lumpur is very different as a result. So, a key course argument about thinking spatially, harnessing the twin concepts of *interconnections* and *juxtapositions*, is neatly summed up by Allen's questioning of the nature of the economic networks operated by, or running through, global cities.

Another example of how we can use a geographical imagination is to examine the ways in which urban spatial configurations are generative, or in other words, help form and develop economic networks over time. What are these spatial configurations and how might you recognize them in the context of the economic theme? Well, you will be pleased to hear that you have already worked with many of them in the course of this chapter, and indeed in this subsection! They are, of course, the proximities and juxtapositions of economic power networks and overlapping economic rhythms. These help to define the essential economic character of cities and produce a range of effects, including the creation of economically marginalized or excluded individuals and groups while other groups may attain an elevated status as part of a 'command centre' in the global economy. These effects can be worked through with reference to course ideas such as community and difference or movement and settlement and can help us to understand how some groups are connected into different economic networks and to different places, whilst others are disconnected. The divisions within the city reflect these patterns of connections and can lead to an even greater degree of segregation and exclusion.

In turn, these effects – as we have seen in **Bk 3 Ch. 2 –** can feed into city images which can constrain attempts to re-shape their economic futures (linked to the notion of order/disorder). In addition, there may be tensions created by negative city images juxtaposed with the notion of an 'economically successful city'. But, we need to be careful that we do not create simple cause-and-effect relationships as we engage with the notion of spatial configurations as generative. There is an 'openness of the outcome', as Doreen Massey explained **(Bk 1 Ch. 4)**. What this can mean in the context of the economic theme is that the trajectories of cities should not be viewed as inevitable and that city responses in managing economic interdependencies through governance regimes and planning may alter outcomes (see **Bk 3 Chs 6** and **7**).

Finally, you will have noticed that the discussion in this section has not been confined to any particular book or chapter. The key theoretical arguments permeate the contributions in all three books. However, different aspects of the economic theme are developed through each book, sometimes explicitly and sometimes implicitly, and you will need to be as wide-ranging as possible in your preparation for the course essay. The next section provides some further guidance and examples on developing cross-course links.

4.4   STAGE 3: MAKING CROSS-COURSE LINKS

To repeat, one of the key elements of a successful course essay will be the way it brings together material from a variety of sources – chapters and readings in Books 1, 2 and 3, the TV programmes, the audiocassettes and material from this theme chapter. Bear in mind that for presentational purposes only in Stage 1 (section 4.2) I followed the structure of the course – i.e. discussing the three books separately. But as you develop your course essay I would encourage you to take a course-wide view and, therefore, you should move freely between the books and other course elements for source material and ideas. If you look quickly back at sections 2 and 3 of this chapter you will see that I have had to do this in order to define the parameters of the economic theme and also engage with course ideas. I include one or two further examples below to hammer home the message on making cross-course links.

You have seen, for example, that a discussion of 'community and citizenship' **(Bk 3 Ch. 7)** will be informed by an understanding of 'one space, two worlds' in **Bk 1 Ch. 3**. The process that provides the link between them is that of social polarization; this, in turn, from the perspective of the economic theme, may be understood in terms of the detachment of individuals from the formal world of work. Approaching the subject from an economic perspective helps us to shed light on the *tensions* and *intensities* that exist in city life.

Michael Pryke **(Bk 2 Ch. 6)** builds an important bridge to Book 1 via the concept of rhythms. He indicates that 'neo-liberalism has its own motives which can rhythm city spaces and times, creating new intensities and experiences' (p.247).

Think about the way you would make the connection to the arguments of Book 1. Pryke sets out the impact of the dominant rhythm – neo-liberalism – on the lives of individuals and communities within cities. Nigel Thrift **(Bk 2 Ch. 7)** also takes up the concept of neo-liberalism and questions its ability to 'govern' the global economy. The concluding section to Thrift sets out some alternative governance structures for global cities. To add to the discussion I would want to investigate the alternatives to western-dominated economic rhythms and their ability to develop different trajectories for certain cities. As noted in the previous subsection, John Allen **(Bk 2 Ch. 5)** is an important source for debates on economic power networks. Finally, questions of the sustainability of economic growth under that dominant rhythm of neo-liberalism come to mind at this point – where would you pick up these debates in the course?

Finally, let me take you back to the *Roissy Express*! I have used the Maspero extracts **(Bk 1 Extracts 2.2 and 2.5; Bk 2 Extracts 3.1–3.3)** before, but they are worth picking up again in the context of making cross-course links. It is clear that we need to draw upon the interpretations of *both* McDowell and Allen to fully understand the implications of the interconnections and economic networks between metropolitan cities and peripheral cities constructed through imperialism or economic exploitation.

4.5   SUMMARY

What I have set out above is a clear structure for you to tackle your course essay. I have not set out to be comprehensive in my coverage of the course material and cross-course connections. There will be chapters, sections of chapters, TV programmes and, of course, your own resource material, that you will want to use which do not appear in my 'map' of the economic material. All I have done is provide examples of how and where you can locate the material for the economic theme. However, you will have quickly realized that the economic theme permeates all three books and that there are important connections to be made between many of the chapters. I have illustrated how course arguments can be drawn upon to make sense of the economies of cities and, most importantly, to answer the specific course essay question in the Course Essay Question Booklet.

5 *Concluding comments*

This chapter on the economic theme has brought together a range of material and arguments from across the course and has also introduced you to new material and arguments contained in the supplementary readings and extracts. You may wish to add to these with current newspaper cuttings, articles and other forms of material that you encounter as you move through the course. Inclusion of this material is not, as Chris Brook was at pains to point out in Chapter 1 of this volume, an essential element of the assessment for the course essay but it may help stimulate your thinking – and add to your interest in – the economies of cities. The sort of materials that you may find helpful are city profiles in sources such as the quality newspaper supplements as well as publications such as the *Financial Times*, *The Urban Age*, *Cities* and *The Economist* – though as good social scientists you will always be careful about identifying the implicit values of the author of the story you are reading! Further, do not forget that we are interested in your *own* views. We want you to think carefully and critically about course ideas and to demonstrate your understanding by applying them in your own thinking.

As flagged on many occasions throughout the course, and again in this chapter, you should use the TV programmes and audiocassettes as an equally important dimension of the resource material available as you tackle the course essay on the economic theme. They will have certainly provided a range of images which will have shocked, informed and helped you to engage with the course arguments.

Having worked your way through this chapter on the economic theme you should now feel confident and able to start the process of developing your own perspective on the economies of cities in response to the particular question asked by the course team. A final word of advice which your tutor will certainly stress to you. Although in preparing the course essay you will have had to put the blinkers on to concentrate on just one of the themes, please do not lose sight of the connections between the economic, social, environmental and political dimensions of city life. They are not separate stories, as some of my illustrations will have indicated, and you should be sensitive to them. The postscript to this book will develop this point more forcefully. All I can say to you now is good luck in the coming couple of months – hopefully the task will be both enjoyable and rewarding!

References

Body-Gendrot, S. (1993) 'Pioneering Moslem women in France' in Fisher, R. and Kling, J. (eds) *Mobilizing the Community: Local Politics in the Era of the Global City*, London, Sage Publications.

Borooah, V.K. and Hart, M. (1995) 'Labour market outcomes and social exclusion', *Regional Studies,* vol.29, no.5, pp.433–8.

Flanagan, W.G. (1993) *Contemporary Urban Sociology*, Cambridge, Cambridge University Press.

Giddens, A. (1990) *The Consequences of Modernity*, Cambridge, Polity Press.

Glyn, A. and Sutcliffe, R. (1992) 'Global but leaderless: the new capitalist order', *Socialist Review 1992*, London, Merlin.

Gray, J. (1998) *False Dawn: The Delusions of Global Capitalism*, London, Granta Books.

Harris, N. (1997) 'Cities in a global economy: structural change and policy reactions', *Urban Studies,* vol.34, no.10, pp.1693–703.

IBRD/World Bank (1991) *Urban Policy and Economic Development: An Agenda for the 1990s*, Washington, DC, IBRD/World Bank.

Knox, P. L. (1995) 'World cities in a world-system' in Knox, P.L. and Taylor, P.J. (eds) *World Cities in a World-system,* Cambridge, Cambridge University Press.

Lovering, J. (1995) 'Creating discourses rather than jobs: the crisis in the cities and the transition fantasies of intellectuals and policy makers' in Healey, P., Cameron, S., Davoudi, S., Graham, S. and Madani-Pour, A. (eds) *Managing Cities: The New Urban Context*, London, John Wiley.

Sassen, S. (1998) 'Whose city is it? Globalization and the formation of new claims' in Pike, A. and Sobers, D. (eds) *New Lifestyles, New Regions,* pp. 33–40, London, Regional Studies Association.

Singh, A. (1992) 'The political economy of growth' in Michie, J. (ed.) *The Economic Legacy, 1979–92*, London, Academic Press.

Resource materials for the economic theme

READING 3A
Nigel Harris: 'Cities in a global economy: structural change and policy reactions'

1 Globalisation and macroeconomic reform

The term 'globalisation' has become popular –
regrettably so, not only because it is a rather ugly
word, but also because overuse encourages an
imprecision which affects the use of the term for
analytical purposes. Here, the term refers to the
implications of three specific and interrelated
processes: trade, capital and labour.

...

In sum, these processes are encouraging the
emergence of a single world economy, superseding
the national parts and resuming a process of
integration that was marked throughout the nineteenth
century and on until 1914. There are many
implications of these changes, of which three are
particularly relevant here.

First, government macroeconomic policy is
increasingly reactive to changes in the external
economic context, rather than initiating. The current
cult of 'sound economic policies' symbolises the
decline in the possibility of alternative approaches in
the area of political discretion or choice ... Instead of
governments 'representing' populations to the world,
they become mediators, transmission belts for external
changes to reach the domestic economy.

Implicit in the first point is a second. In the past,
governments, particularly in larger countries, tended
to strive for self-sufficiency through creating
domestically a fully diversified microcosm of world
productive capacity; imports and the inflow of foreign
capital were to be minimised. The new agenda accepts
that the national economy plays a specialised role in
an international order, that competitive exports
depend upon the cheapest imports, that one should
be neutral as between domestic and foreign capital
(even this overestimates the ability, in a globalised
capital market, to distinguish on any rigorous basis

between the two). Within countries, this change of
emphasis reorganises domestic patterns of
geographical specialisation. The process of transition
from one economy to the other can be painful,
restructuring economies with some violence (seen at
its most painful in sub-Saharan Africa and the
countries of the former Soviet Union).

Thirdly, domestic markets become increasingly
governed by prices determined in world markets, by
international competition, and this accelerates
processes of structural change (or, in conditions of
rigidity, social breakdown). Economic flexibility
(Killick, 1995), the capacity to respond swiftly and
accurately to external changes, is at a premium, both at
national and local levels. Indeed, much of the
macroeconomic reform programme and of
administrative decentralisation is directed at enhancing
flexibility, minimising the time of adjustment.

To exploit the effects of global integration (or more
often, to avoid the disasters of preventing integration),
requires powerful and disturbing reform efforts by
governments, often in the face of considerable
opposition from those interests which most benefited
from the old order ... The resistance is strongest
where the changes are most specific, as in the
privatisation of state enterprises. Privatisation
subordinates an increasing share of activity which was
formerly determined by political discretion (and hence
the direct pressure of lobbies) to markets and
international competition. Similar issues arise in efforts
to make central banks independent of political
decisions. Thus, simultaneously, lobbies lose the
capacity to determine economic outcomes and
governments lose a major part of their power of
patronage – and hence their capacity to secure their
own political survival. Of course, in practice, there
may be substantial compensations – the forms of
privatisation often benefit a selection of the old
'stakeholders', so the old order of state managers
becomes the new private business class (and pays off
the state bureaucrats for this privileged transition).

Given the considerable disadvantages to
governments in macroeconomic reform, it is
remarkable that the new agenda has been embraced
by virtually all governments, even if with different
degrees of reluctance, single-mindedness and delay.

The shift has occurred apparently without reference to the claimed politics of the governments (Williamson, 1994), including Communist regimes (China, Vietnam, Laos, the Soviet Union and eastern Europe), Social Democratic (Australia, New Zealand, Spain, Portugal, France), liberal-conservative (Britain, the US), left-nationalist-populist (the Peronists of Argentina, the PRI of Mexico), and military dictators (Chile, Indonesia after 1965, Turkey in 1980, Ghana in 1983) … Furthermore, the transition to the new agenda was pressed regardless of the level of development. The universality of the process suggests that it is a response to a new global economic context rather than flowing from the peculiarities of any particular country, even though local factors may precipitate the beginning of the change.

…

The emerging global economic order has undermined the political certainties of the last century and a half, leaving considerable confusion. The old corporatist right and the *étatiste* left are both equally undermined by national policy being superseded by a global order. Sovereignty itself becomes equivocal. The concept of 'national interest' becomes opaque, and therefore the political agendas to advance it.

2   Cities and macroeconomic reform

Cities are the most dynamic centres of economic change in national economies. Changes in the world economy thus are likely to have their most radical effects in restructuring the urban economy and in refashioning old settlement patterns. Guangdong province in southern China, the major beneficiary of China's reform programme, exhibits this process most vividly – with, in the 1980s, some 6 million new jobs in manufacturing (and even more in the non-manufacturing sectors) added to the towns and cities of the Pearl River delta. Shenzhen, a decade and half ago a village on the border of Hong Kong, is now a city of over 3 million inhabitants.

Each city, however, is economically peculiar, with, at a disaggregated statistical level, a unique output of goods and services. Aggregated data – like aggregated geographical areas – normally conceal this uniqueness, this degree of specialisation. In addition, each city enters a common liberalisation process from a different resource endowment (of which location is one), different institutional structure, physical features, etc. Inevitably, the effects of macroeconomic changes will therefore be different in different cities – even if it were possible to isolate the effects of macroeconomic policy from many simultaneous changes (for example, changes in important prices, varying points on the business cycle, technological innovations etc.).

Furthermore, it is difficult to know what time-period should be taken for an evaluation – the Chilean reform programme started in the first half of the 1970s, but the country and the city of Santiago experienced a very severe crisis in the early 1980s, and high levels of unemployment continued until 1986 (Daher, 1996). At any time between 1982 and 1986, the temptation was to declare the reform programme a failure even though, after 1986, the Chilean economy attained the highest rate of growth in Latin America and the lowest rate of unemployment on record, and Santiago experienced a striking renewal. It is thus difficult to 'draw lessons', even though in most countries, there are always nationalists who insist on doing so, automatically attributing all negative outcomes to the action of foreigners (imports, immigrants, foreign companies, international agencies).

Evaluation of the effect of reform is rendered more difficult because the programme is not initiated in tranquil circumstances, but usually is impelled by short-term crisis in the balance of payments and/or the public budget. A recession may be occurring simultaneously, and this is then often attributed to the reforms when the reforms are the result of the crisis, not the cause. (For example, many Canadians blamed the North American Free Trade Agreement for a recession that followed the signing, even though the provisions of the treaty could not have had this effect in the time involved.)

On the other hand, recession is the test of the flexibility of the economy and its capacity for incremental change, of the effectiveness of the reform programme. In Europe and North America, the lack of flexibility in the recessions of 1973–75 and 1979–81 is seen as the source of rapid de-industrialisation and the emergence of inner-city dereliction. By contrast, Hong Kong has been through a succession of very rapid economic transformations in the composition of its output (including a rapid decline in manufacturing capacity) without producing these effects; flexibility permitted incremental change that prevented the kind of physical discontinuity embodied in industrial and inner-city dereliction.

Each recession has a different character, affecting differently different sectors and cities. For example, to oversimplify, the older heavy industry cities of the developed countries which had had growing problems for a long time were most badly affected by the first recession of the 1970s – Glasgow, the cities of the Ruhr, Hamburg, Pittsburgh, Gary (Indiana), etc. The recession of 1979–81 affected more powerfully many of the post-war high growth centres, based on the manufacture of vehicles and other engineering goods (Detroit, Birmingham and the West Midlands).

The third, in the early 1990s, seems to have most affected some of the new service industries and white-collar employment in, for example, south-east England. Again, it is not a practicable procedure to make generalisations about the reaction of all cities to reform in general.

3   The issues

What are some of the key implications of reform for cities?

1   The liberalisation of a protectionist regime leads to a staggered and differentiated decline in physical controls on imports and in tariffs, possibly generating intensified import competition for sectors of the city's production (and also cheapening imported inputs to the city's output). Exchange rate policy can exaggerate or offset some of these effects (often under the old economic regime, currencies were overvalued to cheapen vital imports, so a depreciation can offset some of the import competition and encourage export expansion). Since import-substituting industrialisation strategies commonly have the strongest protection of manufactured imports, and manufacturing has tended to be concentrated in and around large cities, this change can force considerable restructuring of the city economy. This obviously affects employment, incomes and different areas of the city (and, at worst, can lead to areas of dereliction). It is often assumed in Europe and North America that urban de-industrialisation was precipitated by liberalisation, but the evidence is not clearcut – liberalisation of imports, like the low profitability and, thus, low investment rates, extend over much longer periods than that of recession and are not easily correlated. Changes in transport costs as the result of the extension of motorways, improvements in vehicles, etc. affecting the costing of alternative locations for manufacturing, also play a role independently of imports. There are also cases where de-industrialisation can be more closely related to reforms – as in Santiago de Chile or Accra. But the conviction does not turn on these cases and is stubbornly held. Even if the causal attribution is erroneous, it assumes a political significance that affects the capacity of governments to act.

2   In the medium term, liberalisation in developing countries can open major opportunities for labour-intensive manufactured exports, facilitated by cheaper imports of skill-intensive equipment and inputs to exports, and an inflow of foreign capital in the hands of companies with long experience of exporting (as in the case of Hong Kong firms relocating to Guangdong province). The extraordinary growth in garment exports from Dhaka in Bangladesh (Rhee and Belot, 1990) parallels the Chinese experience in this respect, as does the growth in manufacturing for export in Mexico's border region after 1982 (Sklair, 1992).

3   A major expansion in manufactured exports, produced in and around big cities, will stimulate rising employment and wages, and increased in-migration of workers both to jobs in manufacturing itself and in the rest of the city economy. Where urban services are publicly provided, without adequate government anticipation of expanding demand, this can exacerbate existing deficiencies in infrastructure.

There is another negative feature. At present, many developing countries have a comparative advantage in energy-intensive manufactured exports. Although these are less and less manufactured in cities, they are usually located close to them. Furthermore, increasing freight movements, a necessary feature of global integration, will almost certainly pass through the transport junctions normally located in cities, with considerable possible threats to the quality of water, soil and air. This is already apparent – while the developed countries are overwhelmingly producers of the largest share of world pollutants, some of the largest concentrations of pollutants occur in the cities of developing countries (Harris, 1992). Increased pollution damages not only the environment; … it decisively afflicts the quality of life and thus many of the new service industries which are replacing manufacturing. An incapacity or failure to combat this is self-destructive for the emerging city economy.

4   The increased importance of manufactured exports forces governments to take seriously the efficiency of transport junctions (the main source of cost in freight movements) lest high costs here eliminate the competitive advantage in pricing local exports. This will accelerate, for example, the need to reform ports and make major increases in investment in cargo-handling, usually in cargo-unitisation (of which containerisation is the most important element). Without this, cargo tends to move to the most efficient port, abandoning the less efficient – thus, Bombay's cargo would tend to be handled in Singapore, and Mexico's to go through Los Angeles or Baltimore. In the reorganisation of ports to accommodate unitisation, there are well-known effects in terms of the relocation of the facilities (often to completely new ports in greenfield sites), the rapid decline in the dock labour force, the closure of dock-related manufacturing and other activities (and the stimulation of activity around inland container terminals), the emergence of large areas of derelict former port land, often close to city centres (the same phenomenon may also affect former railway lands). In many cities – for example Hamburg, New York, Yokohama, Sydney, London, Cape Town (Pentecost, 1992; Turlik, 1992; Ikeda, 1992) – this has been the opportunity for major redevelopment schemes to strengthen the new economic functions of the city.

5 The opening up of national economies confronts a city with the need for increasingly swift reactions to changes in the external economic environment. The introduction of just-in-time stock policies in manufacturing is a good example of practices where any delays in freight movement can have disastrous economic consequences. Thus, the quality of the transport system and the efficiency of its management become crucial in ensuring the reliability of movement, minimising the time lost in junction transfers. The design of multi-modal junctions to minimise the costs of transfer between sea, air, road and rail systems is becoming one way of seeking to minimise the costs of movement. The competition between cities in the provision of transport facilities, is already intense – in east Asia, for example, in container berths between Singapore, Hong Kong, Kiaohsiung, Inchon and Kobe; or in new airports, between Hong Kong, Kansai, Seoul, Taipei, etc.

6 The extraordinary increase in the international flows of capital transforms the former financial quarters of cities. Often, existing centres are part of the oldest parts of the city, quite ill-equipped to expand, and therefore imposing higher costs on financial transactions – to the loss of the national economy. Investment in modern telecommunications becomes crucial in the development of a modern central business district, as the improvement in air facilities is needed to allow increased passenger movement connected to financial activity. Competition between countries and cities also forces deregulation and debureaucratisation. In the case of Guangdong province, local authorities competed for foreign capital and thus sought to eliminate all unnecessary restrictions on investment. On the other hand, a decline in regulation and increasing ease of movement of finance ties cities into externally determined patterns of financial interaction. Renaud (1995) has recently attempted to illustrate the interactions between Japanese credit policy, Tokyo's land market and the escalation – and subsequent collapse – of land and property prices in many cities of the world in the late 1980s. City management becomes very much more difficult in such a context.

7 A subject that has received most attention in the literature is the impact on the poor of macroeconomic reform, particularly the impact of increasing prices for necessities, reduced employment following reductions in public spending and the privatisation of state assets, the effects of cuts in health, education and social security spending, of the removal of consumer subsidies, etc. Although there is a popular conception that the reforms automatically reduce the condition of the poor – and there are clearcut cases where this seems abundantly true – the general evidence is less than clearcut. It is not always clear who were the beneficiaries of the old order, and to what extent, and therefore what the effects of the changes are, particularly in the light of the next factor. However, it would be irresponsible of those managing cities to be complacent in the face of these threats to social conditions, and adequate monitoring of the course of reforms is required to identify where the changes are deleterious so that remedial action can be taken.

8 Whether it is related to macroeconomic reforms or to earlier changes (for example, the major increase in state regulation in the 1970s), an increasing proportion of economic activity seems to be slipping below the threshold of the statistical reporting system; it is becoming 'informal' (though the term is particularly misleading). Again, it is popularly supposed that this represents a deterioration in the conditions of employment and incomes for those involved, although this is, again, not self-evident. Statistically unrecorded activity covers the whole gamut of the city economy, from the above- to the below-average, so generalisation is fraught with problems. The growth of the informal sector is popularly seen as a coping response by the poor to declining incomes, as if labour supply could determine labour demand. But it is equally possible that an important change in labour demand has occurred, leading to the expanded employment, for example, of women. This in turn has in some cases sustained household income in conditions where the official economy appears to be in severe decline. However, the more general point is that an increasing part of the economy is no longer being recorded in the available figures, and alternative routes to the truth – or, at least, sensible guesses – are required.

9 Finally, in terms of city governance, it seems that global economic integration is tending to promote *de factor* or *de jure* administrative decentralisation, a reversal of the long trend towards increased centralisation of the state. There are notable examples – France, Colombia, Spain, India and especially, China. This trend is parallel to a process taking place at the local level, the fragmentation or diversification of responsibility for city governance. One element here is the privatisation of city services; another, the active initiative of business associations, non-government organisations and universities in local urban improvement and management. In Europe and North America, new partnerships or city fora bring together these forces for collaborative projects.

4   Specific reactions

How have cities reacted to the onset of economic restructuring? The most extreme forms of restructuring were experienced in older industrial cities in Europe and North America in the 1970s and 1980s, combining high levels of unemployment, de-industrialisation and the emergence of large areas of dereliction in both inner-city, port and industrial areas. The incapacity for incremental change was violently revealed in terms of physical, social and economic decay.

Initially, national governments and cities endeavoured to finance manufacturing enterprises threatened with closure. (In India, for example, such enterprises were classified as 'sick industries' and became the recipients of subsidies to continue operation with the intention of preserving employment.) At the same time, efforts were made to try to support, often financially, new enterprises and foreign-inward investment. Considerable sums were expended in this way, and national governments and cities in Europe and state governments in the US competed in a quasi-auction to bribe large international companies to invest in their localities. The costs and risks were high, the returns poor, particularly insofar as such efforts were supposedly directed at reducing unemployment. Through a painful process of learning, cities increasingly came to abandon large-scale and mass-assembly manufacturing, the former major employers of city labour forces, and to accept the implicit trends and facilitate the growth of specialised services, now seen in an international rather than regional or national context.

The concentration – in conditions of economic flexibility – shifted the character of planning. Numerous cities formulated 'visions' or scenarios, often linked to the arrival of the second millennium. These were not plans in the old sense since they were not intended to be the subject of statutory provision or to be adhered to regardless of circumstances; they were to be changed according to how events worked out. They were political and promotional rather than technical documents, directed at securing a consensus of city interests. The politics of creating agreement among the city 'stake-holders' (the word itself was a newcomer, presumably designed to avoid the negative connotation of city interests, particularly 'vested interests', although this in effect was what they were) took priority over the technical validity of what was proposed.

In seeking to develop a bundle of specialised services, city authorities did not start with a blank sheet, but rather identified what already existed or was emerging as the result of market demands – for example, finance, producer services (often for manufacturing regions), personal and social services, commercial services, retail and wholesale trade, restaurants and hotels, services in transport, health, education, culture, sports, research and development, etc.

...

Some cities created a complex of interrelated activities in the provision of health services – teaching and research hospitals, university faculties of medicine, specialised clinics, pharmaceutical and medical engineering facilities, as well as specialised medical consultancy services. Barcelona and Bogotá offered package tours for patients, combining in one price, credit facilities, travel, hotels, the costs of treatment and convalescence. The package presupposed a desirable city, an adequate external and internal transport system, cultural facilities, etc.

Cities have set up universities or sought to exploit existing universities as the focus for services, assuming a much wider economic impact from higher education through a significant expansion in local demand for accommodation, foodstuffs, transport, entertainment, etc. With foreign students, this constitutes a major expansion in export earnings ... Furthermore, universities, it is thought, can upgrade local human capital (or attract it from elsewhere), provide research and development for advanced research-based manufacturing, often facilitated by the creation of a science park of the more ambitious technopoles of France and Japan. They also stimulate local cultural life and entertainment, as a basic means to expand tourism. Lyons tried to develop universities on an island in the Rhône river as the nucleus of an attractively designed 'left bank' – a university quarter, with restaurants, theatres, bookshops, etc. – as a means to expand tourism. The idea of a university as the generator of inner-city economic activity is in marked contrast to the American idea of a campus, a relatively isolated entity, often in a greenfield site remote from cities.

'Festivalisation' has also become more fashionable (although, whether consciously or not, many cities have pursued similar projects over a long period of time) – that is, seeking to hold major popular events to provide the pretext for extensive investment in refurbishing the city fabric; expand, albeit temporarily, the market for city output; and leave a permanent stock of physical capital for future growth. In the well-known case of Barcelona (Pons, 1993; Ajuntament de Barcelona, 1990), the Olympic Games of 1992 were employed in this way ...

Other services hold high potential for future growth, particularly in developing countries. The dispersal of formerly unified manufacturing processes between several countries (most notably, between the US and Mexico; east and south-east Asia; or Germany and north Africa and eastern Europe) depended upon the process concerned being 'unbundled' – broken into a discrete set of operations which could be fitted to advantage to the factor endowments of different countries. (At its most primitive, this means locating labour-intensive processes in areas with relatively low labour costs, and skill-intensive processes where skills are abundant.) Something similar has for some time been occurring in services (UNCTAD/World Bank, 1994) which is perhaps why the topic was for the first time included in the Uruguay GATT round of negotiations. This provides significant opportunities for cities. Unfortunately – and notoriously – services are ill-recorded statistically, partly because of conceptual difficulties, so general figures tend to be at such a high level of aggregation that they show little which is analytically illuminating. The opposite extreme leads us to anecdotal evidence which, despite its unsatisfactory character, is the best available.

Data-loading and processing are intrinsically intensive in the use of educated labour and thus suitable for location in those developing countries with an already significant supply of the educated. Airline and banking back-office tasks are prototypes of this – for example, Swiss Air's accounting and ticketing services are located in Bombay, American Airlines in Barbados. The processing of real estate transactions is another example: the largest Japanese real estate company sub-contracts the data processing to Shenzhen in China. Government bureaucratic transactions might move more easily if there was a lesser obsession with security of information (but British criminal records were recently loaded in Manila, courtesy of an Australian intermediary). The loading of library catalogues, of museum collections, of medical or demographic (births, deaths and marriages, for example) records, and indeed, of any other major data sources is likely thus to be relocated in the future. A more skill-intensive example of unbundling has emerged in Bangalore and Bombay which have become centres for software programming for Silicon Valley in California. Satellite technology is likely to make possible many similar kinds of relocations of parts of processes.

Again, it would be unwise to regard many of these activities as isolated sectors. The internationalisation of cities (their increasing dependence on providing services internationally), of which foreign tourism is the most striking and growing example, depends upon an acceptable quality of urban life, transport, security and infrastructure. The old agenda of public services, then seen as simply provisions for the local population – to allow them to manufacture efficiently! – now returns as a precondition for becoming economically viable in the international context. It strengthens the case for effective public authorities in managing and facilitating economic growth and change. Local government, the orphan of modern governmental systems, thus becomes much more important. It is perhaps the coincidence of national and local government in Hong Kong and Singapore (with a very different character of public intervention) which has made for most effective economic management.

A city can only attain the capacity to adjust quickly, to increase the degree of flexibility in response to external changes, if it possesses accurate and timely information – otherwise, people learn of a changed structure only long after it has happened (or through the by-product of rising unemployment, increased in- or out-migration, or urban dereliction). The city economy is unknown terrain for most city officials; they know little of the city's comparative advantages and disadvantages, so management can hardly be other than blind. A symbol of this blindness is the lack of an up-to-date regularly produced statistical yearbook for the city, an instrument both for the city's officials, for promotion and, above all, for the citizens to be effective participants. Hitherto, such information has not been at all important for running cities, and still, even with new responsibilities, many city managers do not see the point of it. However, decentralisation within an open world economy implies that sub-national levels of government acquire responsibilities that were formerly exclusively held by national governments, and correspondingly are required to begin to operate more like national governments – where the supply of information, monitoring and evaluating the performance of key sectors, becomes a critical factor in public action …

Macroeconomic reform, moving towards open economies, involves significant changes at the level of the city – of economic structures, of relationships between local and national governments and local government and the citizens. The emergence of an 'entrepreneurial city' out of the old form of a servicing agency is a far aim for most cities, but where the hammer of recession was most brutal, in the older industrial cities of Europe and North America, it is becoming a more serious phenomenon. The city is, in the final analysis, a concentration not of bricks and mortar (the so-called built environment), nor of capital equipment, but of human intelligence, and it is this which is the key to the employment and incomes of the citizens, to the resources available.

References

Ajuntament de Barcelona (1990) *Pla Estrategic Ecónomie i Social,* Ajuntament, Barcelona, 19 March.

Daher, A. (1996) 'Santiago de Chile: the second turning point' in Harris, N. and Fabricius, I. (eds) *Cities and Structural Adjustment,* pp.214–29, London, UCL Press.

Harris, N. (1992) 'Wastes, the environment and the international economy', *Cities,* August, pp.177–85.

Ikeda, T. (1992) 'Minato Mirai 21 Plan', paper presented to the International Conference on Urban Development Policies and Projects, 19–23 October, Nagoya, Centre for Urban Advancement.

Killick, T. (ed.) (1995) *The Flexible Economy: The Causes and Consequences of the Adaptability of National Economies,* London, Overseas Development Institute.

Pentecost, R.W. (1992) 'Waterfront Development Project: Darling Harbour', paper presented to the International Conference on Urban Development Policies and Projects, 19–23 October, Nagoya, Centre for Urban Advancement.

Pons, J.M. (1993) 'How Barcelona used the 1992 Olympics to rebuild the city', paper presented to the American Planning Association Conference, 1 May, Chicago.

Renaud, B. (1995) *The 1985–94 Global Real Estate Cycle: Its Causes and Consequences,* Policy Research Working Paper 1452, Washington, DC, World Bank.

Rhee, Y.W. and Belot, T. (1990) *Export Catalysts in Low-income Countries: A Review of Eleven Success Stories,* Discussion Paper 72, Washington, DC, World Bank.

Sklair, L. (1992) *Assembling for Development: The Maquila Industry in Mexico and the United States,* Boston, MA, Unwin Hyman Books.

Turlik, P. (1992) 'London Docklands Development Project', paper presented to the International Conference on Urban Development Policies and Projects, 19–23 October, Nagoya, Centre for Urban Advancement.

UNCTAD/World Bank (1994) *Liberalizing International Transactions in Services: A Handbook,* New York and Geneva, United Nations.

Williamson, J. (ed.) (1994) *The Political Economy of Policy Reform,* Washington, DC, Institute of International Economics.

Source: Harris, 1997, pp.1693, 1694–1703

READING 3B
Saskia Sassen: 'Whose city is it? Globalisation and the formation of new claims'

The organising theme is that place is central to the multiple circuits through which economic globalisation is constituted. One strategic type of place for these developments and the one focused on here, is the city. Why does it matter to recover the place in analyses of the global economy, particularly place as constituted in major cities? Because it allows us to see the multiplicity of economies and work cultures in which the global information economy is embedded. It also allows us to recover the concrete, localised processes through which globalisation exists and to argue that much of the multi-culturalism in large cities is as much a part of globalisation as is international finance. Finally, focusing on cities allows us to specify a geography of strategic places at the global scale, places bound to each other by the dynamics of economic globalisation.

I refer to this as a new geography of centrality, and one of the questions it engenders is whether this new transnational geography also is the space for a new transnational politics. Insofar as my economic analysis of the global city recovers the broad array of jobs and work cultures that are part of the global economy though typically not marked as such, it allows me to examine the possibility of a new politics of traditionally disadvantaged actors operating in this new transnational economic geography. This is a politics that arises out of actual participation as workers in the global economy, but under conditions of disadvantage and lack of recognition – whether factory workers in export processing zones or cleaners on Wall Street.

The centrality of place in a context of global processes makes possible a transnational economic and political opening for the formation of new claims and hence for the constitution of entitlements, notably rights to place. At the limit, this could be an opening for new forms of 'citizenship'. The city has indeed emerged as a site for new claims: by global capital which uses the city as an 'organisational commodity', but also by disadvantaged sectors of the urban population, frequently as internationalised a presence in large cities as capital. The de-nationalising of urban space and the formation of new claims by transnational actors, raise the question: whose city is it?

I see this as a type of political opening that contains unifying capacities across national boundaries and sharpening conflicts within such boundaries. Global capital and the new immigrant workforce are two major instances of transnationalised actors that have unifying properties internally and find themselves in contestation with each other inside global cities. Global cites are the sites for the over-valorisation of corporate capital and the devalorisation of disadvantaged workers. The leading sectors of corporate capital are now global, in their organisation and operations. And many of the disadvantaged workers in global cities are women, immigrants, people of colour – men and women whose sense of membership is not necessarily adequately captured in terms of the national, and indeed often evince cross-border solidarities around issues of substance. Both types of actors find in the global city a strategic site for their economic and political operations.

The analysis presented here grounds its interpretation of the new politics made possible by globalisation in a detailed understanding of the economics of globalisation, and specifically in the centrality of place in a context where place is typically seen as neutralised by the capacity for global communications and control. My assumption is that it is important to dissect the economics of globalisation in order to understand whether a new transnational politics can be centred in the new transnational economic geography. Secondly, I think that dissecting the economics of place in the global economy allows us to recover non-corporate components of economic globalisation and to inquire about the possibility of a new type of transnational politics. Is there a transnational politics embedded in the centrality of place and in the new geography of strategic places, such as is for instance the new worldwide grid of global cities? This is a geography that cuts across national borders and the old North-South divide.

Immigration, for instance, is one major process through which a new transnational political economy is being constituted, one which is largely embedded in major cities insofar as most immigrants, whether in the US, Japan or Western Europe are concentrated in major cities. It is, in my reading, one of the constitutive processes of globalisation today, even though not recognised or represented as such in mainstream accounts of the global economy. These are the main issues addressed in this brief paper.

Place and work-process in the global economy

I think of the mainstream account of economic globalisation as a narrative of eviction. Key concepts in that account – globalisation, information economy, and telematics – all suggest that place no longer matters and that the only type of worker that matters is the highly educated professional. It is an account that privileges the capability for global transmission over the material infrastructure that makes such transmission possible; information outputs over the workers producing those outputs, from specialists to secretaries; and the new transnational corporate culture over the multiplicity of work cultures, including immigrant cultures, within which many of the 'other' jobs of the global information economy take place. In brief, the dominant narrative concerns itself with the upper circuits of capital; and particularly with the hypermobility of capital rather than with that which is place-bound.

Massive trends towards the spatial dispersal of economic activities at the metropolitan, national and global level are indeed all taking place, but they represent only half of what is happening. Alongside the well-documented spatial dispersal of economic activities, new forms of territorial centralisation of top-level management and control operations have appeared. National and global markets as well as globally integrated operations require central places where the work of globalisation gets done. Further, information industries require a vast physical infrastructure containing strategic nodes with hyperconcentrations of facilities. Finally, even the most advanced information industries have a work process – that is, a complex of workers, machines and buildings that are more place-bound and are more diversified in their labour inputs than the imagery of information outputs suggests.

Centralised control and management over a geographically dispersed array of economic operations does not come about inevitably as part of a 'world system'. It requires the production of a vast range of highly specialised services, telecommunications infrastructure, and industrial services. These are crucial for the valorisation of what are today leading components of capital. A focus on place and work-process displaces the focus from the power of large corporations over governments and economies to the range of activities and organisational arrangements necessary for the implementation and maintenance of a global network of factories, service operations and markets. These are all processes only partly encompassed by the activities of transnational corporations and banks.

One of the central concerns in my work has been to look at cities as production sites for the leading service industries of our time, and hence to recover the infrastructure of activities, firms and jobs, that is necessary to run the advanced corporate economy. The focus is on the practice of global control: the work of producing and reproducing the organisation and management of a global production system and a global marketplace for finance, both under conditions of economic concentration (see Sassen, 1991, 1994). This allows in turn a focus on the infrastructure of jobs involved in this production, including low-wage, unskilled manual jobs typically not thought of as being part of advanced globalised sectors.

Global cities are centres for the servicing and financing of international trade, investment and headquarter operations. That is to say, the multiplicity of specialised activities present in global cities are crucial in the valorisation, indeed overvalorisation of leading sectors of capital today. And in this sense they are strategic production sites for today's leading economic sectors. This function is reflected in the ascendance of these activities in their economies. Elsewhere (Sassen, 1994, Ch. 4) I have posited that what is specific about the shift to services is not merely the growth in service jobs but, most importantly, the growing service intensity in the organisation of advanced economies: firms in all industries, from mining to wholesale buy more accounting, legal, advertising, financial, economic forecasting services today than they did twenty years ago. Whether at the global or regional level, cities are adequate and often the best production sites for such specialised services. The rapid growth and disproportionate concentration of such services in cities signals that the latter have re-emerged as significant 'production' sites after losing this role in the period when mass manufacturing was the dominant sector of the economy. Under mass manufacturing and Fordism, the strategic spaces of the economy were the large-scale integrated factory and the government through its Fordist/Keynesian functions.

A focus on the work behind command functions, on the actual production process in the finance and services complex, and on global market *places* has the effect of incorporating the material facilities underlying globalisation and the whole infrastructure of jobs typically not marked as belonging to the corporate sector of the economy. An economic configuration very different from that suggested by the concept information economy emerges. We recover the material conditions, production sites, and place-boundedness that are also part of globalisation and the information economy.

We recover the broad range of types of firms, types of workers, types of work cultures, types of residential milieux, that are also part of globalisation processes though never marked, recognised, or represented as such. Nor are they valorised as such. In this regard, the new urban economy is highly problematic. This is perhaps particularly evident in global cities and their regional counterparts. It sets in motion a whole series of new dynamics of inequality (Sassen, 1994, Ch. 5). The new growth sectors – specialised services and finance – contain capabilities for profit making vastly superior to those of more traditional economic sectors. Many of the latter remain essential to the operation of the urban economy and the daily needs of residents, but their survival is threatened in a situation where finance and specialised services can earn super-profits and bid up prices.[1] Polarisation in the profit-making capabilities of different sectors of the economy has always existed. But what we see happening today takes place on another order of magnitude and is engendering massive distortions in the operations of various markets, from housing to labour. We can see this effect; for example, in the retreat of many real estate developers from the low- and medium-income housing market in the wake of the rapidly expanding housing demand by the new highly paid professionals and the possibility for vast overpricing of this housing supply.

What we are seeing is a dynamic of valorisation which has sharply increased the distance between the valorised, indeed overvalorised, sectors of the economy and devalorised sectors even when the latter are part of leading global industries. This devalorisation of growing sectors of the economy has been embedded in a massive demographic transition towards a growing presence of women, African-Americans and 'third world' immigrants in the urban workforce, a subject I return to later.

We see here an interesting correspondence between great concentrations of corporate power and large concentrations of 'others'. Large cities in the highly developed world are the terrain where a multiplicity of globalisation processes assume concrete, localised forms. A focus on cities allows us to capture, further, not only the upper but also the lower circuits of globalisation. These localised forms are, in good part, what globalisation is about. We can then think of cities also as one of the sites for the contradictions of the internationalisation of capital. If we consider, further, that large cities also concentrate a growing share of disadvantaged populations – immigrants in Europe and the United States, African-Americans and Latinos in the United States – then we can see that cities have become a strategic terrain for a whole series of conflicts and contradictions.

Unmooring identities and a new transnational politics

Typically, the analysis about the globalisation of the economy privileges the reconstitution of capital as an internationalised presence; it emphasises the vanguard character of this reconstitution. At the same time it remains absolutely silent about another crucial element of this transnationalisation, one that some, like myself, see as the counterpart of that of capital: this is the transnationalisation of labour. We are still using the language of immigration to describe this process.[2] Secondly, that analysis overlooks the transnationalisation in the formation of identities and loyalties among various population segments that explicitly reject the imagined community of the nation. With this come new solidarities and notions of membership. Major cities have emerged as a strategic site for both the transnationalisation of labour and the formation of transnational identities. In this regard they are a site for new types of political operations.

Cities are the terrains where people from many different countries are most likely to meet and a multiplicity of cultures come together. The international character of major cities lies not only in their telecommunication infrastructure and international firms: it lies also in the many different cultural environments in which these workers exist. One can no longer think of centres for international business and finance simply in terms of the corporate towers and corporate culture at its centre. Today's global cities are in part the spaces of post-colonialism and indeed contain conditions for the formation of a post-colonialist discourse.[3]

The large Western city of today concentrates diversity. Its spaces are inscribed with the dominant corporate culture but also with a multiplicity of other cultures and identities. The slippage is evident: the dominant culture can encompass only part of the city.[4] And while corporate power inscribes these cultures and identities with 'otherness' thereby devaluing them, they are present everywhere. For instance, through immigration a proliferation of originally highly localised cultures now have become presences in many large cities, cities whose elites think of themselves as cosmopolitan, that is transcending any locality. An immense array of cultures from around the world, each rooted in a particular country or village, now are reterritorialised in a few single places, places such as New York, Los Angeles, Paris, London, and most recently Tokyo.[5]

Immigration and ethnicity are too often constituted as 'otherness'. Understanding them as a set of processes whereby global elements are localised, international labour markets are constituted, and cultures from all over the world are deterritorialised, puts them right there at the centre of the stage along with the internationalisation of capital as a fundamental aspect of globalisation today. There has been growing recognition of the formation of an international professional class of workers and of highly internationalised environments due to the presence of foreign firms and personnel, the formation of global markets in the arts, and the international circulation of high culture. What has not been recognised is the possibility that we are seeing an internationalised labour market for low-wage manual and service workers. This process continues to be couched in terms of the 'immigration story', a narrative rooted in an earlier historical period.

I think that there are representations of globality, which have not been recognised as such or are contested representations. Among these is the question of immigration, as well as the multiplicity of cultural environments it contributes in large cities, often subsumed under the notion of ethnicity. What we still narrate in the language of immigration and ethnicity I would argue is actually a series of processes having to do with the globalisation of economic activity, of cultural activity, of identity formation. Immigration and ethnicity are constituted as otherness. Understanding them as a set of processes whereby global elements are localised, international labour markets are constituted, and cultures from all over the world are de- and re-territorialized, puts them right there at the centre along with the internationalisation of capital as a fundamental aspect of globalisation. This way of narrating the migration events of the post-war era captures the ongoing weight of colonialism and post-colonial forms of empire on major processes of globalisation today, and specifically those binding emigration and immigration countries.[6] While the specific genesis and contents of their responsibility will vary from case to case and period to period, none of the major immigration countries are [sic] innocent bystanders.

Making claims on the city

These processes signal that there has been a change in the linkages that bind people and places and in the corresponding formation of claims on the city. It is true that throughout history people have moved and through these movements constituted places. But today the articulation of territory and people is being constituted in a radically different way at least in one regard, and that is the speed with which that articulation can change. One consequence of this speed is the expansion of the space within which actual and possible linkages can happen. The shrinking of distance and of time that characterises the current era finds one of its most extreme forms in electronically based communities of individuals or organisations from all around the globe interacting in real time and simultaneously, as is possible through the internet and kindred electronic networks.

I would argue that another radical form assumed today by the linkage of people to territory is the loosening of identities from what have been traditional sources of identity, such as the nation or the village. This unmooring in the process of identity formation engenders new notions of community, of membership and of entitlement.

The space constituted by the global grid of global cities, a space with new economic and political potentialities, is perhaps one of the most strategic spaces for the formation of transnational identities and communities. This is a space that is both place-centred in that it is embedded in particular and strategic sites; and it is transterritorial because it connects sites that are not geographically proximate yet intensely connected to each other. As I argued earlier, it is not only the transmigration of capital that takes place in this global grid, but also that of people, both rich, i.e. the new transnational professional workforce, and poor, i.e. most migrant workers; and it is a space for the transmigration of cultural forms, for the reterritorialisation of 'local' subcultures. An important question is whether it is also a space for a new politics, one going beyond the politics of culture and identity, though at least partly likely to be embedded in these.

Yet another way of thinking about the political implications of this strategic transnational space is the notion of the formation of new claims on that space. Has economic globalisation at least partly shaped the formation of claims? There are indeed major new actors making claims on these cities, notably foreign firms who have been increasingly entitled to do business through progressive deregulation of national economies and the large increase over the last decade in international business people. These are among the new city users. They have profoundly marked the urban landscape. Their claim to the city is not contested, even though the costs and benefits to cities have barely been examined. These claims contribute to the incipient de-nationalisation dynamics discussed in the previous section which though institutional, tend to have spatial outcomes disproportionately concentrated in global cities.

Perhaps at the other extreme of conventional representations are those who use urban political violence to make their claims on the city, claims that lack the de facto legitimacy enjoyed by the new 'city users'. These are claims made by actors struggling for recognition, entitlement, claiming their rights to the city.[7]

There are two aspects in this formation of new claims that have implications for the new transnational politics. One is sharp and perhaps sharpening differences in the representation of these claims by different sectors, notably international business and the vast population of low income 'others' – African-Americans, immigrants, and women. The second aspect is the increasingly transnational element in both types of claims and claimants. It signals a politics of contestation embedded in specific places – global cities – but transnational in character.

At its most extreme, this divergence assumes the form of (a) an overvalorised corporate centre occupying a smaller terrain and one whose edges are sharper than, for example, in the post-war characterised by a large middle class; and (b) a sharp devalorisation of what is outside the centre, which comes to be read as marginal.

Notes

1 Elsewhere I have tried to show how these new inequalities in profit-making capacities of economic sectors, earnings capacities of households and prices in upscale and downscale markets have contributed to the formation of informal economies in major cities of highly developed countries (see Sassen, 1994). These informal economies negotiate between these new economic trends and regulatory frameworks that were engendered in response to older economic conditions.

2 This language is increasingly constructing immigration as a devalued process in so far as it describes the entry of people from generally poorer, disadvantaged countries, in search of the better lives that the receiving country can offer; it contains an implicit valorisation of the receiving country and a devalorisation of the sending country.

3 In the colonial era, it was the cities in the colonies which were probably the most internationalised.

4 There are many different forms such contestation and 'slippage' can assume. Global mass culture homogenises and is capable of absorbing an immense variety of local cultural elements. But this process is never complete. The opposite is the case in my analysis of data on electronic manufacturing [which] shows that employment in lead sectors no longer inevitably constitutes membership in a labour aristocracy. Thus Third World women working in Export Processing Zones are not empowered: capitalism can work through difference. Yet another case is that of 'illegal' immigrants; here we see that national boundaries have the effect of creating and criminalising difference. These kinds of differentiations are central to the formation of a world economic system (Wallerstein, 1990).

5 Tokyo now has several mostly working-class concentrations of legal and illegal immigrants coming from China, Bangladesh, Pakistan, the Philippines. This is quite remarkable in view of Japan's legal and cultural closure to immigrants. Is this simply a function of poverty in those countries? By itself it is not enough of an explanation, since they have long had poverty. I posit that the internationalisation of the Japanese economy, including specific forms of investment in those countries and Japan's growing cultural influence there have created bridges between those countries and Japan, and have reduced the subjective distance with Japan (see Sassen, 1991, pp.307–15).

6 The specific forms of the internationalisation of capital we see over the last twenty years have contributed to mobilise people into migration streams. They have done so principally through the implantation of western development strategies, from the replacement of small-holder agriculture with export-oriented commerical agriculture and export manufacturing, to the westernisation of educational systems. At the same time the administrative, commercial and development networks of the former European empires and the newer forms these networks assumed under the Pax Americana (international direct foreign investment, export processing zones, wars for democracy) have not only created bridges for the flow of capital, information and high level personnel from the centre to the periphery but, I argue, also for the flow of migrants from the periphery to the centre. The renewal of mass immigration into the US in the 1960s, after five decades of little or no immigration, took place in a context of expanded US economic and military activity in Asia and the Caribbean Basin. Today, the United States is at the heart of an international system of investment and production that has incorporated not only Mexico but areas in the Caribbean and Southeast Asia. In the 1960s and 1970s, the United States played a crucial role in the development of a world economic system. It passed legislation aimed at opening its own and other countries' economies to the flow of capital, good, services and information. The central military, political and economic role the United States played in the emergence of a global economy contributed, I argue, both to the creation of conditions that mobilised people into migrations, whether local or international, and to the formation of links between the United States and other countries that subsequently were to serve as bridges for international migration. Measures commonly thought to deter emigration – foreign investment and the promotion of export-oriented growth in developing countries – seem to have had precisely the opposite effect. Among the leading senders of immigrants to the United States in the 1970s and 1980s have been several of the newly industrialised countries of South and Southeast Asia whose extremely high growth rates are generally recognised to be a result of foreign direct investment in export manufacturing.

7 Body-Gendrot (1993) shows how the city remains a terrain for contest, characterised by the emergence of new actors, often younger and younger. It is a terrain where the constraints placed upon, and the institutional limitations of governments to address the demands for equity, engenders social disorders. She argues that urban political violence should not be interpreted as a coherent ideology but rather as an element of temporary political tactics, which permits vulnerable actors to enter in interaction with the holders of power on terms that will be somewhat more favourable to the weak.

References

Body-Gendrot, S. (1993) 'Pioneering Moslem women in France' in Fisher, R. and Kling, J. (eds) *Mobilizing the Community: Local Politics in the Era of the Global City*, London, Sage Publications.

Sassen, S. (1991) *The Global City: New York, London, Tokyo*, Princeton, NJ, Princeton University Press.

Sassen, S. (1994) *Cities in a World Economy*, Thousand Oaks, CA, Pine Forge/Sage.

Wallerstein , I. (1990) 'Culture as the ideological battleground of the modern world-system' in Featherstone, M. (ed.) *Global Culture: Nationalism, Globalisation and Modernity*, London, Newbury Park and Delhi, Sage.

Source: Sassen, 1998, pp.33–40

READING 3C
Sophie Body-Gendrot:
'Pioneering Moslem women in France'

In democratic countries governed by majority rule, it is crucial to understand how newcomers or people who are distinct from majorities because of their origins, their modes of integration, or their values manage to have their demands taken into account and to become actors per se ...

This chapter will approach the question of how people become actors through the example of minorities within minorities in France, that is, immigrant women of Moslem origin. They are among the least likely to be moving forces. Their culture, their status as immigrants or recent French citizens, their poverty, and the legacy of colonialism weigh against them. Yet I will show that at the beginning of the 1990s theirs are voices that count. Their actions are even more impressive when the importance of the historical context (they are the daughters of 'colonial workers') and of economic changes (they operate in cities in crisis) are emphasized.

In France, there are no structured 'ethnic' or minority neighborhoods in the American sense. Rather, deprived populations from 20 or 30 different countries (with a majority of French) tend to live in the same deindustrialized areas simply because of networks leading them there and cheap rent. In such areas, with a high social homogeneity, yet with differentiated ethnic populations, people, including foreign populations themselves, attempt to create symbolic distances within the spaces of daily life. In those close spaces, hierarchies of social relations appear, founded on social origins, allowing people to compensate for the representation they have of their own marginalization.

In these communities, organizations provide the tools that residents need to mobilize before moving into more secure structures. People resort to what R. Dahrendorf (1963) calls 'political secondary rights', that is, mediating structures such as associations and formal or informal networks. In these organizations, the role of culture as a dimension is inseparable from material demands; it is the key to 'self-created resistance'.

Physical proximity or propinquity in residential communities generates some common interests, in this case reinforced by common gender, ethnic background, and historical experiences. Likewise, geographic concentration facilitates efforts to organize diverse populations of various generations at the community level. Associations such as the ones that will be described here give a sense of empowerment and resources to 'forgotten' inhabitants once state services have abandoned the field. Such residents do not use their voting rights (either because they are not French or, if they are, because, since the decay of the Communist party in the 1980s, there is no collective structure capable of answering their specific problems and needs); they turn, rather, to home-based organizations.

Neither their social adjustment nor their forms of resistance to the existing articulations between capital, class, and ethnicity can be dissociated, therefore, from the spaces out of which these responses emerge. For spaces also give rise to everyday struggles and to innovative strategies. Certainly people experience their determinative productive situations and relations as needs, interests, and antagonisms; but, as E.P. Thompson remarks, they 'handle' their experiences of constraint within their consciousness and their culture and they act on their determinate situation in their turn (Thompson, 1978, p. 164). Or, as Pierre Bourdieu would say, their 'habitus', their inherited dispositions, help them strike the dice and play the game in the semiautonomous subspaces that they occupy in a way favorable to them. However dominated they might be, they perceive that there are stakes that can be called into question and they know that they may possess trump cards that may change the game in their favor. 'The social world, is, to a large extent, what agents make of it, at each moment; but they have no chance of un-making and re-making it except on the basis of realistic knowledge of what it is and what they can do with it from the position that they occupy within it' (Bourdieu, 1985, p.734).

Immigrant Moslem women offer a perfect example of these very sorts of discreet challenges to the existing order that generate social change. Their strategy to create diverse collective forms of resistance and advancement, which lead from the formation of community organizations to community businesses, is especially significant. In their struggle to find voice through independent entrepreneurship, these women cut new and unexplored paths for themselves. Their experiences form the focus of this chapter.

The analysis that follows begins by introducing the context of the Moslem experience in France. It then explores the impact of community organization strategies on the day-to-day life of this population as well as the role played by the central state. Finally, female Moslem community leaders appear as fully committed actors who begin to exercise independence and control over their lives through community-based entrepreneurship.

The historical context of ethnic segregation and tensions

...

The legacy of colonization

In a way, France was the first country to 'invent' the use of proletarian labor from underdeveloped countries for industrial goals (and not for settlement, as in the United States). Colonized Algeria, in return, was the first of all underdeveloped countries to have started and organized rationally, in the beginning, the emigration of those of her men who were available for wage labor abroad and whose departure would not be too disruptive to the daily processes of their communities. What is exceptional, sociologist A. Sayad says, is the precocity of the trend and the mode of political treatment that those emigrants experienced. Algerians were indeed immigrant workers in France while being French. They were not part of a political space that was homogeneous, yet they were not outside of it either. They were therefore in a deeply ambivalent situation, forming a sort of 'experimental population'. While both colonizers and colonized belonged to the same French nationality, no one could deny the hegemony of the first category over the other or the persistence of paternalist attitudes in the treatment of the colonized French in the workplace and the neighborhood in France. At the same time, the haunting question for the foreign workers, one that still persists today, was this: 'How to be French in France without being completely French while nevertheless being French?'

Departing from the national form of individual integration, the French policymakers of the time set forth special welfare institutions that at the same time were under police control. Thus hostels and soup kitchens created specially for isolated Algerian males also provided medical facilities, organized pilgrimages, and took care of the burying of the dead while, at the same time, providing control 'to remove them from the temptation of the bars and of the streets' (Sayad, 1991). There was a consensus shared by the state, the private sector, and charitable organizations to mix welfare and police functions in the 'help' provided to these workers.

This historical account exemplifies a logic of social segregation meant for a special category operating in and through space. A logic that still holds today, it once seemed exceptional, born of necessity. But it was reinforced as the spatial exceptionalism of this category was allowed to deteriorate. The stigmatization of the locale where the workers, and later their children, lived, would have two opposite effects: either to prevent them from mentioning their address or, on the contrary, to push them to defend symbolically their 'community turf'.

The Algerian War and cultural differentiation

The legacy of colonialism continues to activate wounds left by decolonization. Indeed, one of the greatest influences upon racial attitudes in metropolitan France remains that of the Algerian war. This issue is so traumatic that the French are still unable to deal with it, a fact reflected in the bitter and violent revolts in 1991 of young Harkis, the sons of those Algerians that chose to remain with the French when the war ended. The war heightened racial tensions and brought the collapse of the Fourth Republic against a background of civil war and military takeover. Immigrant Moslem workers were the obvious scapegoats for all the negative feelings that a divided French society then experienced. These memories linger only subconsciously and they explain the 'special relationship' of hostility existing in metropolitan society between those who identify with the main ethnic majority and those of Islamic Algerian descent (Silverman, 1991).

...

The new urban context

The xenophobia expressed toward 'Arabs' intensified when family reunification was authorized after the immigration gates closed in 1974. One of the unintended consequences of that political decision was to turn nomadic, single birds of passage of North African origin into sedentary families with numerous children. These families were to remain for good in the low-income periphery or decayed neighborhoods of large French cities like Paris, Lyon, and Marseille. Their visible needs for welfare services triggered the anger of French taxpayers and of those who claimed to have established the best health system in the world – a system for the culturally appropriate, not for (sometimes French) foreigners.

A 'quiet' Islam

The hostility the foreigners could feel in the circumscribed territories where they were assigned explains in part why those first migrants remained usually silent, except for strikes that developed in semipublic workers' hostels (*Sonacotra*) between 1976 and 1980. Revolts occurred due to poor management, ostentatious racism, and the policing of the workers' daily lives in those places. For the first time, these strikes revealed that immigrants could launch an urban social movement and sustain it with success for several months (Body-Gendrot, 1982; de Rudder, 1991). Culturally (and this demand was unnoticed by both the media and the researchers), Moslem workers demanded prayer rooms, just as, in another context, the Moslem fathers living with their families in high-rise projects did.

In a rapidly changing urban environment, these uprooted individuals and families were trying to reconstitute a familiar ground and to find an anchor in religion, all the more as prayer rooms not only provided moral and religious support but established social links in sponsoring multicentered activities and in offering material support, if necessary. In other words, they re-created micro societies populated with familiar figures. Such sites provided support for quiet resistance, building on the reproduction of cultural symbols and on the perception those migrants had of the appropriation of a space of their own.

Islam is the second and fastest growing religion in France. There are 1,000 mosques (few of them have minarets and most of them are not visibly religious from the outside). At the beginning, French local authorities saw in Islam a way to regulate dispersed populations, and building permits were granted to religious leaders. After the Iranian revolution and with the demagoguery of extreme-right French leaders seeking scapegoats for electoral returns, however, Islam, immigration, and insecurity became linked in the public discourses, and the controversies over the building of mosques in large cities like Lyons and Marseille revealed a NIMBY (not-in-my-backyard) syndrome.

Ethnic tensions are also the product of French privatization policies enacted after the oil crisis (Bourdieu and Rosin, 1990). This was the time when it was decided by the central government that subsidies for the building of social housing (*aide à la pierre*) were too costly and should be transformed into financial (and private) support for individual projects (*aide à la personne*), a policy encouraging the building of detached or semidetached houses in the very areas where decayed high-rise projects were stigmatized. Consequently, new tensions rose between, on the one hand, the mobile segments of the French working-class that had access to those houses and that aspired to change the image of their neighborhood and, on the other, the multiracial poorer and newer families who were 'trapped' in the social housing because they had no other option. The malaise generated by these rapid changes is reflected by the social workers working in these tough neighborhoods.

Exclusion: French style

In the 1960s social work aimed at integrating newcomers from rural or Third World areas into the working class. The meaning of this work was the collective promotion of marginal segments at the local level. After 1968 such action changed and became openly critical of bureaucratic procedures, of social reproduction, of law and order. Today a deconstruction process has taken place among those social workers strongly identified with the marginalized poor immigrants who are their clients. They feel unable or refuse to question contradictions, such as troublesome immigrant families who should be expelled at the demand of other residents, or the swelling numbers of African families who provoke an image of 'ghettoization' in the neighborhood. They feel powerless and burnt out …

…

The mobilization of Moslems

Each generation of residents produces its own meanings, constructs its own history and identity, then reacts back upon other spheres. As the networks cross geographic boundaries and endure for generations, those migrant populations have been sustained by collective strategies for survival and accommodation that have proved to be more and more efficient.

… Several factors explain why only recently have Moslems, and Moslem women in particular, been able to take an active part in grass-roots organizations. These factors include the slow decline in the 1980s of moral and financial dependence upon the home countries, the influence of religious and union leaders from abroad, and the cultural dependence of 'colonial workers'.

Demography and destiny

Recent demographic transformations help explain why Moslem women in the French population have become conscious of their potential strength. While between 1975 and 1982 the increase of male immigrants was only 2.1% (the gates were supposed to be closed), the increase in female immigrants was 14% (entries due to family reunification and marriages). From 1982 until 1986, the proportion of foreign women continued to grow (5.6% compared with 3.1% for men) and they represent 44% of the immigrant population, that is, 1,541,600 persons out of 3,462,200 (Bentaïeb, 1991, p.5). To this figure one must add the women of foreign origin who are French because (a) they have been born in France of a French parent, (b) they have lived in the country until they were 18, (c) they have chosen to become French through naturalization, or (d) they were French through the colonization process. A more inclusive figure of foreign women in France therefore totals about 3,170,000. Half of them are under 30 and 65% of them were born in France. North African women form about half of this population.

…

The older the wave of immigration, the more women are part of the labor force. In 1990, 50% of those between 25 and 49 years old worked. Work reflects both a search for autonomy from their traditional family and a desire for social mobility. Despite jobs specifically designated for foreign workers, a complex means of access to the labor market is now in progress: the jobs held by foreigners in the secondary sector have declined from 45% to 36% in the 1980s and in the service sector have increased from 20% to 37.5% and become the major source of employment. Half the workers are now qualified, while only one third were 15 years ago. The young and female forces are well represented in that sector. 'Contraction, feminization, tertiarization': the foreign profile is close to the French one. Strikingly, the number of small companies owned by Portuguese or Maghrebi has doubled within 3 years (Maurin, 1991, no.4). The leading women that we will now look at are representative of this economic emancipation. They are not a majority. Yet they are all the more striking as they represent the embryo of an elite whose numbers will grow in the years to come.

Pioneering Moslem women

It is into space at the neighborhood level that disadvantaged people, as they challenge the existing order, project the discreet practices and tenuous strategies that they develop individually and collectively. The constraints of French political and social life are indeed present and, every day, people continually experience them: racism, bureaucracy, collapsing economic order, disintegration of social units (Bourdieu, 1985; Thompson, 1978). What is impressive, however, is the way the Moslem women of these neighborhoods have relied on practices of their own to engage and interact with these constraints. To mark their identity and mobilize followers, these women, through associations and strategies that vary according to particular social environments, have creatively reappropriated the physical and symbolic spaces in which they live.

...

From grass roots to entrepreneurship

The new trend on the part of many Moslem women is to become entrepreneurs. We can observe the emergence of an important dynamic in the creation of trades and innovative firms started by young North African women, who are eager to use both their know-how and the social capital that they have accumulated as leaders of community organizations. Such organizations serve as the foundation for the creation of restaurants, jewelry stores, dance centers, beauty parlors, *hammams* (Turkish baths), and so on, mixing economic and social goals. Examples abound.

D.A. is an exotic restaurant, created in 1986 by a community organization in an immigrant neighborhood in response to the demands of unskilled immigrant women who wanted to become active. The catering of ethnic meals in this diversified neighborhood in Paris was developed after many months of struggle. The board of the company is composed of Maghrebi, African, and Portuguese women. Another company promoted by French, Algerian, Moroccan, and Spanish women produces fine-quality dresses inspired by the traditional costumes of their home countries and adjusted to French taste. Financial difficulties plague the firm, but important grants help it to survive.

The creation of a beautiful hammam in a difficult neighborhood challenged the poverty-stricken image of a suburb of Lyon, Les Minguettes, where riots had started in 1981. The enterprise required a heavy investment. The decision to develop this hammam was in response to an official demand aimed at maintaining the residents in the neighborhood. It was a deliberate choice to create something aesthetically beautiful at the foot of a high-rise project belonging to the state. Despite the healthy benefits of the hammam, after 2 years the investments' interest created a financial crisis. The Public Office for Social Housing offered to provide its help in exchange for 51% of the shares. The young Moslem woman and her unemployed husband who had conceived the idea of the hammam, and who had invested all their resources in it, refused to yield control over their patrimony. They demanded from the state a 'generous attitude'. The state (SAF) resisted. It is prepared to provide funding for social causes and projects; but an 'economic' approach embarrasses officials who are unaccustomed to this type of enterprise. On the other hand, it is not in the tradition of the private sector in France to take risks and bet on an innovative project of this sort. Obviously a public/private partnership could be a solution but, at this point, it is unlikely that the creator of the hammam will open up her family enterprise to other shareholders. The new actors learn how to change their strategies and tactics, but if their goals and politics do not jibe, the transition can sometimes be painful.

In other cases, know-how and responsibilities have accumulated as organization leaders have given individual entrepreneurs the social qualifications and perspectives necessary to develop their projects. These projects reflect the experience of cultural crisis, changing values, distance toward the immigration experience, and integration within a specific turf. For instance, a hairdresser and former sociologist has opened a beauty parlor that is also a music room. 'Violin and hair-blown-dry; it is the same struggle', she remarks. 'You can't play the violin on an empty stomach and with an empty head … I look to the future, I want to act before the problems occur, before the kids drop out of school. Without music, without culture, a community dies, it has no history, no memory to insert into its daily life and that's dangerous.' Economic enterprises are carried on in an environment in constant flux. Leaders therefore have to foresee what the leisure society will be like in 20 years in order to create new adaptive structures now. Another example – opening a hammam/fitness club – shows the same type of vision. 'Beyond generations, it implies a construction, a duration, roots, making a space, saying at the same time we want to stay but we want to stay with our culture.'

Social concerns over profit

… The jump into entrepreneurship by Moslem women in leadership provides them with a new energy. After the fatigue of organizational life, it provides an increased legitimacy in French society and a clearer recognition of their work, power, and potential. 'How to be French without being completely French' is still the haunting question. Due to their origins, due to their fathers' experiences in France, due to prevailing racism, the need to prove that they are effective actors is extremely important. A Moroccan woman explains it this way: 'For a long time, I was a street social worker. I became conscious of the huge potentialities that were in the neighborhood … At the same time, I was aware that no one thought deeply about the meaning of one's work, that there was a blindness oblivious of people's assets … I became enraged.'

Enraged is a recurrent term used to describe the feeling of waste produced by huge bureaucratic procedures, by fatigue, by stereotypes. It is a feeling that leads to a strategy of self-empowerment. It is understandable that immigrant female leaders, former social workers, or grass-roots leaders should have felt 'enraged', powerless, and ready to try new forms of communication. They sought to substitute relations of autonomy for ones of former dependence on either organizational structures or French society at large. The owner of a Moroccan restaurant explains:

> In commercial transactions such as a restaurant, there is a way to work without submission – equal to equal … There are no longer barriers and misunderstandings between cultures. You can transmit a lot of messages … The making of meals is a cultural message, an image of myself and of the traditional women working with me that I would like my patrons to keep in their mind in order to discard stereotypes.

She now prefers to use her living experience rather than words to accomplish her goal.

Speeding mutants

It may seem strange to defend the virtues of consumerism over and against those of community organizing. But one needs to understand the spirit that pushes these women to undertake such adventures. They have an almost philosophical perception of their creations; they are aware of the complexity of their generation, a generation that they define as neither first nor second but as 'the generation of their age'. In other words, their specific experiences and social trajectories define their identity. It is not a specifically French identity, nor a specifically ethnic one, but universal. They are defined by their will to act and by their urgency to accelerate the evolution of conservative French and immigrant societies. 'We have the feeling that so many things are to be done. Our community [of entrepreneurial women] is like a crossroads. We are all the communities at the same time and all the generations as well.'

Their specific attitudes, in contrast with those of first-generation immigrant women, can partly be explained by the hardships they have gone through. It was difficult to break new ground, to oppose their fathers, their relatives, their friends. As veterans and survivors, they have turned such struggles into assets and have become overmotivated. Their personal itinerary comes as a secondary explanation.

…

Self-interest is not their primary motivation. As they did when they were community organization leaders, they continue to see themselves as linkages. 'What is the interest of escaping alone?' one remarks. In that respect, the embryo of a movement can be perceived. These women feel responsible for the younger generation and act as role models, trying to protect Moslem girls from oppressive families, boys from crisis and from drug temptations. They incorporate the young people into their actions, through initiation to art, ethnic cooking, craftsmanship, and so on. But they also want to rehabilitate their mothers, 'the passive first generation', which is a way for them to enhance their cultural heritage. 'The assertion in terms of continuity of the historical and affective memory with their mothers, beyond individual confrontations taking place inside families, expresses a will to rehabilitate the negative image glued on their mothers, and at the same time, a violent rejection of the protective behaviors they have experienced' (Golub, 1988, p.3). Even if they have much reason to rebel against both their mothers and the women from the home countries who transmit the values of the households, they acknowledge that they are the products of that culture. They recognize that, frequently, from those 'oppressed' mothers they have had instilled into them the motivation not to reproduce the traditional models of their community.

In sum, this new generation of Moslem women, who start with the handicap of being minorities in a society technically and culturally ruled by a historical majority, nevertheless prove that they are creating the elements of a new elite. The future, of course, is most uncertain, as this dialogue reveals: 'We are women, we are immigrés, we are poor, we do not vote ... and you would like us to represent something? Are you dreaming? Maybe in 50 or in 60 years, we will represent something.' To which another interviewee replies: 'In half a century, no one will talk any longer about our integration.'

It indeed remains to be seen whether these women will be able to maintain their empowerment and, through their personal charisma, generate the sorts of mobilizations among younger followers that will eventually improve the status and well-being of the Moslem communities in the cities where they live.

References

Bentaïeb, M. (1991) 'Les femmes étrangéres en France', *Hommes et Migrations*, no.1141, March, pp.4–12.

Body-Gendrot, S. (1982) 'Urban social movements in France and the US' in Fainstein, N. and Fainstein, S. (eds) *Urban Policy under Capitalism,* Beverly Hills, CA, Sage.

Bourdieu, P. (1985) 'The social space and the genesis of groups', *Theory and Society*, vol.14, no.6, pp.723–44.

Bourdieu, P. and Rosin, C. (1990) 'La construction du marché: le champ administratif et la production de la "politique du logement"', *Les Actes de la Recherche en Sciences Sociales,* pp.81–2.

Dahrendorf, R. (1963) 'Recent changes in the class structure of Western European countries' in Craubard, S. (ed.) *A New Europe?,* Boston, MA, Beacon.

de Rudder, V. (1991) 'Housing and immigrant integration in French cities' in Horowitz, D. (ed.) *Immigration and Ethnicity in France,* New York, New York University Press.

Golub, A. (1988) *Femmes Issues de l'immigration Maghrébine dans le Processus d'intégration de la Société Francaise,* unpublished manuscript.

Maurin, E. (1991) 'Les étrangers: une main-d'oeuvres à part?', *Economie et Statistique*, no.242, April, pp.39–50.

Sayad, A. (1991) 'Immigration in France: an "exotic" form of poverty' in McFate, K., Lawson, R. and Wilson, W. (eds) *Urban Marginality and Public Policy in Europe and in America,* Washington, DC, Joint Center for Political Studies.

Silverman, M. (ed.) (1991) *Race, Discourse, and Power in France,* Aldershot, Avebury.

Thompson, E. P. (1978) *The Poverty of Theory and Other Essays,* New York, Longman.

Source: Body-Gendrot, 1993, pp.270–80, 284–90

CHAPTER 4
Cities, environment and sustainability

by Ian Munt

1 *Introduction*

Perhaps, like me, you are fascinated – even overwhelmed – by the array of environmental issues facing cities, by the vast amounts of television coverage, the acres of newspaper articles, the platitudes of politicians and the string of 'global' environment conferences such as the Rio Earth Summit (1992) and the Habitat II conference in Istanbul (1996). From the potential environmental destructiveness of cities globally to the environmental impacts of the nearby superstore, there's no doubting it – environmental issues are big news and have caught the public imagination and mood, especially in the 'developed' western world. But there is an up-side to the urban environment too. Cities can offer unusual, uplifting, environments – environments that can move us, that we can delight in. And in contrast to the gloomy predictions offered by some urban commentators, others suggest that cities offer the principal means of addressing local and global environmental problems and of finding more environmentally 'sustainable' ways of living.

The enormity and importance of city–environment issues, and the way in which they impact daily on our own lives, make writing this guide to the environment theme an exciting challenge for me. And perhaps you feel the same kind of excitement (and even a little dread!) in starting to digest and distil the range of ways in which the course reflects these issues so that you can begin to plan your course essay. But now is the time to begin thinking how you will piece together a story on the environment. I hope this guide will help you on your own journey.

1.1   USING THIS CHAPTER AS A GUIDE

So, what is the main purpose of this chapter? How is it structured and how can you get the most from it?

Our first task is to identify exactly what is meant when the 'environment' is referred to in the context of *Understanding Cities*. Doing so will help remind you of the scope of the environment theme and the way in which this theme is interwoven throughout the course.

Secondly, we shall begin the task of re-visiting the three books and other course materials and of looking at some of the ways in which the environment theme can be traced through them. Some chapters directly address the question of city–environment relationships; others contain useful references to these issues. Some chapters have less to say on this particular topic – although even in these chapters, environmental issues are never far below the surface! This task will therefore help you to review and distil the course material in relation to this theme. But whilst some chapters will be more explicit about environmental issues than others, it is important to embrace the wider course ideas too, including social and economic issues, and consider the ways in which they can be reworked and applied to the environment theme; in respect to this, you may want to take another look at Chapter 1 of this book.

Having mapped some of the ways in which the environment theme appears in the course, our third task is to consider the ways in which you can create 'routes' through the course material ('environment pathways'). This will help you both to identify relevant theoretical arguments and to piece together the way in which the environment theme runs through the whole course. To take just one example, John Allen **(Bk 1 Ch. 5)** provides some fascinating reflections on how power is exercised in cities, although he does not apply this directly to environmental issues. We could, however, apply this thinking to pose questions ranging from how environmental problems are identified, who defines what a problem is and what responses (if any) are used to address these problems, to establishing who benefits from these responses and environmental improvements.

This chapter seeks to cover a lot of ground, demonstrating how ideas on the environment can be drawn together. It begins to interrogate the key arguments that run through the course and how these arguments can assist our understanding of cities in the context of an environmental 'narrative'. You will already be very familiar with these key messages from studying the three course books, the Course Guide and Chapter 1 of this book. They address the geography or *'spatial'* aspects of contemporary cities, the *tensions* that exist within and between cities and the *intensity* of city life. It is worth emphasizing once more that this chapter is only a start, and is only one element of the course materials that it will be necessary for you to draw on. All the course elements – the course books, the theme guides in this book, the TV programmes and audiocassettes – have something to offer. It is worth referring back to Chapter 1 to remind yourself of the scope of this material. Each of these elements will help you to get to grips with this course theme and anchor your work in preparation for the essay.

There are also a number of extra Readings to provide an additional resource for your essay and these are printed at the end of the chapter, as for the previous themes. These complement and build upon the core ideas presented and help to demonstrate further how the course arguments can be applied to environmental questions. I will refer to some of this material as we progress through the chapter.

You may also have already followed the advice of Phil Pinch in the Course Guide and started to build your own 'course file' of relevant and interesting newspaper and magazine snippings. If so, you can also use these as additional materials to draw on and, as Chapter 1 suggests, make the course 'come alive'. You can now decide which of your material is most relevant to the environment theme if you choose this for the course essay. But don't worry if you haven't built a course file – it isn't essential for completing the course essay! Remember, too, that my views and coverage in this chapter are provided just to start you off on the right lines. The challenge and excitement of doing the course essay is in piecing together relevant evidence and arguments for yourself.

The environment is an integral part of our geographical and spatial understanding of cities. I hope this chapter will help you to increase your awareness and understanding of contemporary urban environments and environmental issues, and importantly, support you in thinking through the big ideas – what action is required to make cities and city environments, as Phil Pinch says in the Course Guide, 'more liveable, equitable and sustainable in the future' (p.11).

2 *The scope of the environment theme*

2.1   WHAT IS THE URBAN ENVIRONMENT?

At face value, this seems a rather straightforward question. When thinking of the 'environment', perhaps most of us would immediately think of 'natural' systems, of nature, of green things! Or perhaps we would frame the urban environment as those 'green areas' that are interspersed amongst the 'built' – or what John Allen **(Bk 1 Ch. 2)** refers to as the 'manufactured' – environment.

The environment that makes up the city is all and more of these elements. On the one hand it talks of those buildings, those settled city environments, that give symbolic meaning to cities, just as the Eiffel Tower, the Empire State Building and the Opera House help to define Paris, New York and Sydney respectively. Built environments can also 'include' and 'exclude', not just people but animals, birds and insects as well as trees and plants. Think of shopping malls or private residential areas that seek to keep 'undesirables' out, or those environments in which we feel uncomfortable, out of place, insecure/threatened, or – conversely – welcomed, happy and settled. And these environments are not static. They change. Our experience of them may change with our age, with the amount we earn, even between daylight and darkness. On the other hand, the city is made up of those 'natural' elements, we have already listed: the parks, commons, green spaces, rivers and so on. And yet many of these elements are as manufactured as the 'built environment' itself.

But it is important that we avoid the temptation to divide the 'environment' in this way. It is essential to challenge the tendency, as Steve Hinchliffe **(Bk 2 Ch. 4)** suggests, to draw a distinction between 'cities' and 'nature' and to define environment in terms of the latter. Steve Hinchliffe discusses the concept of city-nature formations which he argues unsettle and challenge traditional ways of thinking about and understanding cities. Thinking in terms of city-nature formations is useful in that it partially rejects the notion that cities must exist at the expense of nature; indeed you may recall David Harvey's thoughts that 'there is nothing *unnatural* about New York city' (Harvey, 1996, p.186; in **Bk 2 Ch. 4** p.171). Also it provides us with the conceptual tools for thinking more positively about what cities have to offer and can achieve in environmental terms.

As Graham Haughton and Colin Hunter, two commentators on urban environmental issues, note: the urban environment is 'richly textured in its interweaving of a mixture of natural, built-form, economic, social and cultural dimensions' (1996, p.15). The environment is about connections and interconnections; the relationships between buildings and open spaces within cities; between city environments and rural environments; between cities and the global environment.

2.2   WHAT ARE URBAN ENVIRONMENTAL ISSUES?

You may well already have given some thought to the environmental issues of cities as you worked your way through the course. Table 4.1 focuses attention on some of the environmental issues associated with cities.

ACTIVTY 4.1   Spend a few moments working through Table 4.1 which is taken from *An Urbanizing World* by the United Nations Centre for Human Settlements. Note the range of urban environmental issues listed in the first column and the way in which these issues vary depending on the level of 'development' experienced by cities (the four categories listed at the top of the table).

As you read through the table, think about the uneven geographical spread of environmental issues and the unequal impact of environmental problems. ◆

TABLE 4.1   *Exploring environmental sustainability and cities*

Environmental problems and influences	Category 1: *Most urban centres in most low-income nations and many middle-income nations*	Category 2: *More prosperous cities in low and middle-income countries – including many that have developed as industrial centres*	Category 3: *Prosperous major cities/metropolitan areas in middle- and upper-income countries*	Category 4: *Cities in upper-income countries*
Access to basic infrastructure and services – water supply and sanitation – drainage – solid-waste collection – primary health care	Many or most of the urban population lacking water piped into the home and adequate sanitation. Also many or most residential areas lacking drainage so such areas often having mud and stagnant pools. Many residential areas at risk from flooding. Many or most residential areas also lacking services for solid-waste collection and health care, especially the poorer and more peripheral areas.	Piped water supplies and sanitation systems reaching a considerable proportion of the population but a large proportion of low-income households not reached, especially those in illegal or informal settlements on the city periphery. Typically, solid-waste collection and health care reaching a higher proportion of the population than in Category 1 but still with between one- and two-thirds of the population unserved.	Generally acceptable water supplies for most of the population. Provision for sanitation, solid-waste collection and primary health care also much improved, although 10–13 per cent of the population still lacking provision (or adequate provision). The proportion of people lacking adequate services generally smaller than in Category 2 but in very large cities, this can still mean millions who lack basic services. In large metropolitan areas, service provision often least adequate in weakest, peripheral municipalities.	Provision of all four services for virtually all the population.

Environmental problems and influences	Category 1: Most urban centres in most low-income nations and many middle-income nations	Category 2: More prosperous cities in low and middle-income countries – including many that have developed as industrial centres	Category 3: Prosperous major cities/metropolitan areas in middle- and upper-income countries	Category 4: Cities in upper-income countries
Pollution & waste – water pollution	The main water 'pollution' problems arise from a lack of provision for sanitation and garbage collection.	Most local rivers and other water bodies polluted from industrial and urban discharges and storm and surface run-off.	Severe problems from untreated or inadequately treated industrial and municipal liquid wastes that are usually dumped without treatment in local water bodies.	Much improved levels of treatment for liquid wastes from homes and productive activities. Concern with amenity values and toxic wastes.
– air pollution	Often serious indoor air pollution, where soft coal or biomass fuels used as domestic fuels – especially where indoor heating is needed.	Often severe problems from industrial and residential emissions. Indoor air pollution in households lessened as households with higher incomes switch to cleaner fuels.	Increasingly important contribution to air pollution from motor vehicles. Perhaps less from industry as city's economic base becomes less pollution intensive and as measures begin to be taken to control industrial emissions.	Motor vehicles becoming the major source of air pollution. Little or no heavy industry remains in the city and the control of air pollution becomes a greater priority for citizens.
– solid-waste disposal	Open dumping of the solid wastes that are collected.	Mostly uncontrolled landfills; mixed wastes.	A proportion of landfills controlled or semi-controlled.	Controlled sanitary landfills, incineration, some recovery.
– hazardous waste management	No capacity but also volumes generally small.	Severe problems; limited capacities to deal with it.	Growing capacity but often still a serious problem.	Moving from remediation to prevention.
Physical and chemical hazards in the home and workplace	The main physical hazards associated with poor-quality living and working environments – especially domestic and workplace accidents. There may be serious occupational hazards among certain small-scale and household enterprises.	A great increase in the problems with occupational health and safety at all levels and scales of industry. Government often not giving occupational health and safety adequate priority. A high proportion of low-income households living in illegal or informal settlements with high risks of accidental injuries – especially if they settle on dangerous sites.	Improved government supervision or worker organization to ensure improved occupational health and safety. Often, a decline in the proportion of the population working in hazardous jobs. A rise in the contribution of traffic accidents to premature death and injury. Improved provision of water, sanitation, drainage and health care lessening physical hazards in residential areas.	A high level of occupational health and safety and active programmes promoting injury reduction for homes and on the roads.

Environmental problems and influences	Category 1: *Most urban centres in most low-income nations and many middle-income nations*	Category 2: *More prosperous cities in low and middle-income countries – including many that have developed as industrial centres*	Category 3: *Prosperous major cities/metropolitan areas in middle- and upper-income countries*	Category 4: *Cities in upper-income countries*
Land	Urban expansion taking place with few or no controls – or where controls exist, they are largely ignored.	Urban expansion continuing to take place with few or no controls; uncontrolled or ineffective land use controls; often rapid growth in illegal or informal settlements, including illegal land sub-divisions for wealthier groups; loss of farmland to expanding urban areas and to demand for building materials and aggregate.	More controls imposed on urban expansion but these often prove ineffective as illegal residential develop-ments continue, in the face of a considerable section of the population unable to afford to buy or rent the cheapest 'legal' land site or house. Different groups often in conflict over use of best located undeveloped land sites or of use of agricultural land for urban purposes.	Land use tightly regulated – perhaps to the point where house prices begin to rise as land supplies for new housing become constrained.
Other environmental hazards	No provision by the public authorities for disaster preparedness. Poor construction practices; low-income settlements in hazardous locations. Recurrent disasters with severe damage and loss of life.	In cities with an industrial base, inadequate provision to guard against industrial disasters and to act to limit the damage and loss of life when they occur.	Good emergency response capacity to natural and industrial disasters.	

Note: UNCHS entries for 'Other environmental hazards' have been amended, based on Bartone *et al.*, 1994.

Source: Based on a table in Bartone, C. *et al.*, 1994. Taken from UNCHS, 1996, Table 8.7, pp.287–8

You will notice how the authors have divided cities into four types according to the per capita income of their populations and have covered a range of problems from water supply and sanitation to the need for land for expanding cities. Table 4.1 emphasizes that environmental problems, and their solutions, are more protracted and difficult the poorer the country. The nature of environmental issues and degree of environmental problems therefore varies between cities.

But just as it is tempting to think about the environment as 'natural' and 'green', it is also tempting to define environmental issues as 'problems' and as 'green issues'. Indeed my initial inclination would be to cite air pollution, traffic congestion or the lack of open space, and think about the actions of environmental and anti-road campaigners who tunnel or occupy trees to protest against road builders. Whilst this is certainly part of the story, it is by no means the only way of framing environmental issues.

As suggested earlier, in exploring the scope of the environment theme and environmental issues relating to cities, we need to think about the relationship between environmental, social and economic issues.

ACTIVITY 4.2   Now take a few moments to consider the potential overlaps with the other course themes – the economic and the social. We suggest you note one example of each. You might decide to note your ideas as a mind map – see Figure 4.1 as an example of my own ideas – or, if you prefer, by simply noting the relationships between the themes. ◆

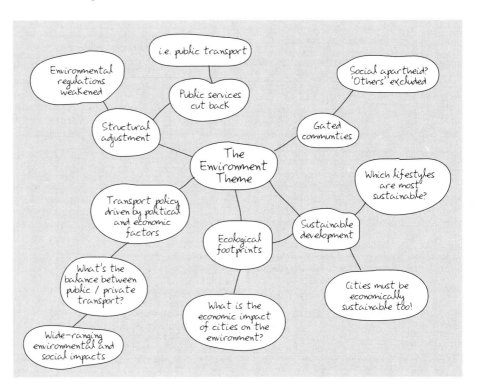

FIGURE 4.1 *What relationships exist between the environment theme and the economic and social themes?*

I decided to explore the relationships with the aid of a mind map. But my thoughts are by no means complete – and you will need to reflect on other interesting relationships.

To take just two examples from my mind map, I noted how neo-liberalism talks of economic and political processes and pressures at a global scale. You may recall that, at its most basic, neo-liberalism seeks to legitimize the idea of individual freedom and the primacy of the private over the public sector and establish the free operation of markets. In particular, neo-liberalism has been pursued through the structural adjustment policies of agencies such as the World Bank and International Monetary Fund and these have impacted upon poorer countries, with significant effects on the environment of cities – for example, by promoting intense urban development or promoting private as opposed to public forms of transport. As Michael Pryke **(Bk 2 Ch. 6)** suggests, we need therefore to 'listen geographically' to the consequences of neo-liberalism: that is, to consider both the environmental and the spatial consequences.

A second example might be the 'private enclaves', 'the sealed-off gated city', that Ash Amin and Stephen Graham **(Bk 2 Ch. 1)** refer to, a discussion that is further developed by Eugene McLaughlin and John Muncie **(Bk 3 Ch. 4)**. This talks of the different spatial effects of creating certain kinds of environments and the manner in which some communities are disconnected, excluded socially and culturally, producing geographically and socially juxtaposed environments. On the one hand there are those communities who have the choice to be kept safe and secure from the supposed dangers of the city by living within guarded compounds. On the other hand, there are 'Others', who are a supposed danger and are to be kept out, excluded from these environments. You may recall how the pursuit of a 'secure environment' results – with an interesting environmental twist – in an 'ecology of fear' **(Bk 3 Reading 3B)**.

2.3 WHAT IS ENVIRONMENTAL SUSTAINABILITY?

There is a further element that we need to be aware of in thinking about the environment theme. You will have noticed the frequency with which the notion of 'sustainability' and 'sustainable development' are referred to in this course. Indeed, perhaps the most pressing question posed by the course is 'are cities of the scale and complexity which we are now facing, sustainable either environmentally or socially?' **(Bk 2 Ch. 4)** – and what actions are required to make them so? As Andy Blowers and Kathy Pain point out **(Bk 3 Ch. 6)**, the notion of sustainability is intimately related to the environment and the Brundtland Report and subsequent Rio Earth Summit were centrally about environmental issues and addressing global environmental problems. There are some advantages to thinking about the environment in terms of sustainability and sustainable development:

1   Although sustainability has been principally concerned with environmental issues and questions, it also helps us to understand the connections between the environment and the social and economic aspects of cities, which we discussed above. Clearly in your course essay you will need to focus on the environmental dimensions but there will be issues, ideas and case studies where there is an overlap.

2   Sustainability and sustainable development tend to focus our attention, not just on environmental problems, but they can also help us to consider the opportunities for cities to address these problems and identify potential policy solutions. Thinking in these terms helps, as Phil Pinch argues in the Course Guide, to 'raise our awareness of the challenges faced by city governments, and people who live in cities, if they are to work toward more humane, liveable and sustainable cities in the future' (section 2.2).

However, as we have seen, sustainability is a 'socially constructed' concept **(Bk 3 Ch. 6)**. It is defined, interpreted and applied differently by governments, by environmentalists, by developers and so on. Sustainability is, therefore, also a contested concept.

ACTIVITY 4.3   Take a few minutes to study Figure 4.2, *Schneckentempo* ('At a snail's pace'), a portrayal of industrialized nations by Walter Hanel. How do you think it reflects different interpretations of sustainability? ◆

FIGURE 4.2   *Walter Hanel:* 'Schneckentempo' *(At a snail's pace)*

The cartoon suggests to me the reluctance of the industrialized nations to come to terms with the environmental consequences of urban development. The author of this cartoon seems to hint at the double standards of the 'developed' world: despite being the greatest consumers of resources and generators of pollution, it is the developed world that defines 'environmental standards' and sustainability – they are the 'apostles of the enviroment'. I also felt it suggests that one city's sustainability, may be at another city's expense: for example, this might happen if wastes are exported elsewhere or if polluting industries are packaged off to Third World cities to take advantage of the cheap labour. The cartoon is, of course, drawn very much from a 'green perspective' and offers quite a depressing interpretation of the role of cities in global pollution. The tugging and heaving taking place to move the snail towards ecology (*Ökologie*) reflects Hanel's principal concern with city–environment relationships as problems.

There is no single interpretation or solution to environmental sustainability and this has triggered off a series of questions in my mind which lead me back to some of the big questions posed by the course:

- Are cities a global hazard?
- Are cities in environmental danger themselves?
- Are cities sustainable?
- Who defines and determines what environmental sustainability is?
- Whose lifestyles does sustainability seek to protect and enhance?
- If cities are not currently environmentally sustainable, can they ever be sustainable and what would be the requirements to achieve this?
- Do individual cities need to be environmentally sustainable, or is the most significant challenge facing cities the one of whether they can collectively help achieve global environmental sustainability?

2.4   THE ENVIRONMENT PATHWAYS

Now we have identified the key aspects of the environment theme, let's start considering the ways in which the environment theme is threaded through the course. We shall begin this by considering how the course materials are reflected in – and can be applied to – the course arguments.

ACTIVITY 4.4   Now turn to Reading 4A, taken from *Cities for A Small Planet* by the renowned architect, Richard Rogers. As you are reading, think about how Rogers' 'populist' narrative reflects some of the course arguments around the issues of environment and sustainability and make a note of these. It's a good idea to have the course materials to hand as you do this so that you can refer back to specific points and flag them. ◆

These are the points that I noted.

The first point that struck me is the intensity with which the urbanization process has proceeded in the twentieth century. Rogers certainly re-emphasizes the scale and scope of urbanization that Massey **(Bk 1 Ch. 4)** and the extract by M. Ishmail Serageldin **(Bk 1 Extract 3.3)** highlight, and the problems and challenges that this presents. I felt quite exhausted after I finished reading Rogers' article. In stressing the enormity of environmental problems, Rogers reflects the key course argument about the *intensity* of relations within and between cities. Cities, as Andy Blowers and Kathy Pain point out **(Bk 3 Ch. 6)**, are characterized by intense and geographically concentrated human activity.

Did you notice how Rogers argues that similar environmental problems are experienced in cities across the world: traffic congestion and the resulting pollution, for example, occur pretty much throughout the urbanized world – indeed, as Kerry Hamilton and Susan Hoyle suggest **(Bk 2 Ch. 2)** the twin problems of traffic congestion and pollution are 'city phenomena'. Social and economic connections between cities have environmental impacts within cities **(Bk 3 Ch. 6)**. The impact of these problems is uneven between cities, between areas within cities and between groups within cities.

And perhaps, like me, you felt Rogers reflects the course interest in the way in which cities are drawn together through a web of global interdependencies. The very title of his book suggests that he has an interest in the interconnections between cities. Global environmental problems can have a particular resonance in cities. Impacts can range from that of rising sea-levels on port and riverside cities to effects of dumping waste outside city limits. Such interdependencies are reflected in the course in a number of ways that you may have noted already. Perhaps the most striking demonstration of this is the concept of the 'ecological footprint' that is referred to at various points in the course and we shall return to this a little later. There are other ways, too, in which interconnections are drawn out by the authors. For example, Steve Pile refers to Lewis Mumford's curious phrase 'geographic plexus' suggesting that cities are made up of 'many networks through which flows, interchanges and interactions take place' (**Bk 1 Ch. 1** p.16) . And Ash Amin and Stephen Graham adopt a 'relational perspective' to emphasize the way in which cities are places where many webs and flows intersect and help shape the physical spaces of cities (**Bk 1 Ch. 1**). As Doreen Massey concludes, 'Each city lives in interconnection with other cities and with non-city areas' (**Bk 1 Ch. 4** p.160).

In both the above respects, it seems to me that Rogers is hinting at the geography – at the spatial impact – of contemporary urbanization. A key element in the Rogers extract is its *spatial narrative*: he is attempting to tell a story about contrasting urban environmental problems and environments, about the interconnections between cities and their futures.

I also felt that Rogers began to touch on the *tensions* that run through the course. For example, you may have noted his comments on the problems of movement in terms of transport within cities and migration to cities (reflecting the movement/settlement tension). And he is concerned with the order of the city and how the technical processes of urban design can produce more ordered, compact and environmentally sensitive cities. Rogers' enthusiasm for the 'compact city' as an answer to the problems of unsustainability reminds us of the way in which 'densification' can disconnect and disrupt city-nature relationships reflecting the order/disorder tension.

Did you also note how Rogers argues that the impacts on some environments and communities are heavier and more detrimental than on others? And it is often the poorer communities that experience the worst impacts, whilst wealthier communities are better able to control their environment and have considerably more scope in choosing where they wish to live. In other words there are marked spatial juxtapositions in the way the environment impacts on communities both within and between cities. This suggests that issues of environment are bound up with questions of power and inequality. I will explore this further below, but examples might range from lower-income communities suffering the effects of a new road being built through their neighbourhood to the exclusionary effects of walled residential enclaves. Rogers appears especially critical of cities in the Third World, referring to these environments as 'appalling'. This view makes me think back to different attitudes to 'urban farming' in Zimbabwe (**Bk 2 Ch. 4**

section 5.1; Bk 2 Reading 6A). Here the authorities in the capital, Harare, have a general distaste for farming in the city, partly for reasonable environmental concerns, but partly due to a technocratic bias against 'rural' land uses in an 'urban' context. In many ways Rogers' work reinforces this sense of city–rural dichotomies. Steve Hinchliffe, however, suggests that city farming represents a progressive form of urban-environmental politics and stands in contrast to the more technocratic approach to the environment of cities adopted by Rogers. This brings us back to the question of who defines what environmental 'problems' actually are, what measures need to be taken and by whom, and who gains most from these measures.

A final, overall impression I was left with, and you may have felt this too, was that although Rogers – like many – starts by viewing cities as an 'environmental liability', there is also, in his opinion, hope for the future. Rogers' shock as an architect that 'mankind's [*sic*] habitat – our cities' should destroy the ecosystem and threaten human survival, reflects his faith in cities and in city life. Indeed he even suggests that perhaps cities are the answer to global environmental sustainability rather than a hindrance. M. Ismail Serageldin **(Bk 1 Extract 3.3)** is of a similar opinion. Imagination, he argues, is necessary to solve these problems, but the question is 'whether we will have the political will to act'. In addition, we might also ask whose imagination and political will could offer solutions, and this search for solutions poses an interesting question. Should we be concerned with the individual sustainability of a city – for example, limiting the ecological footprint of a city like Buenos Aires, Sydney or Johannesburg – or should we be considering the contribution that cities can make to overall global sustainability? Or a bit of both, perhaps: as Steve Pile observes, understanding cities 'requires a geographical imagination capable of looking both beyond the city and within the city' **(Bk 1 Ch. 1** p.49).

Reading Rogers in this way has helped us begin to develop our thinking about three overlapping elements within the environment theme – the urban environment, urban environmental issues and urban environmental sustainability. In doing so we have begun to think about where the material on the environment theme is found in the course and how this material might be pieced together. And we have started to analyse these through three principal course arguments. Let's take this one stage further now, by returning to the course materials and beginning to map the environmental 'routes' (or 'pathways') through *Understanding Cities*. Most importantly, again, we need to find ways of making links between the material on the environment and the course arguments, broader themes and narratives that are developed through the three books, the Course Guide, TV programmes and audiocassettes. In the next activity I will talk you through the way I would set about these tasks.

ACTIVITY 4 .5   Think about the ways in which you could organize your material on the environment theme. This will help you to identify relevant sources, as well as to order and distil your ideas as you plan your course essay. Importantly it will help you reflect on the breadth of the environment theme throughout *Understanding Cities*.

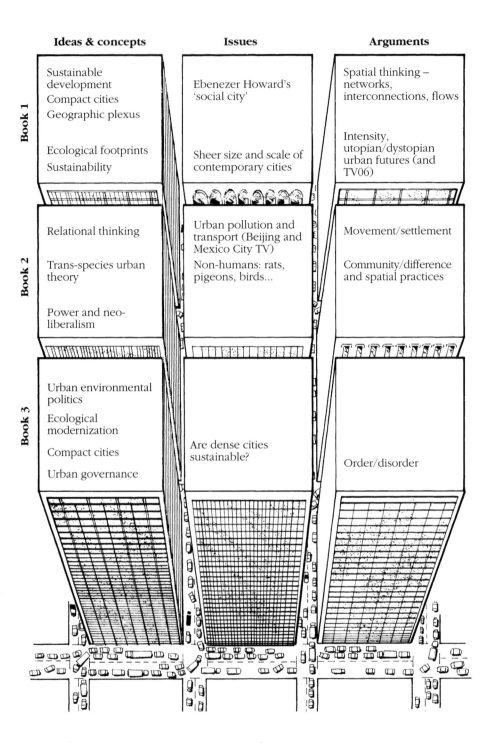

FIGURE 4.3 *Mapping an environment pathway*

I found it useful to construct a kind of table or grid to help me to separate out different aspects of studying the course environmentally, looking at examples from across the course: see Figure 4.3. But this is simply my preference and you may choose other ways of completing this task – using a 'mind map', for example. ◆

This is how I approached this task. Initially, I found it useful to split my notes into three, focusing on the following:

1   the scope of *ideas* and *concepts* that assist our understanding of urban environmental issues and urban environmental sustainability more generally: in other words, I have tried to identify the key *theoretical* arguments;

2   the environmental *issues* identified and what might be included as an environmental issue: this will help identify the main aspects of the environment theme;

3   most importantly, how this material reflects the course *arguments*: tensions, spatiality and intensity.

To begin the task of filling out the table, I then started to skim through my notes and to review the text (in the three books and Course Guide) which I had highlighted with a marker pen. I also found my thinking on the relevant activities useful and you may have made notes on the TV programmes and audiocassettes that you can also add into the table. I have included some of my notes below, but you will notice that I have only started this process and you will need to complete this task for yourself. There are plenty of ideas to draw in here!

It will take a little time to complete this task, and you can return to it as you work your way through this chapter, but I found it very useful in consolidating my knowledge of environmental issues and reflecting on the breadth of environmental material in the course. On a practical level this activity immediately demonstrates that some chapters are more obviously relevant than others; indeed there may be some chapters where it is less easy to include an entry. Nevertheless, as I showed earlier (in relation to **Bk 2 Ch. 5),** there are some chapters that, whilst not dealing with environmental issues directly, do contain ideas that can usefully be applied to the environment theme. Other examples are the 'relational' perspective **(Bk 2 Ch. 1)** which seeks to emphasize the way in which the intersection of social, cultural and technological flows is superimposed on the physical spaces of cities. This not only helps us to explore the way in which urban environments are moulded (New York City is used as an example) but to appreciate the connections formed within and between cities and rural areas. In this way it reflects the ecological footprints of cities. Ash Amin and Stephen Graham refer to this as the 'multiple geographies of cities' and a relational perspective also helps us conceptualize the geographical juxtaposition of two very different New York environments, the Lower East Side and Manhattan. As these authors contend, 'it is a good example of how spaces which are physically close within a city can simultaneously be relationally very distant and relatively disconnected' (p.12). A similar approach could be taken with the discussion of La Paz, Bolivia **(Bk 2 Ch. 6)**. It is important, then, to consider how the material, both in its explicit and implicit forms, can be applied to the environment theme.

Returning to Figure 4.3, I found it helped to identify course ideas and concepts (for example, sustainable development, ecological footprints), course issues (pollution, transport, planning and so on) and how the course arguments are related to these. For example, the concept of city-natures and reference to trans-species urban theory which emphasizes the presence of the non-human in cities (the rats, pigeons, birds and so on) have a clear link with the city tensions argument **(Bk 2 Ch. 4)**. They illustrate the tension between community and difference, and the need for new spatial arrangements to favour the urban practices of these non-human species.

I also found this grid useful in identifying how the course arguments are reflected spatially. Did you note how it underlines the varying ways the environment, environmental issues and environmental sustainability are represented and can be understood spatially? Some processes such as the international trade in polluting industries more obviously connect the 'local' with the 'global'. Other seemingly local issues often need to be viewed in a broader geographical context, such as the causal links between vehicle emissions and global warming.

In the next section we will explore these ideas further and review the key arguments in the course.

3 *Key arguments*

So far so good, I hope! We have identified the parameters of the environment theme and started to map out how the theory and ideas on the environment run through and cut across the course. We need to take this a stage further now by drawing out the relevance of three key sets of arguments in the course and asking how these arguments enrich our understanding of cities and environmental issues and questions.

It is useful at this stage to briefly recall the types of course essay questions that will be posed within the environment theme. Figure 1.1 in Chapter 1 of this book sets out the 'options for the course essay'. The questions themselves will be set out in the Course Essay Question Booklet. You will be asked to work through the course material on the environment by focusing on one of these three key arguments in *Understanding Cities:* exploring the intensity of cities and the environmental impacts arising from this; thinking spatially or geographically about environment and cities; or applying one of three course tensions to the environment.

The following three sections consider each in turn and suggest some ways in which you can draw upon the course material in answering a question. You may find it useful as you progress to return to Activity 4.2 and Activity 4.5, and review and add to the ideas you have already noted. You will also find it helpful to reflect on any other material you may have collected so that you can weave this material into your approach to the environment theme. This will further help you to identify your 'routes' or 'pathways' through the course material, to identify key theoretical arguments and to see how the environment theme cuts through all the course materials.

At the outset, it is important to re-emphasize that my thoughts are only intended to be a start: they are indicative of the material that is available to you, but there are other narratives in the course and different ways in which the environment story can be told. So you will need to add to this process. The questions posed within each of the three sections will help you to reflect on the wider context of the environment theme. There is also a 'sub-plot' that I want to draw out under each of the three headings here and that is about the dimensions of *power* and *inequality* in relation to the environment.

3.1   CITY INTENSITIES

Let's start by grappling with intensity, the first argument running through *Understanding Cities*. You may recall from the outset of the course that the intensification of 'concentrating things in urban space' was identified as perhaps the most significant feature of cities **(Bk 1 Ch. 1)** and the TV programme on Mexico City certainly gets to grips with this. Two types of intensity were identified. The first talks of an *open intensity*, the way in which people, resources, goods and so on flow into, around and out of the city: for example, take the environmental impact arising from the movement of people in cities or the range of resources that are required to build, maintain and feed cities. This concentration of activity produces a second *felt intensity*, and many of us are aware of the daily grime and intensity of airborne pollution that we encounter in the city, the congestion of city roads **(Bk 2 Ch. 1)**, or the excitement created by the intense use of city environments. And perhaps the most striking example of intensification and a way of beginning to grapple with this key course argument is the rate at which cities have grown, both in terms of the numbers of people living there, the physical expansion that has been needed to accommodate urban populations and the range of resources necessary to support these city populations. You may recall that a number of the authors in this course refer to the population of cities, emphasizing the rate of growth and the fact that over half the world's population is now 'urban' (with cities occupying only two per cent of the Earth's land surface) and that by the year 2020 urban population is likely to rise to over 75 per cent of global population **(Bk 3 Ch. 6)**. Table 4.2 and Figure 4.4 quantify and map the distribution of the world's population in the largest cities. In environmental terms, this has placed 'cities on trial'. On the one hand they are lamented and demonized for their supposed environmental destructiveness; on the other, they are promoted as a principal means of achieving environmental sustainability.

TABLE 4.2   *The regional distribution of the world's population in 'million-cities' and the location of the world's largest 100 cities, 1800, 1950 and 1990*

	Proportion of the world's				Number of the world's 100 largest cities in		
	urban population		population in million-cities				
	1950	1990	1950	1990	1800	1950	1990
Africa	4.5	8.8	1.8	7.5	4	3	7
Eastern Africa	0.5	1.7	–	0.8	–	–	–
Middle Africa	0.5	1.0	–	0.8	0	0	1
Northern Africa	1.8	2.8	1.8	3.2	3	2	5
Southern Africa	0.8	0.9	–	0.8	0	1	0
Western Africa	0.9	2.6	–	2.0	1	0	1
Americas	23.7	23.0	30.1	27.8	3	26	27
Caribbean	0.8	0.9	0.6	0.8	1	1	0
Central America	2.0	3.3	1.6	2.7	1	1	3
North America	14.4	9.2	21.2	13.1	0	18	13
South America	6.5	9.7	11.1	1	1	6	11
Asia	32.0	44.5	28.6	45.6	64	33	44
Eastern Asia	15.2	19.7	17.6	22.2	29	18	21
Southeastern Asia	3.7	5.8	3.4	5.6	5	5	8
South-central Asia	11.2	14.8	7.0	14.6	24	9	13
Western Asia	1.8	4.1	0.6	3.3	6	1	2
Europe	38.8	22.8	38.0	17.9	29	36	20
Eastern Europe	11.8	9.3	7.7	6.3	2	7	4
Northern Europe	7.7	3.4	9.0	2.1	6	6	2
Southern Europe	6.5	4.0	6.7	3.2	12	8	6
Western Europe	12.8	6.2	14.6	6.2	9	15	8
Oceana	1.1	0.8	1.6	1.3	0	2	2

Source: UNCHS, 1996, Table 1.6, p.20

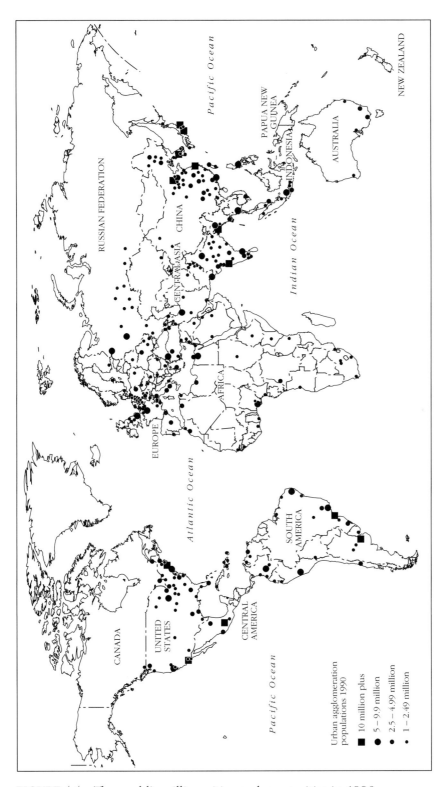

FIGURE 4.4   *The world's million-cities and mega-cities in 1990*

ACTIVITY 4.6   Let's consider these different urban environmental scenarios a little further by working through Reading 4B taken from *Small is Beautiful*, written by one of the most influential early thinkers on the environment and sustainability, E.F. Schumacher.

As you study Reading 4B, note down:

● your overall impression and 'feeling' about Shumacher's approach having studied the *Understanding Cities* course

● the connections that Schumacher makes and how these connections relate to the course-wide argument on city intensities

● the appropriateness of Schumacher's suggested solution to urban problems

● other issues that you think Schumacher fails to take into account. ◆

Overall, I found it pretty disturbing stuff, did you? Much like Doreen Massey's initial reaction to the M. Ismail Serageldin article **(Bk 1 Extract 3.3)**, I felt overwhelmed. This is a thoroughly negative view of urbanization and cities. There were a number of points that struck me.

You may have noted that Schumacher's thinking is dominated by the overall size of the population. We may begin to think of a variety of other factors that challenge the sustainability of cities, such as the level of resources consumed by different social groups in that city, the way in which cities draw their resources from other areas and from other parts of the world, and the way in which city environments are managed and controlled. Overall, I didn't get the impression that Schumacher was concerned by the causes of power and inequality expressed in urban environments or the up-side to the open intensity of cities and positive aspects of city life.

I was shocked by the provocative language employed by Schumacher referring, for example, to 'unprecedented', 'explosive' and 'pathological' population growth. He is offering a particular geographical and spatial imagination of urbanization, especially in the Third World, that demonizes the very populations that inhabit those cities.

Whilst, as Table 3.1 **(Bk 1)** demonstrates, the majority of 'mega-cities' are in the Third World, and this is where the most rapid growth in urbanization is occurring, there appears to be another narrative behind these figures. I stopped to think about the dominant images of Third World cities (and you could glance back at some of the photos used in the course) – and what my geographical imagination of these places consists of. For the most part these are negative images, of intense mega-cities experiencing severe environmental problems – unsanitary living conditions, poor health and the kind of 'disorderly' urban peripheral sprawl that Gerry Mooney refers to **(Bk 3 Ch. 2)**.

Perhaps, like me, you detected the way in which Schumacher seems to blame populations for causing environmental problems, seeing these cities as cauldrons of poverty and hopelessness, their populations as 'parasites'. This poses the question: is it the spatial intensification in certain cities of the Third

World that is causing a global environmental catastrophe? Or is it the differential level of consumption of resources by different social and income groups? In other words, how do social and economic issues impact on what seems to be an environmental problem?

Did you notice how Schumacher's approach seems reminiscent of what Steve Hinchliffe **(Bk 2 Ch. 4)** refers to as 'foundational stories' – that is, tales or stories that people construct about how cities came to be. Schumacher seems to construct a very particular story about this environment, a *degradation/pollution* foundational story where Lima is presented as wreaking havoc on its environment. His narrative, as with that of Simon's 'Mexico City trashed' **(Bk 2 Extract 4.1)**, displays the characteristics of such foundational stories. Of Lima, Schumacher both *idealizes the past* and displays a strong *anti-urbanism*: 'The once beautiful Spanish city is now infested by slums, surrounded by misery-belts that are crawling up the Andes.' It all appears very negative, Schumacher *undercuts the future*, and doesn't provide us with much hope of responding to the environmental problems of cities or finding solutions.

Perhaps you found yourself asking if spatial intensification is a problem, and, if it is, is 'de-intensification' a necessary prerequisite for overcoming urban environmental problems and producing environmentally sustainable cities? What solutions would you advocate for the environmental problems created by cities?

We have begun to think about one of the key debates over the future of cities and one of the big questions that lies behind this course. The open intensity of cities can produce both intense environmental impacts and intense debates, not just about the environmental problems of cities, but also their possibilities. At this point you might want relief from the gloomy – dystopian – views of the likes of Schumacher! Reading 4C by Diana Mitlin and David Satterthwaite is included as an extra resource at the end of this chapter and it takes a very different approach by listing the advantages and potential arising from the intensity of cities.

Now let's pause for a moment to think about how you might apply material from across the course to the course argument of city intensity in relation to the environment theme. We will do this with a particular mock question in mind.

ACTIVITY 4.7   To what extent does the intensity of city life undermine the environmental sustainability of cities?

Take a few moments to jot down your thoughts and consider the issues and sub-questions to which this broad-ranging question gives rise. You might want to do this in note form or by using a mind map. And don't worry if your ideas seem a little 'disordered' at this point: brainstorming is an important stage which will help you identify a way of constructing a well-focused and balanced argument. ◆

When I tried this activity, I was amazed at the breadth of the question and the amount of material I could use from across the course. This is why it is important to get 'behind' the question and explore the specific sub-questions it poses, as well as pulling out the less obvious – but no less important – reflections offered by the course. Here are the questions and ideas that occurred to me.

I started by asking in what ways intensity undermines environmental sustainability. One way of thinking about this is to consider how the 'felt' and 'open' intensities of cities produce environmental problems that work to undermine sustainability. Examples of this can be seen throughout the course, ranging from pollution **(Bk 2 Ch. 2)** to environmental degradation **(Bk 1 Ch. 3**; **TV** programmes on Mexico City and New York), to environmental movements **(Bk 3 Ch. 5)**, to the ways in which cities are part of wider flows and interconnections **(Bk 2 Chs 1 and 2; Bk 3 Ch. 6)**.

I then began to think about less obvious connections. For example, if a key course issue is the way in which intensity can lead to conflict, I wondered about the degree to which conflicts over the environment could compromise environmental sustainability. And there are plenty of examples in the course, ranging from 'nimbyism' **(Bk 3 Ch. 5)** to conflicts over who plans, owns, develops and has access to certain environments – with case studies that include Rainham Marshes **(Bk 2 Ch. 4)**, Tompkins Square **(Bk 2 Ch. 3)** and walled communities (for example, **Bk 2 Chs 1 and 3**).

We might also ask whether all cities and social groups are responsible for undermining environmental sustainability. Are some cities more sustainable than others, and are the consumption patterns of some social groups less polluting than others? To put it another way, is it just intensity that causes environmental problems or are there other factors that we need to take account of, such as affluent lifestyles or the ways in which cities are governed and managed **(Bk 3 Ch. 7)**?

Remember, though, that the question is asking us to look at both sides of the argument and the intensity of cities might also promote environmental sustainability. The more obvious discussion could assess the sustainability of certain types of city, such as 'spread' or 'compact' cities (which crops up through the three texts, the final **TV** programme and **AC** 2 Side A). But again try to think about the initially less obvious course ideas as well: for example, how cities have produced assertive and progressive forms of urban-environmental politics **(Bk 2 Ch. 4; Bk 3 Ch. 5)** and the ways in which city development is leading to a changing ethical relationship between humans and non-humans **(Bk 2 Ch. 4)**. There is more than one future for cities and it is possible to intervene and create these futures!

As you can see, we are dealing with a broad question here, and there is plenty of course material to draw on. I've suggested some ways of tackling this, but there are other approaches and other examples you can use.

3.2   SPATIAL THINKING AND THE ENVIRONMENT

You only need to take a trip to a local supermarket, furniture store or clothes shop to remind yourself that goods are drawn from across the region, country or globe to service our needs and desires in cities. We have already come across the views of Richard Rogers (in Reading 4A) and the web of interconnections and interdependencies that draw cities together to which he alludes. These echo the course emphasis on connections, disconnections and juxtapositions and the way in which, through these, city environments can also be connected, so to speak, by encountering similar environmental problems. In this section we will think a little further about what it means to 'think spatially' about cities in terms of the environment.

Now we are at an advantage here, as Chris Brook has already considered this in part in Chapter 1 in relation to the question: *In what ways does 'thinking spatially' help us to understand environmental issues within cities?'* It is worth spending a few moments reviewing the approach adopted by Chris Brook, and you might want to look again at the mind map constructed by him (Figure 1.1). There are a number of points that stuck in my mind from his approach. For example, Chris Brook starts thinking about the different spatial frames that are relevant here and how these range from the uneven web of global connections to unequal localized impacts. He also questions the spatial inequalities that arise from environmental issues and conflicts, and the social construction and contested nature of environmental issues. You may be familiar with clashes of opinion from your own area (or perhaps from national news) amongst local communities and environmental groups about the appropriateness and impact of new developments such as a new supermarket, housing or a new road, or perhaps the loss of an open space. These are points that we need to think about further here.

A visual way of demonstrating how the environmental impact of cities extends beyond cities is the 'ecological footprint'. Footprints are referenced in a number of places in the course with the idea most fully developed by Andy Blowers and Kathy Pain **(Bk 3 Ch. 6)**. You may remember that the ecological footprint refers to the 'total area of productive land and water required on a continuous basis to produce the resources consumed, and to assimilate the wastes produced, by that population, wherever on Earth that land is located' (Rees, 1997, p.305). Above all else, such concepts help us to acknowledge the nets of interconnections within which cities operate and how distant environments are connected to cities through spatial relations.

But, further than this, footprints emphasize that cities in different parts of the world consume very different levels of resources, and by inference have differential impacts on environments beyond the city. Footprints vary in size: for example, the footprint of Vancouver in British Columbia is estimated at 180 times its own area (see Reading 4D below), while Santiago, the capital of Chile, has a footprint equivalent to just sixteen times its metropolitan area. This points to the uneven environmental consequences of cities and challenges our perceptions of what type of city is responsible for the greatest consumption of resources and production of waste.

ACTIVITY 4.8   Now turn to Reading 4D, 'Is "sustainable city" an oxymoron?' As you read, note Rees's environmental perspective on cities, on the environmental problems they create and the approaches to solving these problems. I also found it helpful to consider the extent to which footprints are useful as a 'spatial tool'. ◆

Did you notice how Rees, like Steve Hinchliffe's discussion of city-nature formations **(Bk 2 Ch. 4)**, seems to challenge a distinction between the urban and the rural (it might be useful to skim that chapter to remind yourself of his arguments). This also challenges the notion of spatial separation of 'nature' from 'cities'. These authors are constructing different ways of representing the city in environmental terms. Rees refers to the dualism that characterizes industrial society, which creates a barrier between city-dwellers and the rest of nature and refers to cities as 'ecological entities' instead. Rees turns the tables, so to speak, in arguing that green plants are the real factories of production and that humans and their economies are 'secondary producers'. And, linking back to the discussion of intensity, you may have noted his reference to cities as '*open* systems' and that in spatial terms 'cities are nodes of intense material consumption and waste discharge'.

I felt the language adopted by Rees, like that of Schumacher, is provocative. He refers to cities as solar collectors, as 'entropic black holes', that sweep up vast areas. He even refers to cities as the 'human equivalent of cattle feedlots'. He, too, rounds on the ever-increasing size, density and interconnectedness of cities. You might also consider the degree to which footprinting reflects the anti-urban foundational stories discussed by Steve Hinchliffe **(Bk 2 Ch. 4)** as reflected in the cartoon that appears in Wackernagel's and Rees' book, *Our Ecological Footprint*: see Figure 4.5.

FIGURE 4.5
A view of the ecological footprint of cities

You may have noted how Rees is also at pains to stress the local interdependencies between cities and the global environment. He assesses the extent to which cities can be sustainable in their own right ('a sustainable city') versus the broader role of cities in collectively contributing to global sustainability. In other words, Rees is arguing that the way in which cities are interconnected in a global web of flows, and the environmental impacts they have beyond their boundaries, has challenged and defeated their ability to be individually sustainable. Sustainable city, he argues, is an oxymoron. But to what extent do you agree with his conclusions?

You will have seen how Rees concludes his paper by suggesting a range of spatial land-use planning actions that could be undertaken to increase the sustainability of cities. Like Richard Rogers, his is a more technocratic solution. His suggestions range from aiming for 'zero impact development', to finding ways to minimize the resource demands of cities. Some of the questions that arose in my mind were: to what extent are his suggestions practicable; in which cities could these be implemented; who would be responsible for implementing such proposals?

But, finally, whilst the footprint is useful in emphasizing the connections between cities and the environment spatially and the differential environmental impact of different types and sizes of cities, I felt it didn't tell me much about the (dis)connections within and between cities. For example, the footprint is certainly no indicator of the relative health or quality of local environments within cities and it doesn't tell us which groups and areas within cities consume the most resources.

From your jottings, the above discussion and Chris Brook's thoughts on spatial issues, you will have begun to consider the range of ways in which spatial thinking helps us to understand environmental issues and cities. Take a few moments more to consider other ways that spatial thinking is reflected in the course materials. You may have noticed how Steve Hinchliffe uses the city-nature formation concept to disrupt the bounded, static and settled way in which city space has been conceived, both in terms of urban theory and in the minds of city planners. The 'spatial logic' of the city plan, Steve tells us, is alien to the spatial transgressions of the 'disordered' or 'differently ordered' fox, or for that matter the movements of all animals, birds and insects through and within the city. Simply, they do not belong and are not contained in one place. So the boundaries that are drawn around cities, and areas within cities, limit rather than add to our understanding of cities.

Thinking about cities spatially helps us to see how connections and disconnections affect cities environmentally. I noted in several places the sharp juxtapositions of wealth and poverty and very different qualities of environments that are experienced by different groups. In Third World cities, from La Paz to Nairobi (for example, in **Bk 2 Ch. 6** and **Bk 1 Ch. 2**), we are reminded of the great contrast between the wealthy élite and urban poor. In some cases, walled and gated communities – 'fortified enclaves' – are created

(Bk 3 Ch. 4) to exclude other urban dwellers. You may also have noted how this 'spatial apartheid' is extended by Jenny Robinson (Bk 3 Ch. 4) to consider the ways in which urban citizens, apparently sharing the same environment, are somehow segregated and therefore experience very different environments. Thinking spatially, as Jenny Robinson reminds us, helps not only in thinking about the borders and boundaries that separate, but also to think about how these environments are connected through the potential of 'crossings'.

It seems to me that these examples and other course material underline the differential power between different social groups, between different cities and between different areas within cities. The following piece by Mathis Wackernagel and Reading 4E by David Satterthwaite (at the end of this chapter) emphasize these environmental spatial inequalities:

> [S]ome (wealthy) cities ... have been able to preserve splendid local settings and restore high water and air quality. Often, however, these cities are only able to protect their local environment thanks to the purchasing power with which they can appropriate additional ecological capacity from somewhere else. From there, they receive the resources to build a sophisticated infrastructure. Or, they use these faraway capacities to absorb their waste. Local air pollution, often misconceived as an 'environmental' problem, is therefore not a matter of ecological capacity, but, equally important, one of quality of life and human health. Sustainable cities must resolve, therefore, the challenge of securing a high quality of life, including a healthy local environment without eroding the ecological capacities beyond its boundaries.

(Wackernagel, 1998, p.20)

Let us conclude this section by revisiting Latin America and thinking about how environmental issues are expressed unequally. It is useful to consider how environmental issues – once again – overlap with the economic and social dimensions of the course. You may have noted discussions of cities in this region in a number of chapters and in the TV series.

ACTIVITY 4.9   To this end, turn to Reading 4F, 'The Latin American metropolis and the growth of inequality ' by Thomas Angotti. As you read, make a note of the principal spatial connections that are affecting the environments of Mexico City and other Latin American cities. You might also want to compare this author's view on the causes of environmental degradation with Julian Simon's (Bk 2 Extract 4.1). ◆

Here are some of my thoughts:

Angotti (as does Richard Rogers) refers to what seem to be generic environmental problems faced by Latin American cities, characterized by mass poverty and severe environmental pollution. In Angotti's words, Mexico City crystallizes the 'urban question in Latin America'. This triggered thoughts for me on the way in which different cities are in some way connected by exposure to similar global processes, and how local environments must face the uneven impacts, albeit translated differently at the local level.

There are also the broader interconnections that Angotti notes, in particular the activities of transnational corporations who gain from the vast pool of surplus labour ('a global assembly-line') in Latin American cities, and the 'austerity policies' of the champions of neo-liberalization, the World Bank and IMF (discussed in **Bk 2 Ch. 6**). I noted Angotti's reference to the 'neo-liberal craze for deregulation' and how this directly affects the environment, in this case in Santiago.

Angotti, like Rees, also offers thoughts on tackling environmental problems and producing what he calls 'liveable cities'. Unlike Rees, however, he urges the need for a 'balanced economic system' that is capable of halting the rural to urban drift. How far do you agree with his analysis? Does the web of interconnections that make up the global economy allow for this? The question remains: who are these environmental improvements for? How can environmental problems be tackled and who formulates these approaches? In thinking about environmental issues and solutions to environmental problems we need to be aware of the foundational stories they reflect.

This section has emphasized the many and varied ways we can think spatially about environmental issues and cities. On the practical side we should bear in mind the fact that there are different and contested views of how to solve urban environmental problems and how to define environmental issues.

3.3 ENVIRONMENTAL TENSIONS

Let's turn now to the final key argument that runs through *Understanding Cities* – 'urban tensions'. You may want to refer back to Book 1, the Course Guide and Chapter 1 of this volume now to remind yourself how this argument is used in the course to capture the ways in which cities are experienced and the ways in which they work. You may have begun to recall how the argument is threaded through the course by completing Activity 4.5. As Chris Brook and Phil Pinch comment, it is important to appreciate that cities and the tensions they produce are paradoxical and ambivalent (Chapter 1 and Course Guide). As we have already seen, there are numerous ways of understanding, experiencing, interpreting and representing city-environments, environmental issues and environmental 'solutions'. As frustrating as it may seem, there are no hard and fast answers here! We are dealing with the social construction of the 'environment' and this inevitably leads to debate, disagreement, tension and conflict.

Here we will think through some of the ways in which this course argument can help our understanding of the environment theme.

ACTIVITY 4.10   Consider one of the three main course tensions – order/ disorder, community/difference and movement/settlement – and show through one or two examples how this might apply to the environment theme. I've tried to take my thinking a stage further by posing the types of questions and issues that these tensions give rise to. This helps to anticipate the kind of ideas that will emerge and the questions you will be asked in the course essay. You can add to these in the list below. ◆

Movement/settlement:

● Do city-nature formations challenge the notion of cities as bounded and settled places? And do 'sustainable cities' demand settled communities?

Community/difference

● Are cities unnatural? How far can difference create more liveable environments?

Order/disorder

● Do ordered cities reduce or increase environmental problems and do disordered cities undermine urban environmental sustainability?

After spending a little time completing this activity, I began to appreciate the breadth of examples from across the course, and the way in which the tensions weave themselves throughout *Understanding Cities*.

For example, I found reflections on the movement/settlement tension in material as diverse as the movements of the urban fox, to the burning contemporary debates over city transport systems. Similarly, the order/disorder tension appears in material ranging from the social construction of what constitutes an acceptable ordering of urban environments (as the cartoon by El Fisgon in Figure 4.6 suggests) to the imposition of western thinking on urban sustainable development – 'ecological modernization'.

FIGURE 4.6   *Urban order/disorder for whom?*

ACTIVITY 4.11   It is also useful to remember how these tensions are present in multiple ways through the course material. I have included two interesting pieces at the end of the chapter: Reading 4G, 'Farming inside and around cities' by Luc Mougeot returns to the issue of 'urban farming' again (discussed in **Bk 2 Chs 4 and 6**) and Reading 4H by Kristin Helmore starts from Bombay and considers new ways of tackling urban problems. As you study Readings 4G and 4H, note down which tensions are relevant here and in what ways. ◆

Perhaps, like me, you detected all three tensions within these pieces. Again, briefly, here are some of my thoughts and you may well have others.

I noted the way in which both authors focus on the social divisions within cities and the way in which this leads to differential environmental impacts and environmental strategies. Mougeot discusses the ways in which urban farming in most Third World countries is a coping strategy for the poor, a way of dealing with economic uncertainty and low incomes. Helmore references not only the way in which environmental impacts are concentrated on the poor, but the ways in which in some cities 'traditional enemies' are attempting to overcome these differences and tackle problems communally. Interestingly, both authors suggest that it is a lack of equity that is one of the key urban problems, but that such problems are also driving solutions, or at least responses, to the fore.

Did you note how the movement/settlement tension is reflected in these readings? Two examples I picked up on were Mougeot's suggestion that much urban farming is a direct result of the in-migration from rural areas, by formerly low-income small farmers. Nature has been asserted in the city, so to speak. By contrast, Akhtar Badshah (of Mega-Cities, a New York-based organization: see Reading 4H) briefly refers to the way in which the poor are pushed to the sprawling peripheries of cities and are further geographically dislocated from work opportunities.

Finally, perhaps you felt that the order/disorder tension is never far from the surface of these pieces. On the one hand there is a fascinating dilemma within urban farming as to whether it should be encouraged and integrated into orderly technocratic plans or whether it is an anathema to the city and should be confined to the countryside. On the other hand, there is the discussion of what form of governance is required to run cities effectively and tackle their environmental problems, and to bring cities back from what this author considers to be the brink of disaster.

I do hope these examples illustrate that it is possible to work through the course material in multiple ways. Let's continue using these tensions to probe environmental issues just a little further. I've chosen to have a crack at the community/difference tension here. At first sight perhaps, like me, you found this tension a little less obviously relevant in environmental terms. A typical question could be:

> Explore how the tension between community and difference can be used to shed light on environmental issues.

Here are my initial thoughts on this question:

I felt I wanted to start by quickly listing what types of environmental issues might be relevant here. My list ranged from the relationship between social equity and environmental impacts, to the nature of urban environmental conflict and politics. One of the key questions I felt compelled to ask was how the community/difference tension helps or hinders urban environmental sustainability.

I asked if, how and why the density of city living results in a distancing both from other people, but more significantly from 'nature'. I considered whether alienation from nature has taken place and whether the dichotomies of urban/rural, city/countryside, natural/constructed encourage a way of reading cities which emphasizes the indifference of cities to nature.

But I also wanted to think about the ways in which indifference is challenged. I found the discussion of 'trans-species urban theory' useful on this front **(Bk 2 Reading 4D)** in attempting to redress the absence of non-human animals in traditional urban theory. From this point I found it helpful to think about city-nature formations and the ways in which they challenge and assert nature in the city. For example, the cultivation of organic foods (on allotments for example) in western cities provides simultaneously for difference and community – an alternative lifestyle movement. **Audiocassette 2** helps us to think about this tension in relation to the environment theme in a positive way.

I also considered how the huge inequalities and differences within and between cities help our understanding of environmental issues. I considered how the course material questions which social groups produce and face the greatest environmental impacts, possess the most environmentally sustainable lifestyles and formulate responses to environmental problems and opportunities. To complement the course material I have included Reading 4I in the resource material at the end of the chapter which returns to the example of Bombay and considers some of these questions.

Perhaps you would have considered the range of urban environmental conflicts from nimbyism **(Bk 3 Ch. 5)** to the protests of poorer communities adversely affected by pollution. Or how the pressure of city living has produced urban-based environmental politics and movements and to what degree this has resulted in more environmentally sensitive and liveable environments. There is plenty of material to draw on from across the course and your task is to focus in on the most relevant and illustrative examples.

That brings us to the end of this guide to the environment theme – though remember to look at the Readings for the chapter, especially those you haven't already studied for Activities. I hope that working through this chapter has helped you to feel not only well prepared but excited about actually preparing and writing your course essay.

Well, it's over to you now. Good luck and I hope you enjoy constructing your own ideas on the environment and cities.

References

Angotti, T. (1995) 'The Latin American metropolis and the growth of inequality', *NACLA Report on the Americas*, vol.XXVIII, no.4, Jan/Feb, pp.13–18.

Bartone, C., Bernstein, J., Leitmann, J. and Eigen, J. (1994) *Towards Environmental Strategies for Cities: Policy Considerations for Urban Environmental Management in Developing Countries*, UNDP/UNCHS/World Bank Urban Management Program no. 18, Washington, DC, World Bank.

Haughton, G. and Hunter, C. (1996) *Sustainable Cities*, London, Jessica Kingsley Publishers and Regional Studies Association.

Harvey, D. (1996) *Justice, Nature and the Geography of Difference*, Oxford, Blackwell.

Helmore, K. (1996) 'Cities on the brink try new tactics', *Choices*, June, New York, United Nations Division of Public Affairs.

Mitlin, D. and Satterthwaite, D. (1994) *Cities and Sustainable Development,* London, IIED.

Mougeot, L.J.A. (1998) 'Farming inside and around cities', *Urban Age*, Winter, pp.18–21.

Rees, W.E. (1997) 'Is "sustainable city" an oxymoron?', *Local Environment*, vol.2, no.3, pp.303–10.

Rogers, R. (1997) *Cities for a Small Planet*, London, Faber & Faber.

Satterthwaite, D. (1997) 'Sustainable cities or cities that contribute to sustainable development?', *Urban Studies*, vol.34, no.10, pp.1667–91.

Schumacher, E. F. (1974) *Small is Beautiful: A Study of Economics As If People Mattered*, London, Abacus.

Seabrook, J. (1993) *Victims of Development: Resistance and Alternatives*, London, Verso.

United Nations Centre for Human Settlements (UNCHS) (1996) *An Urbanizing World: Global Report on Human Settlement,* Oxford, Oxford University Press.

Wackernagel, M. (1998) 'The ecological footprint of Santiago de Chile', *Local Environment,* vol.3, no.1, pp.7–25.

Wackernagel, M. and Rees, W.E. (1996) *Our Ecological Footprint: Reducing Human Impact on the Earth*, Gabriola Island, British Columbia, New Society Publishers.

Resource materials for the environment theme

To help you further with the course essay, here is a range of readings. You will have noticed how I have referenced and worked through most of this material in this chapter. Some pieces I have referenced in passing and included here because the material complements messages developed in the course and may be useful to you in writing your course essay. The material can be applied in multiple ways, and you shouldn't see it as necessarily informing only part of the argument – the point at which I have used it: try to apply it elsewhere in your exploration of the environment theme. Of course, if you decided to develop your own 'course file' you can now decide which of your material is most relevant to this theme, and add it to these additional materials. All in all, a rich bundle of resources to draw upon!

READING 4A
Richard Rogers: 'Cities for a small planet'

In 1957 the first satellite was launched into orbit. It gave us a vantage point from which we could look at ourselves and signalled the beginning of a new global consciousness, a dramatic change in our relationship with the planet. Seen from space, the beauty of the earth's biosphere is striking – but so also is its fragility. The plumes of pollution, the wounds of deforestation, the scars of industrialisation and the sprawl of our cities are all evidence that in our quest for wealth we are systematically plundering every aspect of our life-support system.

…

It is a shocking revelation, especially to an architect, that it is our cities that are driving this environmental crisis. In 1900 only one-tenth of the world's population lived in cities. Today, for the first time in history, half the population lives in cities and in thirty years' time it may rise to as much as three-quarters. The urban population is increasing at a rate of a quarter of a million people per day – roughly the equivalent of a new London every month. The world-wide growth of urban populations and grossly inefficient patterns of living are accelerating the rate of increase of pollution and erosion.

It is ironic that mankind's [sic] habitat – our cities – is the major destroyer of the ecosystem and the greatest threat to humankind's survival on the planet. In the United States, pollution from cities has already reduced crop production by almost 10 per cent. In Japan, waste dumped by Tokyo city amounts to an estimated twenty million tons every year, waste that has already saturated the entire Tokyo bay. Mexico City is literally drinking its two rivers dry, while London's massive traffic congestion causes greater air pollution today than did the burning of coal in the pre-1956 Clean Air Act period. Cities generate the majority of greenhouse gases …

While the need for cities and the inevitability of their continued growth will not diminish, city living *per se* need not lead to civilisation's self-destruction. I passionately believe that the arts of architecture and city planning could be evolved to provide crucial tools for safeguarding our future, creating cities that provide sustainable and civilising environments …

My cause for optimism is derived from three factors: the spread of ecological awareness, of communications technology and of automated production. All are contributing conditions for the development of an environmentally aware and socially responsible post-industrial urban culture. Throughout the world, scientists, philosophers, economists, politicians, planners, artists and citizens are increasingly demanding that the global perspective be integrated into strategies for the future. The United Nations report, *Our Common Future,* proposed the concept of 'sustainable development' as the backbone of global economic policy …

The core of this concept of sustainability is the redefining of wealth to include natural capital: clean air, fresh water, an effective ozone layer, a clean sea, fertile land and the abundant diversity of species. The means proposed to ensure the protection of this natural capital are regulations and, most importantly, an appropriate pricing of the market's use of natural capital, an asset that had been previously considered limitless and therefore cost-free …

Nowhere is the implementation of 'sustainability' more potent and more beneficial than in the city. In fact, the benefits to be derived from this approach are potentially so great that environmental sustainability should become the guiding principle of modern urban design.

If cities are undermining the ecological balance of the planet, it is our patterns of social and economic behaviour that are the root cause of their development in ways that produce environmental imbalance. In both developed and developing worlds the 'carrying' capacity of cities is being stretched to their limit. Cities are increasing in size and at such a rate that conventional patterns of accommodating urban growth have become obsolete. In the developed world the migration of people and activities from city centres to the dream world of suburbia has led to massive suburban development, wide-spread road-building, increased car use, congestion and pollution – best exemplified in the cities of the Western USA like Phoenix and Las Vegas. Meanwhile, in the fast-growing economies of the developing world, new cities are being built at a phenomenal rate and density with little thought for future environmental or social impact. World-wide, there is a mass migration of the rural poor to these new consumerist cities. Everywhere the situation of the poor is largely overlooked. In the developed world the poor fall out of the consumer society and are abandoned and isolated in the inner-city ghettos, while in the developing cities the poor are relegated to the squalor of the swelling shanty towns. 'Unofficial' or illegal residents regularly outnumber the official ones.

Cities are producing disastrous social instability that is further driving environmental decline. Despite global increases in wealth that far outpace increases in population, the world's poor are growing in number and in poverty. Many of these poor are living in the most squalid environments, exposed to extremes of environmental poverty and perpetuating the cycle of erosion and pollution. Cities are destined to house a larger and larger proportion of the world's poor. It should come as no surprise that societies and cities that lack basic equity suffer intense social deprivation and create greater environmental damage – environmental and social issues are interlocked.

Poverty, unemployment, ill-health, poor education, conflict – in short, social injustice in all its forms – undermine a city's capacity to be environmentally sustainable …

…

Today's cities are consuming three-quarters of the world's energy and causing at least three-quarters of global pollution. They are the place of production and consumption of most industrial goods. Cities have become parasites on the landscape – huge organisms draining the world for their sustenance and energy: relentless consumers, relentless polluters.

If the developed world considers its problems of pollution, congestion and inner-city decay are appalling, then consider the changes that are overwhelming the developing world. While in the developed world city populations are effectively stagnating, in the developing world the multiple pressures of urban population explosion, economic development and migration from the countryside are expanding cities at a terrifying rate. In 1990 there were 35 cities with populations over 5 million, 22 of them in the developing world. By the year 2000, it is estimated that there will be 57 cities over the 5-million mark, of which 44 will be in the developing world.

Over the next thirty years, a further 2 billion people are expected to be added to the cities of the developing world. This massive urbanisation will cause an exponential growth in the volume of resources consumed and of pollution created. Yet perversely, at least half of this growing urban population will be living in shanty towns with no running water, no electricity, no sanitation, and little hope. At least 600 million people already live in life-threatening urban environments. Our multiplying cities threaten overwhelming pollution, and a global society polarised into the haves and have-nots.

…

Cities themselves must be viewed as ecological systems and this attitude must inform our approach to designing cities and managing their use of resources. The resources devoured by a city may be measured in terms of its 'ecological footprint' – an area, scattered throughout the world and vastly greater than the physical boundary of the city itself, on which a city depends. These footprints supply the cities' resources and provide sites for the disposal of their waste and pollution. The ecological footprints of existing cities already virtually cover the entire globe. As the new consumerist cities expand so competition for these resource footprints grow. The expansion of urban ecological footprints is taking place simultaneously with the erosion of fertile lands, living seas and virgin rain forests. Given this simple supply constraint, urban ecological footprints must be dramatically reduced and circumscribed.

The urban ecologist Herbert Girardet has argued that the key lies in cities aiming at a circular 'metabolism', where consumption is reduced by implementing efficiencies and where re-use of resources is maximised. We must recycle materials, reduce waste, conserve exhaustible energies and tap into renewable ones. Since the large majority of production and consumption takes place in cities, current linear processes that create pollution from production must be replaced by those that aim at a circular system of use and re-use. These processes increase a city's overall efficiency and reduce its impact on the environment. To achieve this, we must plan our cities to manage their use of resources, and to do this we need to develop a new form of comprehensive holistic urban planning.

The city is a complex and changing matrix of human activities and environmental effects …

Environmental issues are not distinct from social ones. Policies aimed at improving the environment can also improve the social life of citizens. Ecological and social solutions reinforce each other and build healthier, livelier, more open-minded cities …

My own approach to urban sustainability reinterprets and reinvents the 'dense city' model …

…

… I believe we should be investing in the idea of a 'Compact City' – a dense and socially diverse city where economic and social activities overlap and where communities are focused around neighbourhoods.

This concept differs radically from today's dominant urban model, that of the United States: a city zoned by function with downtown office areas, out-of-town shopping and leisure centres, residential suburbs and highways. So powerful is this image and so prevalent are the forces that motivate its creation (set by the market-driven criteria of commercial developers) that the less developed countries are now locked into a trajectory that has already failed the developed countries.

…

The creation of the modern Compact City demands the rejection of single-function development and the dominance of the car. The question is how to design cities in which communities thrive and mobility is increased – how to design for personal mobility without allowing the car to undermine communal life, how to design for and accelerate the use of clean transport systems and re-balance the use of our streets in favour of the pedestrian and the community.

The Compact City addresses these issues. It grows around centres of social and commercial activity located at public transport nodes. These provide the focal points around which neighbourhoods develop. The Compact City is a network of these neighbourhoods, each with its own parks and public spaces and accommodating a diversity of overlapping private and public activities. London's historic structure of towns, villages, squares and parks is typical of a polycentric pattern of development. Most importantly, these neighbourhoods bring work and facilities within convenient reach of the community, and this proximity means less driving for everyday needs …

Sustainable Compact Cities could, I contend, reinstate the city as the ideal habitat for a community-based society.

Source: Rogers, 1997, pp. 3–8, 27–30, 32, 33, 38, 40

READING 4B
E.F. Schumacher: 'Small is beautiful'

What scale is appropriate? It depends on what we are trying to do. The question of scale is extremely crucial today, in political, social and economic affairs just as in almost everything else. What, for instance, is the appropriate size of a city? And also, one might ask, what is the appropriate size of a country? Now these are serious and difficult questions. It is not possible to programme a computer and get the answer. The really serious matters of life cannot be calculated. We cannot directly calculate what is right; but we jolly well know what is wrong! We can recognise right and wrong at the extremes, although we cannot normally judge them finely enough to say: 'This ought to be five per cent more; or that ought to be five per cent less'.

Take the question of size of a city. While one cannot judge these things with precision, I think it is fairly safe to say that the upper limit of what is desirable for the size of a city is probably something of the order of half a million inhabitants. It is quite clear that above such a size nothing is added to the virtue of the city. In places like London, or Tokyo, or New York, the millions do not add to the city's real value but merely create *enormous* problems and produce human degradation. So probably the order of magnitude of 500,000 inhabitants could be looked upon as the upper limit. The question of the lower limit of a real city is much more difficult to judge. The finest cities in history have been very small by twentieth-century standards. The instruments and institutions of city culture depend, no doubt, on a certain accumulation of wealth. But how much wealth has to be accumulated depends on the type of culture pursued. Philosophy, the arts and religion cost very, very little money. Other types of what claims to be 'high culture' – space research or ultra-modern physics – cost a lot of money, but are somewhat remote from the real needs of men [*sic*].

I raise the question of the proper size of cities both for its own sake but also because it is, to my mind, the most relevant point when we come to consider the size of nations.

The idolatry of giantism that I have talked about is possibly one of the causes and certainly one of the effects of modern technology, particularly in matters of transport and communications. A highly developed transport and communications system has one immensely powerful effect: it makes people *footloose*.

Millions of people start moving about, deserting the rural areas and the smaller towns to follow the city lights, to go to the big city, causing a pathological growth. Take the country in which all this is perhaps most exemplified – the United States. Sociologists are studying the problem of 'megalopolis'. The word 'metropolis' is no longer big enough; hence 'megalopolis'. They freely talk about the polarisation of the population of the United States into three immense megalopolitan areas: one extending from Boston to Washington, a continuous built-up area, with sixty million people; one around Chicago, another sixty million; and one on the West Coast, from San Francisco to San Diego, again a continuous built-up area with sixty million people; the rest of the country being left practically empty; deserted provincial towns, and the land cultivated with vast tractors, combine harvesters, and immense amounts of chemicals.

...

... The factor of footlooseness is, therefore, the more serious, the bigger the country. Its destructive effects can be traced both in the rich and in the poor countries. In the rich countries such as the United States of America, it produces, as already mentioned, 'megalopolis'. It also produces a rapidly increasing and ever more intractable problem of 'drop-outs', of people, who, having become footloose, cannot find a place anywhere in society. Directly connected with this, it produces an appalling problem of crime, alienation, stress, social breakdown, right down to the level of the family. In the poor countries, again most severely in the largest ones, it produces mass migration into cities, mass unemployment, and, as vitality is drained out of the rural areas, the threat of famine. The result is a 'dual society' without any inner cohesion, subject to a maximum of political instability.

As an illustration, let me take the case of Peru. The capital city, Lima, situated on the Pacific coast, had a population of 175,000 in the early 1920s, just fifty years ago. Its population is now approaching three million. The once beautiful Spanish city is now infested by slums, surrounded by misery-belts that are crawling up the Andes. But this is not all. People are arriving from the rural areas at the rate of a thousand a day – and nobody knows what to do with them. The social or psychological structure of life in the hinterland has collapsed; people have become footloose and arrive in the capital city at the rate of a thousand a day to squat on some empty land, against the police who come to beat them out, to build their mud hovels and look for a job. *And nobody knows what to do about them.* Nobody knows how to stop the drift.

Source: Schumacher, 1974, pp.60–62, 64

READING 4C
Diana Mitlin and David Satterthwaite: 'The advantages and potentials of cities'

... [C]ities have some obvious advantages or potential advantages for meeting sustainable development goals over rural settlements or dispersed populations ... It is worth considering these advantages in more detail, in relation to each of the main goals of sustainable development.

In terms of social and health needs, cities permit a much lower cost per person or per household than rural settlements or dispersed populations for most forms of infrastructure and services, including piped water, sewers and drains, garbage collection and most forms of health, educational and emergency services. The concentration of employment in cities reduces the cost of enforcing regulations on occupational health and safety while the concentration of industries and other businesses also cheapens the cost of enforcing environmental legislation, including pollution control.

In terms of minimizing the use or waste of non-renewable resources, cities provide a greater range and possibility for post-consumer material reclamation, recycling and re-use while their concentration of demand also cheapens the promotion of re-usable containers. Cities reduce the cost of many specialized services and waste-handling facilities by concentrating demand for them – including those that reduce waste levels or which recover materials from waste streams for re-use or recycling. The physical concentration of demand for space heating in residential, commercial and industrial enterprises in cities in temperate or sub-tropical zones (or in cities at high altitudes where space heating is necessary) often provides economies of scale in heating – for instance through the use of district heating or heat and power stations. Larger buildings (including terraces) also have considerable potential advantages over smaller freestanding houses for reducing the fuel needed for space heating. With regard to fossil fuel use in transport, cities provide a much greater potential for walking or the use of bicycles for a significant number of all trips made and a much greater potential demand for public transport.

In terms of sustainable use of renewable resources, cities have a much higher population concentration which reduces the demand for land relative to population. In most countries, the area taken up by cities and towns is less than one per cent of the total surface area of the nation. Although cities are often criticized for expanding over prime farmland, the problem is more the expansion of low density outer suburbs. If urban expansion took place at densities approaching those of high class inner-city residential areas – say in compact, nucleated settlements, the encroachment on farmland would be much less … There is also great potential within cities for recycling waste water to cut down on the draw on freshwater resources – and often to leave more for agricultural use.

With regard to keeping wastes generated by city producers and consumers within the absorptive capacity of local and global sinks, again cities have many potential advantages ranging from those mentioned above that help cut down on fossil fuel use (and thus on greenhouse gas emissions) to cheaper unit costs for many measures to promote re-use of containers or to collect chlorofluorocarbons from fridges and other forms of cooling equipment. The concentration of households and enterprises in cities also makes it easier for the public authorities to implement sustainable development policies – including the collection of taxes and charges for public services.

In prosperous cities there is a larger revenue base, a greater demand and a greater capacity to pay. This same concentration of people can make easier their full involvement in electing governments at local and city level and in taking an active part in decisions and actions within their own district or neighbourhood.

Source: Mitlin and Satterthwaite, 1994, pp.6–7

READING 4D
William E. Rees: 'Is "sustainable city' an oxymoron?'

Despite the two Habitat conferences (Vancouver in 1976 and Istanbul in 1996) cities – particularly northern high-income cities – have also been given short shrift in the mainstream sustainability debate. The World Conservation Strategy of 1980, which apparently first explicitly used the term 'sustainable development', gave no special attention to accelerating urbanisation. The Brundtland Report did discuss global urbanisation, but the main emphasis was on the 'urban crisis in developing countries' (WCED, 1987, p.8).

This relative neglect of cities is difficult to reconcile with physical reality … In short, half the people and three-quarters of the world's environmental problems reside in cities, and rich cities, mainly in the developed North, impose by far the greater load on the ecosphere and global commons.
…

The human ecology of cities

Just what is a city? …

… The city is … an ecological entity. This fact is generally ignored, perhaps because it is obscured by the very process of urbanisation itself. Living in the city distances people both spatially and psychologically from the land that supports them. Urbanisation thus reinforces the Cartesian dualism that permeates industrial society, creating a mental barrier between people and the rest of nature …

The important question is: what are the critical material relationships between people and the other components of their supportive ecosystems? …

Economic production is consumption

Economists and ecologists would agree that human beings function as consumer organisms in both the economy and the ecosphere. In fact, in today's increasingly market-based society people are as likely to be called 'consumers' as they are citizens … In addition to our biological metabolism, the human enterprise is characterised by an industrial metabolism. All the artefacts of industrial culture – buildings, equipment, infrastructure, tools and toys (the human-made 'capital' of economists) – are 'the exosomatic equivalent of organs' and, like bodily organs, require continuous flows of energy and material to and from 'the environment' for their production and operation (Sterrer, 1993).

Economists and ecologists also both see humans as producers. However, there is a fundamental difference between production in nature and production in the economy. In nature, green plants are the factories. Using the simplest of low-grade inorganic chemicals (mainly water, carbon dioxide and a few mineral nutrients) and an extra-terrestrial source of relatively low-grade energy, light from the sun, plants assemble the high-grade fats, carbohydrates, proteins and nucleic acids upon which most other life forms and the functioning of the ecosphere are dependent. Because they are essentially self-feeding and use only dispersed (high entropy) substances for their growth and maintenance, green plants are called *primary* producers.

By contrast, human beings and their economies are strictly *secondary* producers. As noted, the production and maintenance of our bodies, our human-made capital, and all the products of human factories require enormous inputs of high-grade energy and material resources from the rest of the ecosphere. That is, all economic output requires the consumption of a vastly larger quantity of available energy and material *first produced by nature*. As little as 1% or 2% of the material extracted for the economic production process actually winds up in the final product (Hawken, 1997), and 100% of the energy and material involved is ultimately dissipated back into the ecosphere as waste …

Cities and the Second Law

Because the economic process is a secondary process, the entire human enterprise in all its diversity and complexity is a dependent sub-system of the ecosphere. The structural hierarchy implicit in this relationship is critically important to urban sustainability …

The second law [of thermodynamics] states that … any isolated system becomes increasingly unstructured and disordered … However, *open* systems, like cities, can maintain themselves and grow by importing high-grade energy and material from their host environments and by exporting entropy (degraded energy and material) back into those environments.[1] Our cities can produce 'the wealth of nations' only by consuming the products and services of the ecosphere. This interpretation shows that in thermodynamic and spatial terms, cities are nodes of intense material consumption and waste discharge within a diffuse and increasingly global human ecosystem.

The ecological footprints of cities

If cities are the nodes of consumption in a spreading human net, just how much productive land/water

(ecosystem) area is required for the corresponding production? … We call this aggregate area the population's true 'ecological footprint (EF)': the total area of productive land and water required on a continuous basis to produce the resources consumed, and to assimilate the wastes produced, by that population, *wherever on Earth the land is located*. …

Our results show that the citizens of high-income countries typically use the output of between three and seven hectares of ecologically productive land per capita.[2] …

For example, the Canadian city of Vancouver … uses the productive output of a land area nearly 180 times larger than its political area to maintain its consumer lifestyle …

These results are fairly typical. The UK's International Institute of Environment and Development estimates that London's ecological footprint for just food, forest products and carbon assimilation to be 120 times the surface area of the city proper (IIED, 1995) … Similarly, Carl Folke and his team at Stockholm University report that the aggregate consumption of wood, paper, fibre and food (including seafood) by the inhabitants of 29 cities in the Baltic Sea drainage basin appropriates an ecosystem area 200 times larger than the cities themselves (this study did not include an energy component) (Folke *et al.*, 1995).

In light of these data it will come as no surprise that most high-income countries in Europe have ecological footprints several times larger than their domestic territories (Wackernagel and Rees, 1995). Even those countries with trade and current account surpluses are running massive 'ecological deficits' with the rest of the world and imposing a massive burden on the global commons (Rees, 1996).

Cities and sustainability

These studies reveal several dimensions of the sustainability crisis that are transparent to conventional perceptions and analyses … [T]hey show that as a result of enormous technology-induced increases in energy and material consumption per capita, and growing dependence on trade, *the ecological locations of urban regions no longer coincide with their geographic locations*. Without taking anything away from cities as economic engines and cultural hotbeds, we must recognise that they also resemble entropic black holes, sweeping up the output of areas of the ecosphere vastly larger than themselves. In this respect, cities are the human equivalent of cattle feedlots. Perhaps the most important insight from this result is that *no city or urban region can be sustainable on its own*.

'Sustainable city' – at least as we presently define cities – is an oxymoron. Regardless of local land use and environmental policies, a prerequisite for sustainable cities is the sustainability of the global hinterland.

...

Self-reliance, once a noble virtue, has become anathema to the free-trading world of today. However, in an era of real or incipient ecological change, it may be time to reconsider our development values. Cities are increasingly vulnerable to the potentially disastrous consequences of over-consumption and global ecological mismanagement. How economically and socially secure can a city of 10 million be if distant sources of food, water, energy or other critical resources are threatened by accelerating ecospheric change, increasing competition and dwindling supplies? ...

To reduce their dependence on external flows, urban regions may choose to implement policies to rehabilitate their own natural capital stocks and to promote the use of local fisheries, forests, agricultural land, etc. In this context, we should remember that cities as presently conceived are incomplete systems, typically occupying less than 1% of the ecosystem area upon which they draw. Should we not be reconsidering how we define city systems, both conceptually and in spatial terms? Perhaps it is time to think of cities as whole systems – as such, they comprise not just the node of concentrated activity as presently conceived, but also the entire supportive hinterland.

Short of so great a conceptual leap, there is much that can be done incrementally to increase the sustainability of our cities. For example, in the domain of land-use planning, planners and politicians should find ways to:

- integrate planning for city size/form, urban density and settlement (nodal) patterns in ways that minimise the energy, material and land use requirements of cities and their inhabitants;

- capitalise on the multifunctionality of green areas (e.g. aesthetic, carbon sink, climate modification, food production, functions) both within and outside the city;

- integrate open-space planning with other policies to increase local self-reliance in respect of food production, forest products, water supply, carbon sinks, etc. For example, domestic waste systems should be designed to enable the recycling of compost back onto regional agricultural and forest lands;

- protect the integrity and productivity of local ecosystems to reduce the ecological load imposed on distant systems and the global common pool;

- strive for zero-impact development. The destruction of ecosystems and related biophysical services due to urban growth in one area should be compensated for by equivalent ecosystem rehabilitation in another.

Land use aside, ecological footprint analysis supports other studies that suggest that we must reduce resource use and environmental impact per unit consumption in high-income countries by up to 90% by 2040 ... Fortunately, the sheer concentration of population and consumption gives cities considerable leverage in reducing the ecological footprints of their citizens ...

Epilogue

The human ecological approach offers one final lesson for consideration by the eco-cities movement. The ecological footprint of any high-income city is attributable largely to final demand, i.e. to personal consumption by its inhabitants. In short, much of the ecological impact that can be traced *to* cities has little to do with the structure, infrastructure, form, or other inherent properties *of* cities *per se*. Rather, it is a reflection of individual values and behaviour and would occur whatever the settlement pattern. For example, if an individual's fixed consumption appropriates the continuous output of 3 ha of land scattered about the globe it does not much matter where that individual resides. This means that efforts to green our cities may gain more from attention to changing personal consumption patterns than from the prevailing focus on city-level factors – post-consumer waste management, public infrastructure, urban greenways, etc. In short, we should focus less on trying to fix our cities and more on fixing ourselves. The best-designed and most sensitively administered city cannot be sustainable if its inhabitants live unsustainable lifestyles.

Notes

1 This means, in effect, that every sub-system in a given hierarchy exists in a potentially parasitic relationship with the next level up in that hierarchy. If a sub-system grows without check, it will reach a point at which its own vitality is purchased at the expense of of the vitality of its host. (This may be a sufficient explanation for the onset of global ecological change.)

2 These data reflect the growing ecological inequity between rich and poor. There are only about 1.5–1.7 ha of ecological productive land per capita on Earth.

References

Folke, C., Larsson, J. and Sweitzer, J. (1995) 'Renewable resource appropriation by cities', draft chapter prepared for *Getting Down to Earth* (Washington, Island Press [1996]).

Hawken, P. (1997) 'Natural capitalism', *Mother Jones*, April.

IIED (1995) *Citizen Action to Lighten Britain's Ecological Footprint,* report prepared by the International Institute for Environment and Development for the UK Department of the Environment, London, International Institute for Environment and Development.

Rees, W.E. (1996) 'Revisiting carrying capacity: area-based indicators of sustainability', *Population and Environment*, vol.17, no.3, pp.195–215.

Sterrer, W. (1993) 'Human economics: a non-human perspective', *Ecological Economics,* vol.7, pp.183–202.

Wackernagel, M. and Rees, W. E. (1995[6]) *Our Ecological Footprint: Reducing Human Impact on the Earth*, Gabriola Island, BC, New Society Publishers.

WCED (1987) *Our Common Future*, Report of the [UN] World Commission on Environment and Development, Oxford, Oxford University Press.

Source: Rees, 1997, pp.303–310

READING 4E
David Satterthwaite: 'Sustainable cities or cities that contribute to sustainable development?'

The discussion of sustainable development in regard to cities has … gained greater official recognition. For instance, the terms 'sustainable cities' and 'sustainable human settlements' were much in evidence at Habitat II, the second UN Conference on Human Settlements (also known as the City Summit) held in Istanbul in June 1996. Despite the disagreements between the different groups represented at the Conference … all government delegations appeared to support the idea of 'sustainable human settlements' or 'sustainable urban development'.

But this apparent unanimity is misleading because there was no clear, agreed definition as to what the terms 'sustainable cities' and 'sustainable human settlements' mean … For instance, one reason why the environmental quality of wealthy cities can improve is because the consumers and producers they concentrate can import all the goods whose production requires high levels of resource use and usually includes high levels of waste (including serious problems with hazardous wastes), pollution and environmental risk for their workforce (Satterthwaite, 1997).

Governments in the world's wealthiest nations can also support the notion of 'sustainable cities' without admitting that it is consumers and enterprises in their cities that need to make the largest reductions in resource use and waste generation …

This lack of progress among the nations in 'the North' discourages progress among nations in 'the South'. The fact that 'the South' includes three-quarters of the world's population and a large and growing share of its economic activity and high-level consumers also means a large and growing share in global resource use, waste generation and greenhouse gas emissions. But despite the diversity of nations within 'the South', they can collectively point not only to higher levels of resource use, waste and greenhouse gas emissions per person in the North, but also to much higher historical contributions to these problems …

The ambiguity as to what 'sustainable cities' or 'sustainable human settlements' means also allows many of the large international agencies to claim that they are the leaders in promoting sustainable cities when, in reality, they have contributed much to the growth of cities where sustainable development goals are not met. For instance, most international agencies give a low priority to meeting directly human needs – for example, in supporting provision of safe and sufficient supplies of water and provision for sanitation, primary education and health care. Most, also give a low priority (or allocate nothing) to improving garbage collection and disposal, energy conservation and public transport in cities, despite their importance for the achievement of sustainable development goals.[1]

...

A framework for considering the environmental performance of cities

The difficulties of comparing environmental performance between diverse urban centres

Perhaps the main difficulty facing any researcher or institution intent on comparing the environmental performance of different cities (including those in the North and in the South) is the range of problems that are 'environmental'. For instance, from the perspective of environmental health, cities in the North perform much better for their inhabitants than most cities in the South, as can be seen in the much smaller role of environmental hazards in illness, injury and premature death (WHO, 1996; UNCHS, 1996). But from the perspective of average levels of resource use or waste or greenhouse gas emissions per person, most cities in the South have much lower levels than cities in the North (Hardoy *et al.*, 1992; UNCHS, 1996).

There is also the difficulty of knowing how to judge the environmental performance of cities when the achievement of a high-quality environment in many cities is in part achieved by transferring environmental problems to other people or locations. For instance, sewage and drainage systems that take the sewage and waste water out of the city bring major environmental advantages to city-dwellers and city businesses. However, the disposal of untreated waste water in nearby water bodies usually brings serious environmental and economic costs to others – for instance, through damage to local fisheries or to water bodies that are then unfit for use by communities downstream. The transfer of environmental costs can also be over much greater distances or into the future.

This suggests the need to distinguish between different kinds of environmental problem when making comparisons between cities, so that like can be compared with like. But there is a danger that this reduces inter-city comparisons on environmental performance to those indicators that are easily measured. For instance, it is easier to get information on the concentration of certain air pollutants such as

sulphur dioxide in major cities in the South than the proportion of their population with adequate provision for piped water and sanitation or the contribution of motor vehicle accidents to injury and premature death. This means that discussions of sulphur dioxide concentrations probably get more prominence than they deserve within the discussions of environmental hazards in cities, while the inadequacies in provision for water and sanitation and in limiting traffic accidents get insufficient attention. In assessing the environmental performance of cities, there is a need both to distinguish between different environmental problems and to seek a more comprehensive coverage of all environmental problems including those for which there are often few data. There is also a need to ensure that improved environmental performance in one area is not at the expense of improved performance in another.

Within a commitment to sustainable development, there are five broad categories of environmental action within which the performance of all cities should be assessed. These are:

1 Controlling infectious and parasitic diseases and the health burden they take on urban populations, including reducing the urban population's vulnerability to them. This is often termed the 'brown agenda' or the sanitary agenda as it includes the need to ensure adequate provision for water, sanitation, drainage and garbage collection for all city-dwellers and businesses. It should include more than this – for instance, in controlling the infectious and parasitic diseases that are not associated with inadequate water and sanitation, including acute respiratory infections (the single largest cause of death worldwide) and tuberculosis (the single largest cause of adult death worldwide) and the many diseases that are transmitted by insect or animal vectors.

2 Reducing chemical and physical hazards within the home, the workplace and the wider city.

3 Achieving a high-quality urban environment for all urban inhabitants – for instance, in terms of the amount and quality of open space per person (parks, public squares/plazas, provision for sport, provision for children's play) and the protection of the natural and cultural heritage.

4 Minimising the transfer of environmental costs to the inhabitants and ecosystems surrounding the city.

5 Ensuring progress towards what is often termed 'sustainable consumption' – i.e. ensuring that the goods and services required to meet everyone's consumption needs are delivered without undermining the environmental capital of nations and the

world. This implies a use of resources, a consumption of goods imported into the city and a generation and disposal of wastes by city enterprises and city-dwellers that are compatible with the limits of natural capital and are not transferring environmental costs on to other people (including future generations).

The first three categories can be considered as the environmental aspects of meeting city-dwellers' needs. These fit within the conventional mandate of local authorities – although there is great variety in the ways in which local authorities promote their achievement. The fourth and fifth are more problematic since they are concerned with environmental impacts that generally occur outside the jurisdiction of the local authorities with responsibility for environmental management in cities.

Separating a consideration of the environmental performance of cities into these five categories allows a consideration of the common elements that all cities share within an understanding of how priorities must differ. For instance, perhaps the main environmental priority in most cities in the North is to reduce levels of resource use, wastes and greenhouse gas emissions while also maintaining or improving the quality of the urban environment. But this does not mean neglecting the other aspects – for instance, in most cities, much remains to be done to reduce physical hazards (such as those caused by motor vehicles) and chemical pollutants – and, as outlined below, there are also new threats to be confronted in the control of infectious diseases. In addition, in most cities in the North, there [is] still a proportion of the population that live or work with unacceptable levels of environmental risk. By contrast, the environmental priorities in most small cities in the lower-income countries of the South will centre on the first two categories – although building into their urban plans a concern for a high-quality urban environment, efficient resource use, good management of liquid and solid wastes and a minimising of greenhouse gas emissions will bring many long-term advantages. Considering cities' environmental performance across the five categories also helps to clarify how environmental problems change for cities that become increasingly large and/or wealthy (see Bartone *et al.,* 1994; Satterthwaite, 1997).

…

This distinction between these five categories is also useful in considering the political economy of environmental problems since there are differences between the categories in terms of who is responsible for the problems; who is most affected by them; the possibilities for those who are affected to get the problems addressed; how the problems are addressed;

and by whom …

One important institutional difficulty arises if environmental problems or costs are being transferred from one area to another and the local authority structure is made up of different, largely autonomous local authorities with no mechanisms to manage inter-municipality disputes and resource transfers. The transfer of environmental costs from richer to poorer areas within nations or regions is what underlies what is often termed 'environmental racism' as polluting industries or wastes are systematically located in lower-income areas …

…

One of the more contentious issues in discussions of 'sustainable development' is what the 'sustainable' refers to. A review of the literature on sustainable development found that much of it was almost exclusively concerned with ecological sustainability, with little or no mention of 'development' in the sense of the meeting of human needs (Mitlin, 1992) … Perhaps what makes the Brundtland Commission's statement so important is its insistence that meeting human needs must be combined with ecological sustainability – to meet 'the needs of the present without compromising the ability of future generations to meet their own needs' (World Commission on Environment and Development, 1987, p.8).

In previous work with Jorge Hardoy and Diana Mitlin, we suggested that the 'sustainable' part of sustainable development be considered as avoiding the depletion of environmental capital (or concentrating on ecological sustainability) while the 'development' part of sustainable development be considered the meeting of human needs (see, for instance, Hardoy, *et al.,* 1992; Mitlin and Satterthwaite, 1996). This led to an elaboration of the social, economic and political goals, based on the Brundtland Commission's statement given above – within a commitment to limit or stop the depletion of the four kinds of environmental capital (see Box 1). The upper part of this table summarises the social, economic and political goals inherent in meeting human needs; these will not be elaborated here, since the purpose of this paper is to concentrate on the environmental aspects of sustainable development.[2]

…

Phrases such as 'sustainable cities', 'sustainable human settlements' and 'sustainable urbanisation' are also unclear for similar reasons.[3] It is not cities or urbanisation that sustainable development seeks to sustain, but to meet human needs in settlements of all sizes without depleting environmental capital. This means seeking the institutional and regulatory framework in which democratic and accountable urban and municipal authorities ensure that the needs

BOX 1 The multiple goals of sustainable development as applied to cities

Meeting the needs of the present ...

Economic needs – includes access to an adequate livelihood or productive assets; also economic security when unemployed, ill, disabled or otherwise unable to secure a livelihood.

Social, cultural and health needs – includes a shelter which is healthy, safe, affordable and secure, within a neighbourhood with provision for piped water, sanitation, drainage, transport, health care, education and child development. Also, a home, workplace and living environment protected from environmental hazards, including chemical pollution. Also important are needs related to people's choice and control – including homes and neighbourhoods which they value and where their social and cultural priorities are met. Shelters and services must meet the specific needs of children and of adults responsible for most child-rearing (usually women). Achieving this implies a more equitable distribution of income between nations and, in most cases, within nations.

Political needs – includes freedom to participate in national and local politics and in decisions regarding management and development of one's home and neighbourhood – within a broader framework which ensures respect for civil and political rights and the implementation of environmental legislation.

... without compromising the ability of future generations to meet their own needs

Minimising use or waste of non-renewable resources – includes minimising the consumption of fossil fuels in housing, commerce, industry and transport plus substituting renewable sources where feasible. Also, minimising waste of scarce mineral resources (reduce use, re-use, recycle, reclaim). There are also cultural, historical and natural assets within cities that are irreplaceable and thus non-renewable – for instance, historical districts and parks and natural landscapes which provide space for play, recreation and access to nature.

Sustainable use of finite renewable resources – cities drawing on fresh-water resources at levels which can be sustained (with recycling and re-use promoted). Keeping to a sustainable ecological footprint in terms of land area on which city-based producers and consumers draw for agricultural and forest products and biomass fuels.

Biodegradable wastes not overtaxing capacities of renewable sinks (e.g. capacity of a river to break down biodegradable wastes without ecological degradation).

Non-biodegradable wastes/emissions not overtaxing (finite) capacity of local and global sinks to absorb or dilute them without adverse effects (e.g persistent pesticides, greenhouse gases and stratospheric ozone-depleting chemicals).

Source: Developed from Mitlin and Satterthwaite (1994)

of the people within their boundaries are addressed while minimising the transferring of environmental costs to other people or ecosystems or into the future. This in turn requires consideration of the kinds of national policies and legal and institutional frameworks and the kinds of international agreements that encourage urban and municipal authorities in this direction.

...

The biggest gap in the Istanbul discussions was the lack of progress in operationalizing the notion of environmentally sustainable development ... While the term 'sustainable development' was mentioned repeatedly, little progress was made in suggesting how it could be operationally applied to urban areas. (Cohen, 1996, p.4)

...

There is also considerable confusion within the Habitat II documents as to what sustainable development is meant to sustain – whether it is settlements or settlement policies or particular activities within settlements. This was not a confusion that arose from the search for consensus at the Conference itself, for it was present in earlier drafts of what became the Habitat Agenda. Within the text, sometimes, it is human settlements that are to be sustainable – for instance, 'sustainable human settlements' or 'sustainable urban centres' or 'sustainable communities' – or aggregates of human settlements, as in sustainable spatial development patterns. In other instances, it is society in general or living conditions that are to be 'sustainable'. In others, it is particular activities within urban areas that are to be sustainable – as in sustainable shelter markets and land development or sustainable transport, sustainable agriculture, sustainable livelihoods, sustainable resource use, sustainable water supply or sustainable energy use. 'Sustained economic growth and equity' are also mentioned as part of sustainable development; clearly, 'sustained economic growth' is not part of sustainable development, although one suspects that what the delegates meant was that the promotion of sustainable development should not inhibit lower-income countries achieving higher incomes and greater economic prosperity and stability.

The worry of government delegates from the South that environmental measures might be the means by which the North inhibits their economic development is still strong in these global meetings – after surfacing as long ago as the 1972 UN Conference on the Human Environment in Stockholm which initiated the cycle of global UN conferences on environment and development issues. The closest the Habitat II documents come to addressing the loss of environmental capital arising from high-consumption lifestyles is several references to 'unsustainable consumption and production patterns, particularly in industrialized countries' (Istanbul Declaration, para. 4), but these are not addressed in the recommendations. And despite the length of the Habitat II documents, there is no mention of the dangers posed to settlements by global warming or of the need to curb greenhouse gas emissions. Perhaps the delegates felt that this was unnecessary, since the Habitat II documentation endorsed the recommendations of previous conferences, and that this was an issue covered by Agenda 21, coming out of the Earth Summit (the UN Conference on Environment and Development in 1992).

The Habitat II documents also have many examples of where it is not human settlements or activities in human settlements, but the development of human settlements that should be sustainable – or particular human settlements policies as in sustainable land-use policies or more sustainable population policies. Sometimes it is broader than this as in sustainable economic development and social development activities. In regard to what constitutes sustainable development, the documents often refer to this being a combination of economic development, social development and environmental protection.[4] These are mentioned as 'interdependent and mutually reinforcing components of sustainable development'.[5] This highlights another flaw in the documents – the assumption that a concern for environmental quality within cities is all that is needed to achieve the environmental component of sustainable development goals. What this misses is the many means by which enterprises and those with high-consumption lifestyles

transfer some of their environmental costs to other people, other regions or into the future, as outlined in earlier sections.

…

Given the tendency for many environmentalists to view cities only as places which generate environmental costs, a greater attention to cities' environmental problems might also ignore the benefits that city-based enterprises and consumers provide (or can provide) for people, natural resources and ecosystems outside their boundaries. Of course, these include the goods purchased by city businesses, governments and consumers which provide incomes from those living outside the city and the goods and services provided by city-enterprises to those living outside the city. Also, care must be taken in ascribing blame to 'cities' for environmental costs transferred from within cities to other ecosystems or people, in that it is particular groups in cities (mostly the higher-income groups) and particular enterprises who are responsible for most such costs.

In addition, the inherent advantages that cities have or can have for combining high-quality living conditions with low levels of resource use, waste and greenhouse gas emissions per person should not be forgotten (Mitlin and Satterthwaite, 1996; UNCHS, 1996). Nor must we forget the fact that wealthy rural or suburban households generally have higher levels of resource use and waste generation than their counterparts living in cities – they own more automobiles, use them more often and have higher levels of energy use within their homes.

Notes

1   IIED monitors the priority given by international agencies to addressing basic needs and to urban development. A summary of the findings of its work in this regard was published in UNCHS (1996).

2   The social, economic and political aspects are described in more detail in Mitlin and Satterthwaite (1996).

3   The justifcation for avoiding this is discussed in more detail in Mitlin and Satterthwaite (1996).

4   See paragraph 3 of the Istanbul Declaration; also paragraph 4 and paragraph 43(b) of the Habitat Agenda. Paragraph 29 talks of sustainable human settlements development ensuring 'economic development', employment opportunities and social progress, in harmony with the environment'.

5   Paragraph 3 of the Istanbul Declaration; this is also repeated in paragraph 1 of the Habitat Agenda, then again in paragraph 8 and paragraph 43(b);

paragraph 21 talks of 'economic development, social development and environmental protection' being 'indispensable and mutually reinforcing components of sustainable development'.

References

Bartone, C., Bernstein, J., Leitmann, J. and Etgen, J. (1994) *Towards Environmental Strategies for Cities: Policy Considerations for Urban Environmental Management in Developing Countries*. UNDP/ UNCHS/World Bank Urban Management Program No.18, Washington, DC, World Bank.

Cohen, M. (1996) *Reflections on Habitat II*, Working Group on Habitat II of the Woodrow Wilson Center, Washington, DC.

Hardoy, J. E., Mitlin, D. and Satterthwaite, D. (1992) *Environmental Problems in Third World Cities*, London, Earthscan.

Mitlin, D. (1992) 'Sustainable development: a guide to the literature', *Environment and Urbanization*, vol.4, no.1, pp.111–24.

Mitlin, D and Satterthwaite, D. (1994) *Cities and Sustainable Development*, Background paper for Global Forum '94, Manchester, Manchester City Council.

Mitlin, D. and Satterthwaite, D. (1996) 'Sustainable development and cities' in Pugh, C. (ed.) *Sustainability, the Environment and Urbanization,* pp.23–61, London, Earthscan Publications.

Satterthwaite, D. (1997) 'Environmental transformations in cities as they get larger, wealthier and better managed', *The Geographical Journal*, vol.163, no.2, pp.216–224, July.

UNCHS (1996) *An Urbanizing World: Global Report on Human Settlements 1996*, Oxford, Oxford University Press.

WHO (1996) *Creating Healthy Cities in the 21st Century,* Background paper prepared for the Dialogue on Health in Human Settlements for Habitat II, Geneva, World Health Organization.

World Commission on Environment and Development (1987) *Our Common Future*, Oxford, Oxford University Press.

Source: Satterthwaite, 1997, pp.1667–71, 1678–88

READING 4F
Thomas Angotti: 'The Latin American metropolis and the growth of inequality'

At the edge of Mexico City, east of the airport, lies Nezahualcóyotl, a sprawling shantytown of two million people located on the bed of what was once Lake Texcoco. It is one of the many self-built neighborhoods that house the majority of the metropolitan area's 20 million people – neighborhoods where it is hard to find decent housing, good jobs, clean water, or parks

...

Mexico City's problems crystallize the urban question in Latin America, not so much because of its size, but because of its economic and social inequalities, and its declining quality of life. The Latin American metropolis is characterized by mass poverty and severe environmental pollution on a scale generally unparalleled in the North.

...

Latin America is now the most urbanized of 'Third World' regions, a fact that bears some relation to the region's economic dependency on North America, itself the most urbanized region in the world ...

...

Poverty and informality may not have been created by transnational corporations, but they serve their interests well. The majority of the population in Latin American cities survives at a level of subsistence far below North American standards. This allows for the suppression of wage levels in the North as well as the South. Latin American workers make up a ready labor reserve for transnationals ... Through the austerity policies of the International Monetary Fund (IMF) and World Bank, Northern capital discourages national governments from making expenditures that would substantially improve the urban quality of life in Latin America, thereby sustaining the low level of subsistence that corresponds with low wages. Indeed, urban consumption levels declined in the last decade as a result of austerity measures undertaken to meet debt obligations. This led to the 'IMF riots' in Buenos Aires, Lima, Santo Domingo, Caracas and elsewhere.

Thus, the Latin American metropolis is an integral part of the global urban network dominated by the North. The *barriadas, favelas* and *ranchos* are ready reserves for international capital to utilize in its global assembly line ...

Despite the widespread perception that the large cities of Latin America are unplanned and unmanageable, there has been considerable planning by government agencies as well as by the private sector.

This planning, however, has mostly benefited the wealthy and powerful. The first urban planning regulations in Latin America, promulgated by the Spanish Crown in the sixteenth century 'Laws of the Indies', established rules for the organization of urban space around the central plaza, which became the seat of political and economic power. Located on the perimeter of the plaza were the representatives of the Crown, the Church, and civil authorities. Urbanization by other colonists near the plaza was regulated, but areas occupied by the indigenous masses were unaffected by planning.

In the twentieth century, the modernist downtown models of Europe and North America replaced the Laws of the Indies. The colonial neglect of the indigenous neighborhoods was supplanted by North America's *laissez-faire* approach to real-estate development. The downtown skylines of the major metropolitan areas in Latin America offer stark images of the influence of the Manhattan model, where central real-estate values combine with official urban-renewal plans to produce monumental business districts …

The planning of Latin American cities has thus reinforced many of the social problems of unequal development. The Latin American metropolis was planned in the image of the North, but without the resources and unique conditions of the North, which has flourished by importing capital and labor to build a diversified consumer economy. Unlike its Northern counterpart, the Latin American metropolis has grown unevenly by exporting its labor and resources. The North American metropolitan area is typically auto-oriented, sprawled over a large territory, and has sharp economic and social divisions between central city and suburbs. The real-estate market is loosely regulated, reinforcing the tendencies toward concentration in the central business district, displacement of low-rent activities, and expansion at the periphery. This model has greatly influenced Latin American planners.

Many Latin American cities have strict master plans, and rent, subdivision and zoning regulations that theoretically govern urban development. However, without the resources and institutions to implement these regulations, they are ignored or easily violated. Thus, an urban system designed to work with Northern wealth falls apart in Southern poverty … As in the colonial era, the masses remain outside the orbit of planning.

…

Mexico, like Venezuela and Brazil and a number of other Latin American countries, is locked into a regime of accumulation that forces it to rely on environmen-tally damaging petroleum energy. A large part of its national surplus and export earnings comes from petroleum, so any restrictions on this sector are looked upon with disdain. Mexico emulates the model of sprawled, auto-based metropolitan growth of the United States, but lacks the resources to control its disastrous ecological consequences. Latin American economies crippled with foreign debt can barely afford the institutional infrastructure – urban planning and a coherent set of regulatory mechanisms – to enforce environmental standards, much less maintain physical infrastructure like highways and bridges.

The neoliberal craze for deregulation could further worsen air quality. In Santiago, air pollution got worse during the years of the Pinochet dictatorship, in large measure because deregulation of the bus system encouraged the importation of used buses. A huge squad of some 11,000 diesel buses now spews black fumes into the air.

Contamination of water and soil are also critical environmental problems. In São Paulo, as in most other large cities, most sewage is discharged without treatment into rivers and streams, only a small fraction of solid waste is treated, and air quality is extremely poor. The city is becoming even less sustainable as real-estate development favors new construction over preservation, and wasteful low-density sprawl over more compact forms of growth.

Urban strategies that have been favored throughout the region often target cities themselves as the problem, and seek to stop urban growth instead of improving the urban – and rural – quality of life. There has been much talk, for example, about 'spatial deconcentration' – the dispersal of the urban population from megacities to small cities and towns …

…

The only way to achieve a balanced urban system and urban equality is to have a balanced economic system, one that is not dependent on a bloated export sector. In a balanced economy, a significant proportion of the national surplus can be used to improve the quality of urban life, and to provide a national social safety net so that large numbers of people are no longer forced out of rural areas. These resources can support the growing network of grassroots community organizations, and responsive local governments. They can foster sustainable forms of urban development and transportation based on indigenous traditions and appropriate technology. These resources can also supplement the enormous reservoir of self-help with socially responsible urban strategies. In the last analysis, the city is anchored in the regional economy. There is no way around the fact that livable cities require sustainable economic development.

Source: Angotti, 1995, pp.13, 14, 16–18

READING 4G
Luc J.A. Mougeot: 'Farming inside and around cities'

Throughout most of our history, across contrasting cultures and climates, we have been producing some of our food within or on the edge of our cities. Urban agriculture (UA) – the growing or raising, processing and distributing of food and other products through the intensive plant cultivation and animal husbandry in (intra-urban) and around (peri-urban) cities – is as old as cities ourselves [sic].

...

The divorce of agriculture, of food production, from our urban economies is really a very recent development in urban history ...

Surveys and projects in cities with half a million or more people show UA to be practised on a much smaller scale and to be more dispersed than most rural agriculture. The advantage that UA enjoys is that it taps into economies of agglomeration that are unparalleled in most rural areas. On the other hand, it suffers from greater economic and ecological pressure than is the case with most rural agriculture, and requires more intensive and better controlled production to stay competitive and safe.

In recent years, UA has regained the attention of city planners and managers. Since the late 1950s, the Chinese have incorporated food production into their city planning. Asian city-states such as Hong Kong and Singapore have evolved highly organized production-consumption systems; UA is expanding in other Asian metropolises. In newly independent African countries, governments have advocated greater food self-reliance for city populations. Since the late 1970s, urban community gardening and urban waste use into peri-urban farming are resurging in North American and European cities.

Today, it is estimated that roughly 800 million people are engaged in UA worldwide. Proponents of UA believe it can be incorporated into comprehensive strategies for food security, reducing poverty, increasing employment, and managing land and waste products.

Many causes

The growth of UA in LDCs results from factors that affect both market supply of and demand for food in cities. The need to obtain hard currency through exports often dictates a country's crop choices, agricultural credit programs and incentives, research, and distribution networks. Controlled food pricing has favored urban wage-earners and discouraged rural

production. Subsidies are less frequent today but their removal often exacerbates price fluctuations. High transaction costs may discourage producers from supplying formal or critical markets, and institutional frameworks may not be in place for markets to operate effectively. Products formerly common to local diets are now being diverted to more attractive export markets for longer periods of the year ...

...

... [M]ost urban farmers are low-income men and women who grow food largely for self-consumption, on small plots they do not own, with little if any support or protection. They tend to come from smaller towns, and a majority are not recent arrivals. In a 1994 survey of three different sectors of Nairobi, over 60 per cent of 177 interviewees had moved to the city before 1985. Although women predominate in most surveys, gender ratios vary greatly from city to city, depending on cultural context, production system and economic climate. Men are the majority of market vegetable growers in Addis Ababa (1991), Santiago (1997), Accra (1997).

All sizes

Urban agriculture uses areas of all sizes, from spaces as small as windowsills and rooftops to recreational grounds, rights-of-way or suburban estates. Plots may extend to thousands of square meters along transportation corridors, particularly in suburban wedge areas. Urban farmers may use different spaces in a complementary way. Year-round home gardens often serve as nurseries for rain-fed, off-plot fields (Lusaka), while a field may carry vegetables in the dry season and grain crops in the rainy season (Brazzaville). Working several fields at different locations ensures stability in the face of theft or eviction from any given plot (Nairobi).

Urban agriculture often spreads despite the intentions of public planners and technocrats. Colonial bylaws and international standards are often unenforceable or inappropriate to local conditions. The interpretation and application of laws and norms have had to compromise with survival options available to the growing urban poor. Information campaigns have been promoted among urban producers, and undeveloped public arable land has been assigned to organized groups for fixed periods of time. Urban agriculture has been tolerated as an interim or permanent land use in public housing schemes (Zimbabwe), and bylaws have been revised to authorize specific production systems in residential areas (Uganda). New capital cities, as in Ivory Coast and Tanzania, have been designed to include UA. Countries have institutionalized programs and agencies to exploit flexible zoning, offer purpose-specific leaseholds (Argentina), promote UA for national school catering programs (Costa Rica), endorse organized groups of urban farmers for credit and technical assistance (Nigeria). Public utilities have leased out land, have partnered up with producers, or have become producers themselves.

International support

Bilateral and multilateral development agencies are promoting UA more actively since the late 1980s. Bilaterals include American, British, Canadian, Danish, Dutch, German, Swedish and Swiss agencies. The World Bank recently funded projects recommending inclusion of UA as legitimate land usage in new city master plans, and commissioned an assessment for comprehensive Bank support to UA in sub-Saharan Africa. Many agencies and international NGOs participated in the formation of a Support Group on Urban Agriculture (SGUA) in 1996 to coordinate future support delivery in a variety of programs.

Little literature so far has overtly risen against UA; the debate likely will heat up as UA grows and affects interests tangibly. Local opposition to UA is usually stronger at the outset, then shifts to tolerance, selective support, and issue management. Using public open spaces for UA is usually more an issue than when private residential space only is involved. Animal husbandry on public or private land is more opposed than is plant cultivation, and growing food plants raises more worries than growing other types of plants, such as ornamentals. The arguments against UA tend to fall into three categories:

- **Urban planning** – Agriculture should be confined to rural areas: it can interfere with more productive uses.

- **Public health** – Nuisances, safety hazards, pollution, contamination, and the harboring and spread of diseases arise from unregulated production, carried out at the wrong places or in the wrong way. This is particularly true of animal husbandry, but also applies to risks posed by UA foodstuffs grown with polluted inputs or handled inappropriately.

- **Environmental conservation** – Visual untidiness, soil erosion, destruction of vegetation, siltation, depletion, and agrochemical pollution of water all form the basis for opposition by nearby residents and businesses.

People engaged in some form of UA for some part of the year vary between 15 and 70 per cent of households in cities surveyed in Africa, Russia, and eastern Europe. Urban agriculture is the largest land user (23 per cent of city region: 34,000 hectares turning out ca.100,000 tons of food annually in 1988) and the second largest employer (20 per cent of those employed) in Dar-es-Salaam. Agriculture provided the highest self-employment earnings in small-scale enterprises in Nairobi, and the third highest earnings in all of urban Kenya. Cultivated open spaces within the city limits of Harare have doubled between 1990 and 1994 to more than 8,000 hectares. The city of Dakar saw its market vegetable paddies grow from 1000 to 2506 hectares between 1980 and 1990, supplying 18 percent of the country's vegetables.

Production reached $4 million

Donald Freeman estimated that in Nairobi open-space farmers' 1987 annual production alone reached $4 million. In Dar, some ten thousand UA enterprises averaged a net profit 1.6 times equal to the minimum salary in 1991. Cost-benefit analyses of market vegetable crops in Lome and Bissau have shown that net incomes largely depend on low-input practices, and that profit margins are higher where there are fewer middlemen. The International Livestock Research Institute found that dairy production is affordable in Kenya even by resource or technology poor farmers.

Source: Mougeot, 1998, pp.18–20

READING 4H
Kristin Helmore: 'Cities on the brink try new tactics'

For half her life, ten-year-old Bilkish has lived in a hut of black plastic on a sidewalk in central Bombay. It's a small space, about three by four metres, and too low for an adult to stand in. Nine people live there: Bilkish and her five brothers and sisters, her parents and her father's brother. The hut's only opening is the "door," a dirty quilt draped over a rope. There is no other ventilation or source of light, and even in the breezy Bombay winters black plastic makes a hot, dark and airless home.

Every morning at five o'clock, Bilkish and her sisters line up at a communal water-tap several blocks away. After waiting more than an hour, they stagger home with sloshing pails of water on their heads: a day's supply for bathing, washing, cooking, drinking and making tea. There is also a public toilet several blocks away, but using it costs more money than the family can afford …

This family's situation is multiplied by hundreds of millions in cities throughout the developing world, from Rio de Janeiro to Nairobi to Manila …

… for many observers it is not the growth of cities that is disturbing, it is the glaring disparities between the lives of the poor and those who are better off. "These are two different worlds," says Akhtar Badshah, director of programmes at Mega-Cities, a New York-based organization that promotes replicable solutions to urban problems. "The conditions of the poor are getting worse and worse, because governments are simply unable to keep pace with the level of services that is needed. As a result, the ill effects of city life are concentrated among the poor." He cites as an example the appalling environmental conditions in many cities that cause harm to the poor. They lack the luxury of air-conditioners or even the option of closing windows against the miasma of leaded-fuel emissions, smoke and dust that passes for air in many cities. Nor can the poor stay healthy by buying bottled water or maintaining hygienic conditions in their homes.

"The gap is widening dramatically," says Badshah. "For example, the poor are often pushed farther and farther onto the fringes of cities where there is industrial pollution. Yet transport is not keeping pace with the needs, so the poor often take longer and longer to get to work, if they can get there at all, or if they can find work in the first place." Indeed, services in cities today are a problem for all levels of society. But the list of basic services to which the poor have little or no access in the over-stretched cities of the developing world is virtually endless. They suffer disproportionately from lack of basics, such as health care, schools, job opportunities, food, transport, training, adequate housing, security, information and access to the justice system and the rule of law.

Equity, participation, decentralization

These inequities represent not only a moral crisis of staggering portions, but the potential for political chaos and large economic losses. "If cities don't function properly, the productivity of an entire country is negatively affected," says Shabbir Cheema, director of the management, development and governance division at the United Nations Development Programme (UNDP), pointing out that cities are the major engines of economic growth in developing countries. "And if the poor are deprived of services, this can have a negative effect on political stability."

The dangers are so acute, in fact, that they are forcing new thinking about the problems of cities, and new approaches to development in general. More and more development professionals agree that lack of equity is the core problem of urban poverty, and that traditional, hierarchical systems of city management cannot meet the needs of cities today and in the future.

Development planners insist that political decentralization is essential to ensure that those in power are accountable to citizens at every level of society and responsive to their needs. "How do we create cities that work for everybody – asks Robertson Work, a senior programme officer at UNDP. "It is possible. But it's got to be neighbourhood by neighbourhood, community by community. You can't stand at the top and order change."

Indeed, the very crisis of overcrowding, poverty and environmental decay that is driving cities to the brink of disaster also provides the incentive for those in power to get their house in order, to try new solutions to complex problems and to begin to share responsibility – and decision-making power– with city dwellers themselves.

One of the most innovative aspects of this new approach is the concept that all sectors – even traditional "enemies" such as slum-dwellers and real estate speculators – can, and must, learn to identify common goals and work together to achieve them. Many development strategies today, including those supported by UNDP, take as their starting point the building of partnerships among diverse groups – officials from national and municipal governments, the business community and community-based organizations – to help define problems and bring about solutions …

Initiatives for change are as diverse as the cities that are spawning them, yet they all point to a global trend toward equity, participation and democracy. Increasingly it is recognized that the role of ousiders, including international organizations, is not to impose solutions. Rather it is to promote dialogue and cooperation and to bring to the attention of local actors a menu of examples of success from which they can shape their own, home-grown strategies for renewal. One positive change, says Mega Cities' Akhtar Badshah, is that development thinkers are beginning to turn away from the old paradigm of studying problems, to studying solutions instead. "Traditional research tries to figure out what is not working and what the problems are," he says. "Instead, we need to look at what is working – to value strengths, to envision what might be."

Source: Helmore, 1996

READING 4I
Jeremy Seabrook: 'The unsustainable city: Bombay'

Bombay appears to be a city constantly on the edge of collapse. The complaints of the middle class evoke a place barely capable, it seems, of supporting life. It is no longer possible to travel by train, because of the overcrowding. You can't travel by taxi either, because the traffic is at a standstill for most of the day …

Yet the city doesn't collapse. Materially, it is sustained by the pressure it places for resources on an ever-extending hinterland. Bombay creates a widening ring of desolation around itself – including the polluted Arabian Sea. Its survival is at the cost of extractable surpluses from the countryside, which leads to an intensifying chemicalized agriculture there. At the same time, its industrial estates eat more and more deeply into the desertified landscapes along the dusty road to Ahmedabad, with its choking fumes, treeless dust and poisoned waters.

The slums of Bombay are seen by the rich as polluting the city. Yet slum dwellers are negligible polluters compared to those who live in the high-rise flats. The millions of bricks required for the construction of apartments are made from the topsoil of thousands of hectares of fertile fields within a radius of 70 or 80 kilometres of Bombay. With wood no longer available for the production of charcoal for the brick kilns, paddy-husks and vegetable matter are used for fuel, instead of being recycled in the fields, and this leads to a further erosion of fertility. The quarrying of limestone for cement has destroyed the watersheds for which the porous limestone rocks serve as storage reservoirs. With wood supplies around Bombay depleted, big builders were, until recently, obtaining much of their requirement from the Himalayan foothills. Now, that area also being denuded, they find it cheaper to import from other South Asian countries. One developer imports 10,000 tons of timber from Malaysia each year. The sand needed for the preparation of concrete has led to the dredging of several thousand cubic metres each day at Kasheli, which in turn has resulted in the erosion and loss of adjoining agricultural land.

Most of Bombay's water comes from artificial lakes constructed more than 100 kilometres from the city. Huge dams have been built for this purpose, which have displaced many *Adivasis* (tribal people). While the urban population – especially in the rich suburbs – receives an assured water supply for baths, fountains, lawns and private swimming pools, rural districts suffer severe water shortages. The sewage produced

187

by those privileged enough to be connected to Bombay's municipal system is discharged into the sea, along with industrial pollutants and wastes. These have damaged and decreased the catch of the beleaguered fishing communities which still cling defiantly to the foreshore in parts of the city. Excessive nitrogen and phosphates in the sewage lead to a profusion of algae, but when these die, they kill much of the marine, mangrove and tidal life. Indeed, compared to those linked to the sewage system, the poor who defecate on open land are less polluting, for there, the wastes are quickly converted by insects into food for themselves and fertilizer for the soil. Vegetable patches brighten with vivid green all the available spaces in the city, especially between the railways slums and the tracks.

Every year, the monsoon causes floods in Bombay, sweeping away the homes and belongings of thousands of poor people. While Rs200 crores (over £50 million), with World Bank aid, are being spent on anti-flood measures in Bombay, this will help little, since the cause of the floods is not addressed: the covering of land by buildings, roads and concrete is so total that it prevents rainwater from seeping into the soil. It simply runs off into low-lying areas, where the poor live.

Agricultural products from the rural areas taken to Bombay represent an export of soil fertility, since the 'wastes' do not return to the village. Grass and oilcakes from the countryside feed the cows and buffaloes of Jogeshwari, which provide milk for the urban consumer, while the dung they produce pollutes rather than fertilizes. It is claimed that the industrial products of the city more than compensate for this draining and mining of the countryside. The theory is that what comes into the city is transformed into something of enhanced value. While this may be true in monetary terms, in reality the true costs are borne by the impoverished of the city, the environment and especially by the poor of the rural hinterland.

In this sense, Bombay – or any other major world city – is a symbol of the 'development' process. The creation of wealth involves passing on the real, as opposed to the merely monetary, costs elsewhere. How the earth and the people which have to absorb and deal with these costs respond, struggle, live and die, does not trouble those whose business it is to manage this increasingly devastating and destructive model.

Source: Seabrook, 1993, pp.89–90

POSTSCRIPT
A final word on cities

by the Book 4 editors and theme authors

1 *Parting thoughts*

The city, half-imagined (yet wholly real), begins and ends in us, lodged in our memory.

(Laurence Durrell)

Now you have reached the end of *Understanding Cities,* we would like to leave you with some parting thoughts. First, we take a brief look back at what you have accomplished in studying the course and writing the course essay, then we take a look out from the course and onwards …

We hope you'll agree that studying the course has offered a way of understanding cities that is new and stimulating. Throughout the course, you have been challenged to think differently about cities and to imagine cities in new ways. The TV series also gave you a glimpse of the diversity and colour of cities around the world. Probably, like us, you are left with a feeling of the mix of excitement and danger that cities offer. In studying the course, at times we hope that you could almost feel the rhythms of the cityscapes visited along the way. Hopefully you can now appreciate why we find cities and city life so exciting to study.

Ultimately, the course essay has given you the opportunity to take a step back from the course, to re-visit the central course questions and arguments, and to reflect on some of the big issues facing cities in relation to one of three themes. The course essay will have given you an opportunity to think through, and use, your understanding of cities and will have helped you to build a range of key skills that you can use in other contexts. You will now have extended your skills beyond those required to answer more narrowly based assignments. The course essay has required you to explore and marshal material on a course-wide basis, to engage with a particular theme, and to apply your understanding of the course in relation to this theme. These skills are not particular to DD304, but are valuable transferable skills that can be used in many capacities, roles and activities outside the course. More generally, you should now feel confident in questioning the day-to-day media images and stories that you see, hear and read about cities and city life, both at home and abroad, in a more informed way. So, studying the course will have helped you to develop skills and knowledge which can be applied to urban issues outside the course, and in your life more generally.

2 *Looking back*

Understanding Cities has built a picture of cities as places that are *open*, places of *intensity*, places of cultural *mixing*, places that give rise to *tensions*, and places that lie at the heart of complex webs of global *interconnection*. We have looked at cities through a *spatial* lens and we have tried to imagine a geography of cities in the world that looks within and beyond the city. In the course essay you have directed this lens in a particular way by focusing on one of the three themes. These three themes – the social, the economic and the environmental – were chosen by the course team for in-depth study because they represent key aspects of city life and have particular significance for the future of cities. Studying just one theme has given you an opportunity to focus in on some of the vitally important issues and dilemmas for cities, the really big policy debates that governments, agencies and non-governmental organizations are addressing. But at the same time, you will have been aware that the three themes are, in reality, far from separate, self-contained aspects of city life.

Throughout the course we have seen how social, economic and environmental processes are intimately connected; if anything, it is the symbiosis and balance between these elements that might form the basis of sustainable futures for cities. For example, the discussion on ecological modernization and the city in Andrew Blowers' and Kathy Pain's chapter **(Bk 3 Ch. 6)** provides a number of illustrations of the way in which economic growth, the market economy, environmental needs and the social inequalities within and between cities are intrinsically linked. Too often, it seems, the primacy of the economy and the market 'pushes out' these other social and environmental interests. The question as to whether contemporary cities are sustainable – socially, economically, environmentally – is fundamental to this course.

3 *Looking out and on*

In *Understanding Cities* it has been argued that, through the making and unmaking of connections within and between cities, just as cities have no single past, they also have no, one, single future. As Doreen Massey emphasizes **(Bk 1 Ch. 4)**, it is the interdependence of cities that will enable them to pursue their distinctive individual trajectories and, as we have seen throughout the course, the spatial configuration of cities will play a key part in the construction and re-construction of the connections, disconnections and juxtapositions that are crucial to cities' survival and success.

Given the dynamic order of cities, their governance and planning cannot, as Doreen Massey goes on to say, work with an assumption of 'some final, formal plan, nor work with an assumption of a reachable permanent harmony or peace' **(Bk 1** p.161). *Understanding Cities* has encouraged you to think about the future of cities in terms of their fluidity, openness, and density of interaction: 'a thinking about process' (*ibid.*). This means thinking about the elements that structure cities – social, economic and environmental – as processes that through their interconnections help to shape the future of cities.

If we are to address one of the key course questions – cities for whom? – we need to understand the geography of inequality, of economic resources and of environmental issues. Cities offer a mix of excitement and danger, inclusion and exclusion, diversity and difference. They are spatial arenas for the changing nature of society. They raise expectations and concerns and pose important questions and dilemmas for us all. Cities have a fundamental function in the organization of human society and they can be a positive element in its future. However, this requires political will and informed commitment. Understanding cities will have a key role to play in making this possible.

CB, MH, IM, KP, JS

Acknowledgements

Grateful acknowledgement is made to the following sources for permission to reproduce material in this book:

Text

Palin, M. (1992) *Pole to Pole*, BBC Books; *Reading 2A:* Back, L. (1996) *New Ethnicities and Urban Culture: Racisms and Multiculture in Young Lives*, UCL Press Ltd; *Reading 2B:* Marks, K. (1998) 'Asian youth cynical about city policing', *The Independent,* 21 October 1998; *Reading 2C:* Reprinted by permission of Transaction Publishers, 'The bubbling cauldron: global and local interactions in New York City restaurants', by Amdur, L. *et al*., Comparative Urban and Community Research, vol.4, 1995. Copyright © 1992 by Transaction Publishers, New Brunswick, New Jersey 08903; All rights reserved; *Reading 2D:* Excerpted and reprinted from chapters 2 and 4 of *Urban Danger: Life in a Neighborhood of Strangers* by Sally Engle Merry by permission of Temple University Press. © 1981 by Temple University. All rights reserved; *Reading 2E:* Stansfield, K. (1997) 'Poverty has a woman's face', *Housing Agenda*, vol.2/2, November 1997, National Housing Federation; *Reading 2F:* Gray, P. (1996) 'Renewal in a divided city', *Housing Review*, 45(4), Housing Centre Trust, London; *Reading 2G:* Smith, N. (1996) 'Tompkins Square Park and beyond', in King, A.D. (ed.) *Re-Presenting the City: Ethnicity, Capital and Culture in the Twenty First Century Metropolis*, Macmillan Press Ltd, © Neil Smith 1996; *Readings 2H and 2N:* Helmore, K. (1997) 'Out of the tunnel of urban childhood: helping the children of the urban poor emerge into a brighter future'and 'Facts and figures', *Urban Age*, 5(1). Reprinted with permission, Urban Age magazine, 1999; *Reading 2I:* 'City of the child catchers', *Observer Review*, 23 February 1997; *Reading 2J:* Bergen, M. (1997) 'Children in the city: an interview with the Mayor of Rio de Janeiro', *Urban Age*, 1997. Reprinted with permission, Urban Age magazine, 1999; *Reading 2L:* Baudrillard, J. in Turner, C. (trans.) (1988) *America*, Verso, London.

Flanagan, W. G. (1993) *Contemporary Urban Sociology*, Cambridge University Press; *Reading 3A:* Harris, N. (1997) 'Cities in a global economy: structural change and policy reactions', *Urban Studies*, 34, © 1997 The Editors of Urban Studies. Carfax Publishing Company Ltd, PO Box 25, Abingdon, Oxfordshire, OX14 3UE; *Reading 3B:* Sassen, S. (1998) *Globalisation and Its Discontents*, The New Press, © Saskia Sassen; *Reading 3C:* Sophie Body-Gendrot, 'Pioneering Moslem women in France', in Fisher and Kling (eds) *Mobilizing the Community: Local Politics in the Era of the Global City*, pp.270-290. Copyright © 1993 by Sage Publications, Inc. Reprinted by permission of Sage Publications, Inc.

Reading 4A: Rogers, R. (1997) *Cities for a Small Planet*, Faber and Faber Ltd; *Reading 4B:* pages 60-62, 64 from *Small is Beautiful: A Study of Economics as if People Mattered*, by E.F. Schumacher. Copyright © 1973 E.F. Schumacher. Reprinted by permission of HarperCollins Publishers, Inc. and Blond and Briggs; *Reading 4C:* Mitlin, D. and Satterthwaite, D. (1994) *Cities and Sustainable*

Figures

Tables

Cover